I0225133

ABOUT MY FATHER'S BUSINESS

PROFESSIONAL MINISTRY FOR KINGDOM LEADERS

Dr. Lee Ann B. Marino, Ph.D., D.Min., D.D.

ABOUT MY FATHER'S BUSINESS

PROFESSIONAL MINISTRY FOR KINGDOM LEADERS

Dr. Lee Ann B. Marino, Ph.D., D.Min., D.D.

Published by:
RIGHTEOUS PEN PUBLICATIONS
(The Righteousness of God shall guide my pen)
www.righteouspenpublications.com

All rights reserved. No part of this book may
be reproduced or transmitted in any form or by any means,
electronic or mechanical, or information storage and retrieval
system without written permission from the author.

Scriptures taken from the Holy Bible,
New International Version®, NIV®
Copyright © 1973, 1978, 1984 by Biblica, Inc™.
Used by permission of Zondervan.
All rights reserved worldwide.

Scriptures marked KJV are from the Authorized King James
Version of the Holy Bible, Public Domain.

Scriptures marked ERV are taken from the HOLY BIBLE:
EASY-TO-READ VERSION
© 2014 by World Bible Translation Center, Inc.
Used by permission.

Copyright © 2014, 2022 by Lee Ann B. Marino.

ISBN: 1940197090
13-Digit: 978-1-940197-09-8

Printed in the United States of America.

And He said unto them,
How is it that ye sought Me?
Wist ye not that I must be about
My Father's business?

- Luke 2:49 (KJV)

TABLE OF CONTENTS

Introduction

Do You Have a Vision?

THE modern church talks a lot about vision from God. We hear about what a vision is, getting a vision, having a vision, and how God wants us to be victorious in that vision. We talk about the vision. We verbally share the vision. We make promises based on the vision. We are encouraged to pursue the vision at any cost. Many today are in debt over their vision. Several have run ahead of God, or handled things with total and complete disorder. As a result, their vision, no matter how God-ordained, does not become a reality.

What we don't hear a lot about in today's church is how to make a vision a reality. That is where we, as a church, are failing in vision. It is true that God gives us a vision, but it is also true that we need to do specific things in order to become the executors of that vision.

Passing from imagination to realities

Ministry sounds like an admirable idea...it sounds powerful and purposed...but being in ministry is more than just a nice idea, vision, and concept. Ministry takes work, thought, and effort. If ministry is to be more than just something pursued as a hobby, it must pass from vision to professional action. While the conditions and requirements of ministry today are different in some ways than in years past, the underlying principle that ministry must be approached in a certain way transcends the ages.

Ministry in every age is not just a matter of vision. It's great to have a vision and yes, we must begin with something when we attempt to start out, but it is not enough to just hold on to a random promise and hope everything else will work out. In order to bring a vision to pass in any day or

1

age, we must become agents of Kingdom business. Some people take issue with applying the word "business" to God's Kingdom, but business is a part of running any successful ministry. If we look at Jesus and His disciples, He had a treasurer to keep watch over the money. He had individuals whom He trained for specific things and brought to a specific place of revelation. Those whom He was closest to were sent out to accomplish the work of God with specific instructions that related to both the spiritual and the practical. Kingdom business is a reference to the practical side of ministry: finances, organization, purpose, clarity, and direction. Such enhances the spiritual side of ministry because when we are rightly organized, we can flow better in the Spirit.

Business is not something to fear. Business is "busy-ness" – it is the essence of what keeps us occupied and purposeful. While the ins and outs of business can seem intimidating in the beginning, we are people called to walk in order. Business gives us the ability to walk in the order of God and bring forth the vision in a way that will bless and benefit all who are part of it or touch it.

We cannot expect everything we do in ministry to be all about spiritual gifts or anointing. I've met many people who tell me, "People will see my anointing and follow me because of it." That may very well be true. People are very taken in by spiritual displays, whether or not those displays are of God. Whether that is true or not, a ministry needs to have the staying power to keep people following and engaged in a ministry for as long as God appoints them to be there. We also need to be organized enough to fulfill our promises, teach, train, and edify those who come to our ministry so they can get the teaching that is needed to change and impact their lives.

Professionalism

Akin to business is professionalism. Professionalism is the quality of being professional, reflecting the purpose and ethics of a specified profession. When I was first a Christian back in 1999, we saw something known as "professional ministry." All leaders of churches – no matter the denomination – were classified as "clergy" and were in their respective positions full-time. As a result, being a church leader was considered a job, and thus, certain things went along with it. Beyond just being something someone was called to do, being a minister was also a source of livelihood and a means by which ministers had to adapt to certain rules, regulations, and criteria. It was not as simple as putting a title in front of one's name on the internet. Most ministers studied through Bible college, a four-year program, or seminary, depending on their denomination's or affiliation's regulations. As with most jobs, that was just the beginning. Ministers also had to be licensed and ordained – under no circumstances was a minister calling themselves any such thing without the proper documentation. There were a host of other rules and guidelines ministers had to follow in order to keep their licenses and ordinations valid within their denominations. If something changed and ministers failed to follow the rules – regardless of what they might be – ministers lost the right to operate in their respective ministries within their associations or denominations. When such happened, it was often difficult to obtain another license or ordination, even with another organization (unless the reason was considerably minor as pertains to doctrinal disagreement). Ministers were expected to dress in a certain way, carry themselves in a certain way, and preach within certain confines of their organizations.

Somewhere in here, professional ministry disappeared. It is rare to meet a minister in full-time ministry anymore. Most ministers treat ministry as a second job or a side hobby, something they pursue after they fulfill their main job. For some, this is the result of waning numbers and lack of financial support, but for others, it is due to a wrong mentality about ministry in general. Some people feel ministry is a secondary calling, something to be pursued after other things. Many ministers operate without license and ordination (or the proper license and ordination credentials) and avoid organizations, networks, or denominations that require any semblance of rules. Dress codes are gone in favor of jeans and T-shirts, or we see the opposite extreme of robes, rings, and liturgical wear. In the world of no rules, regulations, order, or authority...what has happened to ministry professionalism?

If ministers want to be respected, they must be respectable. If we are to be respectable, we must bring back professional order and structure within our ranks. We have to stop treating ministry as if it is a random pipe-dream and start approaching our ministerial function as a business endeavor, with professional conduct and professional operation.

The purpose of this book

The purpose of this book is to bridge business and professionalism, all the while incorporating these important facets into modern ministry. With the rise of the internet, cell phones, tablets, and other forms of modern technology, older methods and means of ministry tend to seem outdated. I want us to realize that yes, some things have changed, but with those things that have changed, new protocol and order must be set for their proper form and execution. We cannot hope that abandoning professionalism and protocol will result in a solidified church; on the contrary, we must recognize rules and regulations to give us the necessary establishment to function properly and rightly. There are reasons policies and protocols have emerged throughout history. While some need updating and changing, the reality remains that standing for time-honored protocol never goes out of style. If we want our ministries to change and get better – and, most of all, grow into viable Kingdom endeavors – we must set ourselves to follow Kingdom protocol and submit to Kingdom order.

Through this book, we will look at the business and professional sides of ministry and how to develop a strong business sense in ministry, because having such will help to further the vision God has given unto you. In it, you will learn how to create a business plan; uphold business essentials; understand business documents; dress for ministry; handle conflicts and bring about resolutions; handle interactions with others; learn about non-profit status; and beyond. Through this program, you will learn all there is to know about being in professional ministry as a professional minister.

SECTION I

WRITE THE VISION

CHAPTER ONE

PLANNING FOR MINISTRY

The plans of the diligent lead to profit
as surely as haste leads to poverty.
(Proverbs 21:5)

MANY people claim to be called to ministry. They will talk about what they believe God has given to them to anyone who will hear. They spend a lot of time thinking about the vision, dreaming about the vision, and positively speaking over that vision. They will tell people where they want the vision to go and what they want it to accomplish. It's all about the vision: seeing it, figuring out where to fit in it, what to do with it. They want to run with this vision and see it happen...

All of this sounds good and fun. It sounds empowering to run with a vision. It's awesome to have a vision....yet there is one thing that most do not tend to do: they do not write the vision.

When it comes to planning ministry, God doesn't tell us to speak the vision, talk about the vision, run with the vision, confess the vision, or dream about the vision. He tells us to write the vision, and make it plain (Habakkuk 2:2). There are a few reasons why it is so important to write the vision:

- **Writing a vision makes it clear what we are about, so there is no confusion** – Visions from God can seem complicated, convoluted, and excessively detailed. We don't always have twelve hours to explain to others what God is speaking to us and what He is working through us. Not everyone is interested to see the bigger picture of what we may be doing or what God may have promised, especially if it has in no way come to pass as of yet. That is why it is essential to write out whatever it is that He is giving to us so we can break it down by various levels and make it appropriate for the needed understanding at the time.

- **Writing a vision helps us to sort things out, because we can see what God is speaking to us in a different way** – Visions are wonderful, powerful, encouraging things…but we need to organize that vision. The visions God gives to us are meant to become a record and a pathway that we will take as we bring it to pass. They aren't just fairy tales or nice thoughts to get us through our days. The organization we need to have to manifest a vision comes as we sort things out and come to a clearer understanding in the purpose of the vision.

- **Writing a vision helps bring purpose to our vision** – Visions are only powerful when they are purposeful. If we can't make a vision practical, it is not going to do anyone any good. Writing a vision makes it practical and doable.

- **Writing a vision helps us to 'chart' our vision** – When we are given a vision, we need to know where to start. We need to know and recognize our first steps and step out in faith to make the vision a reality. Writing it out helps us know where to start and helps us identify practical steps we can take to move forward with the vision as more details of the vision manifest and unfold.

Writing a vision doesn't have to be a long, drawn-out,

complicated process. Sometimes I think people avoid writing visions because they think they have to write out a five-hundred-page dissertation. This isn't like writing an essay at school or a report for a job, but it is just as important. We must set to the task and give ourselves a deadline, if necessary, to complete the project. We can always add something else later, but we can't delay the first steps to bringing forth God's vision in our lives and purpose.

CHAPTER TWO

WHAT YOU NEED TO WRITE

Write down the revelation and make it plain on tablets
so that a herald may run with it.
(Habakkuk 2:2)

IN order to write a vision from God, one doesn't need to be the next great American novelist. If we look at the different scribal gifts present throughout the Bible, we see some individuals who wrote many words, and others who wrote a few. The point of all those words isn't how long they were, but that they established and presented the vision God gave them in the manner best for that vision. All one needs to do is have a few basic stills and be able to write a few pages. The major components of a good plan are a vision statement, mission statement, statement of faith, statement of activities and operations, and bylaws.

It is essential we are able to write in different ways for the purpose and productivity of business writing. Some people have a very hard time making things plain and concise. This is because leaders in the church have given us the idea we need to use a lot of words to sound relevant. This could not be farther from the truth! In most circumstances, using too many words causes things to become irrelevant to others and can, in the long-run, hurt our point because people stop reading or listening.

The goal for writing in a Kingdom-business style is simple. We need to be able to express our point in one to three sentences, three to eight sentences, one to five pages, and in the form of about five to ten pages. Business writing is purposed to answer the five "w"s of matters: the who, the what, the where, the when, and the why.

- **Vision Statement** – A vision statement is a short statement defining the reason why an organization exists. In a vision statement, one covers the general overview of that vision, rather than being specific in detail. It is approximately one to three sentences long and tells the "what" an organization does what they do in that short statement.

- **Mission Statement** – A mission statement is a little longer than a vision statement, usually anywhere from three to eight sentences long. The purpose of a mission statement is to set forth the mission, or purpose, of an organization. This answers the "who" the organization is for and the "what" in terms of the purpose.

- **Statement of Faith** – A statement of faith is a selection of pinpoints the organization stands for and the guiding belief system behind its vision and mission. A statement of faith for a ministry typically outlines their belief in God, the revelation of God, the Word of God, the Christian life, the reason for rites (such as baptism and communion), their reason for believing ministry is essential today, and why they reach out as they do. This document can be anywhere from one to five pages. A statement of faith answers the 'why' an organization does what they do.

- **Statement of Activities and Operations** – This is where the organization starts to hit paper and the discipline comes forth. As concisely as possible, a statement of activities and operations outlines the specific things a ministry will do as part of their work. A statement of activities and operations needs to be more detailed than a vision or mission statement, but not too wordy, somewhere between one and five pages. What is required under this heading may vary by the need for its purpose (a grant, for example). Examples of such can be found online.

- **Bylaws** – Bylaws are laws of governance as pertain to the board of an organization and organizational function. Bylaws can be of varying length, as requirements for bylaws can vary by state. You can find samples of bylaws as pertain to the state in which you live online.

These items can be simply written, but should be well-written. It is important that, in writing them, you use proper grammar, spelling, and syntax. Spell-check is a great resource and available on all major word processing systems. They should be written in a standard font, ten to twelve point in size, and clearly readable. Bylaws should be bound and kept in their own compilation, and the rest of the aforementioned documents should be kept together. We will discuss more about what will be combined with these documents a little later.

CHAPTER THREE

PREPARING A BUDGET

The blessing of the LORD brings wealth,
and He adds no trouble to it.
(Proverbs 10:22)

IF you are anything like most ministers, you probably dread the idea of budgeting. Most ministers just want to get out and reach people. Doing a lot of paperwork is a serious drag and takes a lot of time – and then we have the area of budgeting, which takes even more time.

It is not uncommon to find ministers who are vastly unfamiliar with budgeting and budgeting software. A large portion of these ministers are intimidated to learn the necessary procedures, believing it to be too challenging or technical. Other ministers may dislike the idea of budgeting, thinking that it somehow defies the concept of trusting God for finances.

The majority of ministries that don't budget fail within the first few years of establishment. This is for a few reasons. The first reason is obvious: it is difficult to plan a ministry and events for a ministry without a record of the finances. Ministry costs money, whether we want to admit it or not; and not knowing how much money a group has is detrimental to the purpose of a vision at hand. The second reason is simple: it is impossible to run a ministry without a rough idea of how much a group will spend in different areas. The third reason is also simple: ministries need to control their spending. The reality of every single ministry is that it typically doesn't start out with a one billion dollar budget to frivolously spend here and there. Ministers, in keeping with right attitudes of Kingdom business, need to be careful about spending and watchful of finances.

This becomes essential, especially in light of becoming a federally recognized non-profit entity. Budgeting is a part of the application process, and bookkeeping and budgeting are both a part of maintaining status and receiving funding from grant organizations and donors alike.

In order to create a budget, one must be familiar with either Microsoft Excel or another budgeting software, such as QuickBooks. Some bookkeeping software makes the process extremely easy, but the budgeting layout is not always easily accessible for emailing or business plans. For the sake of this book, we are going to do a brief introduction to Microsoft Excel and how to create a budget using Microsoft Excel. It is often sold as part of a Microsoft Office package, which means most computers containing MSOffice have Microsoft Excel on them. If you do not have MS Excel, it is essential you purchase it, or use a free open source program that is comparable in function.

Microsoft Excel is a spreadsheet program. This means when you open up the Excel program, a screen will appear with many smaller boxes and divisions on it, much like a grid. Although using it at first looks very intimidating, using Excel greatly eases the process of making and maintaining a budget as later changes arise.

Associatedcontent.com has outlined an excellent step-by-step process for the creation of a budget with MS Excel. I am providing their information below to help you get started:

- To begin you will need to open a new Microsoft Excel Worksheet. First, click on "My Documents". Then click on "File", then click on "New". Next click on "Microsoft Excel Worksheet". You now have a blank Microsoft Excel worksheet to input your budget into.

- You will notice that each column of the Microsoft Excel worksheet is labeled with the letters of the alphabet and each row is labeled with consecutive numbers. In this way, each individual cell is referred to by its corresponding letter and number. For example, the first cell is referred to as A1. You can move your location around on the worksheet either by using your mouse or your arrow keys. You will notice that as you move around the worksheet, the cell reference indicated at the top of the worksheet will change according to your location.

- You should begin by listing your expenses in the first column of your Microsoft Excel worksheet. For a basic budget you might begin with putting the name of your first expense in cell A5. To do this you would simply arrow over to cell A5 and type in the name of your first expense and hit "enter". Then type in your next expense in cell A6 and continue down the column entering in the names of all of your expenses. When you have completed entering the names of all of your expenses you should enter "total" as the name of the last cell in the column. Next you should label the top of each column with the months of the year. Begin by typing in "Jan". in cell B4, then "Feb." in cell B4. Continue labeling all the months of the year and then label the top of the next column "total".

- Now the labels of your budget are complete and you can begin to enter in your budget figures. If your first expense is "mortgage", fill in the budgeted amount for that category in each column for every month of the year. Then continue down until all of the budgeted expense amounts have been entered for every month.

- You are now ready to calculate the totals of each of your columns and rows. Let's begin by calculating the total expenses for each month. In the first cell next to the "total" label, you will enter a formula that will calculate the total of all of your January expenses. The great thing about this formula is that if you later change one of your expense figures for January, the total will automatically be updated.

- The formula you enter will vary slightly depending on how many expenses you have. If you had a total of 20 different expenses, this is the formula you would type in "=SUM(B4.B23)" and then hit "enter". You will notice that this cell will now contain the sum of all of the numbers entered in the column from cell B4 through B23. If you had more expenses you would change the B23 to whatever cell contained the last of your expense figures. Next you will copy this formula from the cell of the Jan. total to the cells for the totals for each month of the year. Begin by making sure you are on the cell you want to copy. Next, click on "Edit" on the toolbar at the top of your page. Then click on "Copy". The cell you are on will now be flashing. Now hold down your "Shift" key and arrow over highlighting all of the cells you want to copy the formula into. Lastly hit "enter" and your formula will now be copied into each of the cells. These cells will now show the totals of each of your expenses by month.

- Next you will want to calculate the yearly total of each of your expenses. To do this, go to the row after Dec. labeled "total". In this cell, type in this formula: "=SUM(B4+B5+B6+B7+B8+B9+B10+B11+B12+B13+B14+B15)" and then hit "enter". You will notice that this cell now contains the sum of all expenses for your first category for each month of the year. Next you will copy this formula into all the cells of that column.

- You now have your complete budget with monthly totals and totals for each expense category. You can save your budget by clicking on "File", then "Save As". A small window will appear where you can type in the name of your Microsoft Excel worksheet. A good name might be "2007 Budget". Next, click "enter" and your worksheet will be saved.[1]

Following the above instructions, one step at a time, will set you right to start budgeting and track finances within a ministry setting.

Things to include in a budget for ministry include:

- Rent or mortgage on a building
- Overhead costs, such as electricity, gas, etc.
- Furniture
- Office supplies
- Office equipment
- Service/sound equipment
- Ministry supplies (textbooks, VBS packets, etc.)
- Church or ministry-sponsored events
- Travel
- Printing/copying costs
- Radio/TV airtime
- Event costs
- Salaries (if applicable)

Because each individual church or ministry has their own unique set of circumstances, each group will have its own unique set of finances. An organization with a church has a different overhead than a ministry that operates via travelling and conference hosting. Different types of ministries even have different needs: for example, what a youth ministry needs to have varies greatly from what a prison ministry needs to have.

There are three types of budgets: a projected budget, and an actual budget, and an estimated budget. A projected budget is an estimated budget for a specific period of time. When a non-profit applies for a grant, a projected budget gives the grant organization an idea of how the non-profit will spend the grant money. This proves to a grant organization that a non-profit has given thought to what they will do if they receive the money and that the money will go to its allocated purpose. When making a projected budget, the funds used are projected rather than an actual statement of one's financial situation. When constructing an actual budget, one is working with their current finances and expenses, and seeking to gain a total of both expenses and finances. The way the budget is constructed is the same for both. The only difference between an actual and projected budget is the specification of finances. With a projected budget, it is usually required for an organization to spend a certain amount through their budget, while an actual budget does not have this requirement.

An estimated budget is somewhere between a projected budget and actual budget. An estimated budget is a long-term budget (at least five years) based on the current earnings and expenses of an organization. When creating an estimated budget, an organization considers growth, both financial and supportive, as well as additional expenses and needs, over the years in question. An estimated budget is based on projected finances that may or may become actual, but are based on current earnings and expenses as opposed to receiving a lump sum from a grant organization. In formatting an estimated budget, the formatting is the same as it is for a projected budget and actual budget.

In dealing with budgeting and plans, all three types of budgeting are essential for ministry vision and planning. Showing that we can work with different finances and both plan and project our finances proves we have a vision beyond right now and the immediate.

CHAPTER FOUR

PREPARING YOUR BUSINESS/PROPOSAL PACKAGE

*I no longer call you servants, because a servant does not know
his master's business. Instead, I have called you friends,
for everything that I learned from My Father I have made known to you.
(John 15:15)*

CONGRATULATIONS! If you have worked the projects found thus far in this book, you should have the following documents prepared:

- Mission Statement
- Vision Statement
- Statement of Activities and Operations
- Statement of Faith
- Budget

Now we're going to work on the assembly of these documents into your business proposal/package.

The first major thing you need to do is proofread your documents. Check for spelling and grammatical errors, and take care to correct any errors. Remember, these documents are the first business impression many will have of your ministry and the quality of what you do. If you don't have a head for spelling and grammar, have someone else check it for you and make any necessary changes.

Next, take your documents and make sure they are in a clear, easy-to-read standard font, and consistently in size 10-

12 in the text size. Headings that identify the sections (such as Mission Statement, etc.) may be a text size to two text sizes larger than the text body. Arrange each heading item on its own page. Then make a cover page that says the name of your ministry followed by the words "Business Package." In the lower right hand corner, put the ministry address, telephone number, email address, and website.

Lastly, combine all the pages of each document into one singular booklet (called a package). Bind or staple the documents together. Congratulations, you have now created the basics for a business proposal or business package. When applying for grants, providing information to apply for non-profit status, and just holding to good practice when the information is necessary, the business proposal/package is supplied. Bylaws, as stated earlier, are bound and kept separately – and, in some instances, may be also supplied along with a business proposal. These documents should remain together and only copies issued to relevant parties upon request, as these documents show forth the written foundation to a powerful vision.

Additional requirements for a business proposal or package may vary depending on the specific type of grant or situation required. Most business proposals require the materials above, plus additional information that may pertain to the specific writing or information requested. Some additional things required for a business proposal or package include:

- Property valuation
- Zoning regulations
- Proof of or eligibility for insurance
- Local demographics
- Property tax information
- Survey of property plans surrounding a property within the next five to ten years

CHAPTER FIVE

THE MEDIA KIT

Therefore, since through God's mercy we have this ministry,
we do not lose heart. Rather, we have renounced secret and shameful ways;
we do not use deception, nor do we distort the word of God. On the contrary,
by setting forth the truth plainly we commend ourselves to every man's
conscience in the sight of God.
(2 Corinthians 4:1-2)

I
F a minister intends to do ministry work beyond a local church or ever work in a media setting, such as on television, internet podcasting, or on the radio, a minister will need a media kit. A media kit is a basic document package that provides information on a minister and their ministry experience, especially their experiences in ministry as pertain to media exposure. While the contents of media kits may vary depending upon request, a basic media kit includes the following documents:

- **An introduction letter** – An introduction letter is a short, one-page letter providing the basic overview of the minister's ministry, what is important to that ministry, and some brief descriptive words about the ways that ministry is reflecting what is most important to them. The letter should end with an invitation to the reviewer to contact the ministry if they believe the ministry can be of service.

- **Minister's biography** – A minister's biography (usually what is found on a website) provides a basic overview of the minister leading the ministry, pinpoints along the way, a few major accomplishments, and things that minister is doing as part of ministry work. This biography should be no longer than two total pages in length, and should include a photo of the minister. A minister's biography should be professional, showcasing God's ministry work within the individual. It is not appropriate for a minister's biography to include lengthy details about private affairs. A professional minister's biography is not a place to detail married life, children, pets, street addresses, and every life ailment. When thinking biography, think about wide-scope: information that will reach a large audience on all levels, both understandable by the average person and enticing to a professional audience as well. Biographies must be professional in nature, as succinct as possible, ordered, and to-the-point.

- **Minister's media profile** – A one-to-two page listing of the different media exposure a minister has had through the years in ministry. This includes features in magazines, newspapers, books one has written for or is author of, radio programs, internet podcasts, and television exposure. It can also include major conference events or other events that one participated in, also generating media exposure. Please note: media profiles do not include being "famous" on Instagram or posting many pictures or statuses on Facebook.

- **Minister's academic profile** – A one-to-two page listing of the academic contributions a minister has made to ministry, if a minister has qualifying academic contributions. This not as much about degrees received (although that can certainly be included), but more about educational programs and achievements done through ministry work. For example, founding or leading a Bible institute, school of the prophets, ordination program, or class would be listed here. So would instituting a seminar or founding a program that educates the church or community. Applicable business information, such as founding a Kingdom-based business or acting as a publisher, would also apply here.

- **About the ministry** – This should encompass no more than five to seven pages and should include contact information (including address, phone number, websites, and social networking sites), some basic divisions of your ministry (kind of along the lines of your Statement of Activities and Operations), your ministry mission statement, and two to three references who can verify your ministry. One reference should be your covering, another reference should be someone you work closely with in a mentioned project within your statement of activities of operations, and an additional reference can be someone who knows you and is familiar with your ministry work. References should never be family members.

Because media kits are submitted for a media purpose, a media kit should have eye appeal. It does not need to be elaborately decorated, but should be assembled on a stationery design that includes a consistent color theme and design on each page and should use a basic, easy-to-read font for the text and a fancier font for the headings. On the first page ministry overview letter, ministry letterhead should be used with the consistent themed color design on the remainder of the page.

Chapter Six

RESUME AND CV PREPARATION

All hard work brings a profit,
but mere talk leads only to poverty.
(Proverbs 14:23)

MOST people familiar with the business world know what a resume is. A resume is an individual's professional summary, prepared for employment purposes. Resumes are a staple of the business world and carefully constructed. They are typically no longer than one to two pages and include an objective (statement of reason for a resume), an education summary (degrees earned, places attended from high school on), job history for the past ten years with positions and job duties, applicable skills, volunteer work or leisure activities/hobbies, and references.

Resumes

There are numerous ways a resume can be constructed, based on the job at hand or the situation required. As a result, there are numerous debates about the correct way to format a resume or to present a resume. When building a resume, there are a few key things to keep in mind:

- A resume should contain your first and last names with middle initial, mailing address, telephone number, email address, and website, if applicable.

- A resume is a summary, not a detailed explanation. Do not think you need to include every little detail. Think short phrases and descriptive terms, not long, wordy passages. Too many details cause a resume to be thrown out.

- If you have more than one type of work and the information and details are too numerous to contain in one resume, have more than one resume. For example: if you have a ministry and a for-profit business, have one resume for your ministry experience and a separate resume for your for-profit business.

- Resumes are not about one's personal testimony and should not include personal information. On a resume, it is irrelevant if you are married or not; if you have children; if you have a pet; what you want out of your life; and details of your personal testimony. Including such will insure you are passed over on a professional level.

- Resumes should show job experience in a positive light. If you have a job that doesn't do that, even in ministry (i.e., you were fired from it), leave it off the resume.

- If you are working in ministry, include your current ministry position, even if it is not financially lucrative. There is more to a job than just the amount of money one makes. If you are working in ministry, actively working in service in some area of ministry (not just sitting on the internet playing games), you are working. Be sure to include skills acquired in ministry development!

- Resumes must include references. References are a sore spot for many potential employees. Most companies seek three references on a resume: a former employer or boss, a co-worker, and a friend. References should never be family members. Ministry references would be your covering or leader, a minister you work closely with in ministry, and a friend who is a believer, who may or may not be in ministry.

Ministers should have a current resume, for a number of reasons. If a minister intends to work for a Bible school, university, school of the prophets, or run any number of programs that may require a grant, a resume is recommended. Sometimes ministry schools or new coverings require a resume from those interested in coming under their ministry. This is so they can trace ministry history and establish a good pattern of ministry commitment and service. Ministers also need to keep resumes on hand if they will be working for other ministries, seek positions within a church, or if they desire to seek a position in any type of arena.

There are number of templates available on the internet and through most computer programs that can help you to find the right resume style for the right situation and occasion. Stick to formatting, remembering that formatting is essential for a resume; do not be excessively wordy; and keep to the necessary information at hand.

Curriculum Vitae

The *curriculum vitae* is similar to a resume, but it is specifically for a specified job or theme. Traditionally nicknamed a "teacher's resume," everything on a *curriculum vitae* (or CV, as it is commonly called) is about one's specific experience as relates to a job, position, or work. In terms of ministry, a curriculum vitae would be a specific resume that relates exclusively to ministry. The main components to a *curriculum vitae* are:

- Your first and last names with middle initial and ministry title, mailing address, telephone number, email address, and website, if applicable.

- Remember that once again, you are providing a summary listing, not paragraph details.

- At the beginning of a *curriculum vitae*, be sure to include a brief description of your ministry vision. At the end, include a brief description of your ministry values.

- A *curriculum vitae* relates specifically to ministry experiences. Do not litter it up with a lot of experiences and job work unrelated to ministry.

- A *curriculum vitae* is not a personal testimony. You need to focus on ministry education, experience, major events, and work rather than personal ministry encounters and perspectives.

Be sure to include references on a CV. Ministry references for a CV are: your covering or leader, other ministers who you work closely with, or those who are under your covering (also leaders) who can attest to your ministry call and experience.

CHAPTER SEVEN

WRITING LETTERS AND EMAILS

So then, brothers, stand firm and hold to the teachings
we passed on to you, whether by word of mouth or by letter.
(2 Thessalonians 2:15)

ANYONE who has read the Bible has read a letter –
actually, they have read several letters. Letter-writing is a long-standing tradition within Kingdom history, as it was the main means of communication between people at a distance for millenniums. Letter-writing was considered an art form, an essential means to convey important messages that, with the right preservation, could be passed down from generation to generation. Letters were also important because they could be circulated among more than one group of people (Esther 9:20, Esther 9:30, Jeremiah 29:1, Acts 15:23-30, 1 Corinthians 16:3, Colossians 4:16, 1 Thessalonians 5:27), and the teaching or information contained in one letter could reach many instead of having to start over again with each new group each time. As a result, the ability to write a letter was considered essential for leaders, educators, and those with a message to deliver.

In our modern day and age, letter writing has gone out of vogue. It is amazing the vast number of people who do not know the basics of writing a good letter. What we fail to realize is letter writing applies to all areas of ministry: greeting leaders, announcements, email, private messaging, applications, and disciplinary writing. Being able to construct a well-written letter helps us deliver information in a variety of areas, and also relates to our presentation as ministers. Here are the basics of good letter-writing:

- Ministry letters should always be written on ministry stationery, complete with ministry name, contact information (address, email, telephone, website), and a closing salutation, complete with signature, typed name, and ministry title.

- Letters contain a few basic elements. Professional letters contain the recipient's address and date of the letter in the upper left-hand corner. There is a line of space left blank and then the appropriate salutation for the individual. A salutation is usually "Dear" followed by the name of the individual (using their title, if appropriate, such as "Dear Apostle Jones," followed by a colon. The enter key then is hit twice to leave another line of space. The body of the letter begins here, with a brief introduction on the reason for the letter, details about what the letter is about, and any pertinent information as related to the intent. New paragraphs are inserted as necessary for continuity and flow of information. The body of a letter is closed with a short concluding paragraph to bring the entire purpose of a letter to a close. The letter should then have another line of space with a closing greeting (such as "Sincerely," or "Yours Truly," followed by four lines of space, and the sender's name with title, office, and then the ministry name underneath.

- As representatives of the Kingdom, letters should follow business form in tone, refrain from vulgar, nasty, or slang terminology, and should uphold courtesy and dignity.

- When letters are used for disciplinary measures, they should include the reason or reasons for the disciplinary action and should be well-structured and ordered. Within a disciplinary letter should be the end result of the letter (one's termination, a warning, etc.) and either the opening for further communication or the cessation therein.

- While emails do not require the same level of formality as letters (including addresses and such), emails should still maintain the same basic form of a salutation, introductory paragraph, details, closing paragraph, closing salutation, a typed name, and title with ministry. Emails should also include the sender's contact information (sometimes called a "signature" in various email programs) at the end of an email rather than at the beginning. Emails should remain polite, upholding courtesy and dignity, as letters do as well. Below are some guidelines for constructing effective emails:

- Emails should never be used to handle formal matters, such as disciplinary action, dismissal from ministry, notification of disassociation, or other formal actions for three reasons. The first is that email is not a perfect science, and emails can be lost or undelivered. The second reason is because it can be difficult to read tone in an email or in electronic media, and the severity of a situation can be misread or misapplied. The third reason is because formal matters need to be handled according to formal order. If that cannot be done or conveyed in person, they need to be handled via formal letter, in keeping with the standard of the Word.

- Emails should be used for electronic newsletters, ministry updates, initial and new inquiries, and to keep in contact with fans, friends, co-workers, people you cover, your covering, and other interested parties with whom you work regularly.

- Make sure your software and email systems are up-to-date. A hacked email used to send out hacker spam is a good way to lose ministry interest because people start blocking your email address.

As we've learned in this section of this book, writing for ministry does not have to be intimidating. Writing the basics is an essential aspect of ministry work and can prove to be a great foundational blessing to any ministry, especially one that is growing. By writing for our ministries, we make the vision plain, that the herald of this ministry may run forth with it.

SECTION II

ORGANIZE THE VISION

CHAPTER EIGHT

THE ESSENCE OF ORGANIZATION

For though I am absent from you in body,
I am present with you in spirit
and delight to see how orderly you are
and how firm your faith in Christ is.
(Colossians 2:5)

WRITING the vision is the first essential step to organizing God's vision. It's an undeniably important step, but it is not where organization begins and ends. Now that we have written the vision, we must move into the next stages of organizing the vision.

Organization is not something one will hear much about in preaching or even in most Bible colleges or training programs. Behind organization is the heart of God's order within our work. One consistent theme I have noted through many years of ministry is the disordered nature of most ministries. We will note their disorder in attitudes of defiance and disrespect, but it manifests in non-verbal areas, as well. They may not function well in events, schedule many events and cancel them at the last minute, have difficulty speaking for other people, or fail to bring visions to pass, time after time. In order to bring events to pass, host successful events, or manifest various visions within a ministry, there must be a sense of order manifest through organization.

Ministers often believe God will help them bring

ministry to pass through some sort of mystical experience. Everything will work out because God is behind it, and they won't have to take initiative or do anything themselves to bring their visions to pass. It is true that God does bring ministry events to pass, and that He does help us. The way He does it is not mystical or mysterious: it is through us. It is through the applied working of the saints. If we apply His principles, precepts, and are obedient to Him and understanding His organization, our business working will be far more effective than if we just wait and hope a miracle will occur. Nobody likes paperwork. Every minister I know would rather be out working in the field in the harvest of souls as opposed to working out legal matters and checking financial issues. What we must step back and recognize is that we will be far more effective at the tasks we do take on if we will only apply ourselves to organization in ministry.

This lack of organization is another reason why most ministries fail within the first few years of establishment. A disordered ministry is an unsuccessful and ineffective ministry. God calls His people to operate in decency and order (1 Corinthians 14:40), which means we are going to organize the vision He gives us. We can't charge full-steam ahead without proper organization and plans. Ministry events don't come to fruition without months of proper planning and notification. We too must organize whatever divisions of ministry God has appointed for us to establish.

Organizing a vision takes on both business and spiritual aspects for its powerful implementation. Here we will be looking at several major areas of organization: ministry logistics, federal 501(c)(3) non-profit status, charitable status around the world, documents every minister must have, necessary business skills, business arrangements, making decisions about ministry direction, things we're not supposed to say about being in ministry, time management, and establishing ministry support, following, and all about events.

CHAPTER NINE

MINISTRY LOGISTICS

At that time the Kingdom of heaven will be like ten virgins
who took their lamps and went out to meet the bridegroom.
Five of them were foolish and five were wise.
The foolish ones took their lamps but did not take any oil with them.
The wise, however, took oil in jars along with their lamps.
The bridegroom was a long time in coming,
and they all became drowsy and fell asleep.
At midnight the cry rang out: 'Here's the bridegroom! Come out to meet him!'
"Then all the virgins woke up and trimmed their lamps.
The foolish ones said to the wise, 'Give us some of your oil;
our lamps are going out.' 'No,' they replied,
'there may not be enough for both us and you.
Instead, go to those who sell oil and buy some for yourselves.'
But while they were on their way to buy the oil, the bridegroom arrived.
The virgins who were ready went in with him to the wedding banquet.
And the door was shut.
(Matthew 25:1-10)

EVERY minister wants to be successful at ministry. Even though ministers may have different understandings of success, every minister wants to be good at what they do and see God's vision come to pass. Ministers envision the day when they will hear the words, *"Well done, good and faithful servant: you have been faithful with few things, so I will put you in charge of many things"* (Matthew 25:21). There aren't many secrets to becoming an effective and successful minister. The foundations of all successful ministries are an active, effective anointing, and good planning.

Success in ministry – by any standards – has, unfortunately, become uncommon. It is not that the church lacks anointing; on the contrary, there are many well-equipped and anointed ministers who are graced by God for ministry. There are many who are unsuccessful, however, because they do not discipline themselves unto making ministry an effective, productive means of Gospel proclamation. This does not happen by anointing alone, but also happens by good planning. One of the most important ways we see good planning in effect is by effective business operation in ministry, commonly called logistics.

The word "logistics" is a business term. According to wikipedia.com, "Logistics is the management of the flow of goods between the point of origin and the point of destination in order to meet the requirements of customers or corporations. Logistics involves the integration of information, transportation, inventory, warehousing, material handling, and packaging, and often security. Today the complexity of production logistics can be modeled, analyzed, visualized and optimized by plant simulation software, but is constantly changing. This can involve anything from consumer goods such as food, to IT materials, to aerospace and defense equipment. The term logistics comes from the Greek logos (λόγος), meaning "speech, reason, ratio, rationality, language, phrase", and more specifically from the Greek word logistiki (λογιστική), meaning accounting and financial organization."[1] To explain this a little bit simpler, logistics is the chain of supply and demand. It starts with the most basic of understandings about existence, production, and getting desired production to the desired consumer. Businesses spend several million dollars annually in the study of logistics. The goal within a business setting is to keep the flow of logistics moving because it is the key to productivity. Within the business world, there is also the intense push to expedite the logistics process, so consumers can receive the product in less time.

The people who do not seem to understand the basic principles of logistics are ministers. We should be very attentive to the notation of logistics, because the word *logos* is foundational to its understanding. The word *logos* is the root for the word *logistiki*, which relates to accounting and financial organization. This means that the *Logos* – Jesus – is the foundation of all types of organization, organizational flow, organizational purpose, and yes, even order in flow and business. Functional, empowering ministry operates by logistics as much as any business does. In order to be successful in ministry, we must understand and operate in logistics, because they are the practical side of God's operation of order.

Creation is a process

Theologians, Bible scholars, and religious professionals of various world religions have spent thousands of years trying to uncover the message in the story of creation found in Genesis 1 and 2. Depending on their level of study, all of them have walked away with differing opinions. Some believe the story is literal, some believe it is figurative, some think the story is about cycles of work and rest, and still others believe there is any number of different precepts hidden within its contents. One of the most obvious – glaringly obvious – precepts found in the Biblical account of creation is that of process. In recounting the story of creation, God is letting His people know that creating anything comes about by process, because creation is a process. The same is true for anything we co-create with God: it happens by process. Creation doesn't happen by accident, without planning, and without proper preparation.

Ministry logistics prove creation is a process, and the creation of a ministry is, likewise a process of creation. In ministry today many are trying to bring about ministry via a means of "accident." They are waiting for God to drop a divine miracle in their lap and the ministry to blossom from it. This is contrary to God's principle of creation by process. Ministries don't happen by accident, nor do great ministers happen by accident; they happen because people walk with God through the process of ministry creation. If we better understand logistics, we can understand them as an essential part of the process of our ministry creation, maintenance, and success. Creation is an ongoing process. God is always creating new people, birthing forth new people in ministry, and bringing forth new revelation and purpose in His people. In ministry, as in the Spirit, creation continues to require process and planning as God's minister moves forward in Christ.

The wise and foolish virgins: A story illustrating good and bad logistics

I open this chapter with the Bible passage about the wise and foolish virgins for one reason: it is, in essence, a story of logistics. The wise virgins didn't rely on other people to get the job done for them or the "kindness of strangers;" they knew the bridegroom was coming and they needed to be prepared for his arrival. The foolish virgins relied on the hope that when the bridegroom came, someone else could help them out of their spot. While the wise virgins relied on good sense and themselves, the foolish virgins didn't plan things out for themselves to the very end.

If statistics are any indication, most ministries today fall in the category of the foolish virgins. They believe that help will come for whatever they need, but take no steps toward facilitating projects and ministry visions themselves. Yes, in ministry, we need a good staff, we need assistance from time to time, and we need help. However, we need to stop thinking all our problems in ministry will be solved if we had more help, more money, or a bigger following. The wise virgins worked with what they had, and it was more than enough. They carefully planned out the amount of oil they had and made a point to bring whatever was going to be needed. The foolish virgins didn't think about the future, or how they would get to the bridegroom if he came forth late. This is where we are missing the boat in modern ministry. We need to think in terms of persistence until Jesus gets back. This means we plan our ministries accordingly, from start to finish. Each project, each event, each assignment given to us from the Lord must be properly carried out, so we will have enough stamina, resources, and vision to see us through from start to finish.

The concept of ministry is simple enough to most: we seek to get our message out. With a simple concept comes great planning. We have to stop relying on the kindness or hopes of others to do what God has told us to do. We have to stop avoiding business mindsets, proper planning, and decent order when it comes to the assignments of the heavenly Father. If we are to be about our Father's business, we must have plenty of oil for that lamp, and that is accomplished through working logistics in ministry from start to finish.

Logistics in Gospel proclamation

If we think of logistics as the chain of supply and demand, the principles of logistics apply to every area of ministry. Ministry is, in its essence, a form of communicating the Gospel through God's service. If we understand ministry in these parameters, the bottom line of ministry is communication. In ministry, we are communicating the Gospel message however God graces us to communicate it. Some people preach, some people minister through counseling or social service, some people write, some people teach, some people do all of the above, and still others minister in a way that may be different from these. In understanding logistics to Gospel proclamation in the example of preaching, the "chain of supply and demand" could be explained like this:

- Ministry starts with God's call to minister in the individual.

- The individual discerns the ministry call.

- The individual is prepared for ministry by God working in them and the educational opportunities God provides for them.

- The individual is licensed, ordained, or both.

- The individual completes the necessary legal steps to operate their ministry within their domicile.

- The individual promotes the ministry and advertises its purpose.

- The individual receives an invitation to minister and accepts the invitation.

- Arrangements are made on behalf of the individual to travel to the location to accept the invitation

- The individual spends time preparing the message in order to preach the message: research, sermon preparation, etc.

- As the date approaches, the individual prepares in other ways, such as preparing in packing, grooming, dressing, and spiritually preparing through prayer and seeking God.

- The invited minister then makes the trip to the location where they will minister. From this point on, they stay where they will be lodged, prepare for the meeting, are transported to the meeting location, and deliver the Word and minister. They are then paid for their service in the form of an offering.

This is a clear picture within the chain of logistics: the minister has gone from invitation to fulfillment in the various steps above. The process may take days, weeks, months, or sometimes, even years, but the process itself remains the same. That process, from beginning to end, is logistics.

Logistics as apply to Gospel proclamation also apply in any facet of ministry that involves planning and procedure. Often we make the mistake of thinking we can pull off ministry events and productions with God on our side and the Holy Spirit's inspiration. I don't question for a second that God is on our side or that the Holy Spirit inspires our work. I also would remind everyone who thinks an event just comes together by the snap of faith and no hard work that God does things with decency and order. From the beginning of creation, God has shown us that all things Kingdom come together by process. God's encouragement and the Holy Spirit's inspiration show in our process – i.e., in our logistics. Logistics shows that we have thought things through, examined possible steps and facets, and continued on in the process, through to the very end. If we are going to operate street ministry, we need to know the various steps involved in having a street ministry: volunteers, dress code, purchasing materials to hand out, practice and role-playing training, dates and times for street ministry, and a post-event meet up for discussion among the participants. Even church services and ministry event services need to follow a certain order of protocol, seeing to it that things are done from start to finish.

Some basic principles to help develop productivity in ministry logistics

The concept of logistics is relatively obvious, but getting from start to finish can be challenging for ministers who don't understand some underlying principles to help launch logistical process. Here are some keys to developing a vision purposed for logistics:

- **Identify your audience** – The general statement for ministry is simple: "I want to reach the world" or "God gave me the vision to go to the nations." That's great, but it is not specific enough for marketing. Ministry, just like anything else, has to be marketed properly and to the proper audience. Who is it within those nations, within the world, that God wants you to reach? "Everybody" is not the right answer; it is, yet again, too non-specific. Let's say you run a ministry that specializes in healing and deliverance. Is 'everybody' in need of healing and deliverance? Maybe, but the correct answer for logistical purposes is that your audience is to "people in need of healing and deliverance." If we are to be more specific, you could say that your ministry is for "those who have been hurt, rejected, abused, mistreated, or wounded." You could go further, depending on your ministry, to say that the ministry is for "those who have been physically, emotionally, mentally, or sexually abused." In the case of deliverance, you could say that your ministry is for "those who have experienced situations in their lives causing them to deal with demonic possession, strongholds, and issues of spiritual, mental, or physical captivity." Someone who is called to work with women needs to specify that purpose of their ministry. When dealing with a ministry with multiple divisions that are each for a different audience, each division should properly identify their audience. For example, my ministry is Spitfire Apostolic Ministries. Within that heading, we have Apostolic University (for education and leaders), the Ephesians 4:11 Missions Society (for missionaries) and Sanctuary International Fellowship Tabernacle - SIFT (our church division). My main ministry identity is the general ministry work we do, and each of these divisions focuses on specific areas of ministry work.

- **Relate to your audience** – Once you know your audience, it's important that your ministry work relates to your audience. For example, a youth minister would never host a youth gathering at a country club or golf course. Doing so would show the youth minister doesn't have the first clue about youth, what they need, and what they are looking for. A women's minister would never hold a women's luncheon at a strip club, because this would show they didn't have the first clue about women, what they need, and what they are looking for. These are obvious signs that a minister isn't relating to their audience, but it is amazing to note the many little ways which a minister often comes across as judgmental or insincere with their target audience. It's important to relate to your audience because people need to believe you understand where they are coming from in order to believe you have an answer to the problem or circumstance they may find themselves in. If you don't do this, your audience won't be receptive to the message you have. Relating to your audience encompasses the entire spectrum of how you will be perceived by them, from how you dress, to how you carry yourself, to where you hold a meeting, to who your guest speakers are, to how you speak, to what you share with them, and to the style and manner in which you carry yourself during times of ministering (such as laying on of hands) and offering. How you carry yourself should tap into reaching your audience as much as your message does.

- **Identify the needs of the audience** – Identifying the needs of the group you are called to minister to is essential for effective ministry marketing and the probably logistical steps for each phase of ministry. The needs of homeless people are radically different than the needs of a childhood sexual abuse victim who is now an adult, married and with children of her own. What kind of teaching does your audience need? How can you effectively communicate the message of hope your audience needs to receive? What kind of events, support, counseling, material items, etc. are needed for this audience? If you know the needs of your audience, it is far easier to plan the logistical steps to meet those needs. Don't guess, don't presume, and don't establish the needs based only on your own personal experience. Doing an examination of your ministry work, talking to people about it or those who are participating in it, getting feedback from those who attend or participate in events, taking surveys, getting testimonies, and watching the general 'type' of person who follows your ministry helps you to know more about the needs you are meeting, and delve deeper into the needs that exist in their lives.

- **Don't attempt to "over produce" a number of products in too many different directions** – We all know major name brands for no more than a few items they have come to produce, and produce well. For example: Land O'Lakes is known for butter, not cars. Nabisco makes crackers, not jet fuel. Ministers often feel they need to expand the ministry in as many directions as possible, even if those ministries aren't really needed. If your ministry only has a handful of people and none of them are children, there is no need to preoccupy yourself with a nursery team. If a ministry has no singles, a singles' ministry should not be a priority. Focus on what your ministry is good at and is working for your ministry, and expand out as necessary. Don't try to be in so many different directions that the basic needs of the ministry get ignored.

- **Don't ignore the basics of general marketing** – Logistics are the production of marketing. They pertain to the entire process by which an item, good, message, service, or anything else makes it from concept to consumer. In this process are extensive marketing basics that help the desired recipient know the product exists. I know we do ministry by the grace of God and with His anointing...but people still need to know that your organization exists to meet their need. God doesn't send out personal invitations to every person in the world who needs to benefit from your ministry work! Knowing your audience and how to relate to your audience gives you the ability to reach out to your audience. Flyers, teaching CDs and DVDs, books, postcards, posters, internet marketing, word-of-mouth, and more all give people the opportunity to receive the message you seek to give to them. Advertising as part of logistics and logistics in general are steps to reach those people – a bridge, if you will – that crosses time and space and makes your audience reachable rather than distant.

- **Know what is important to your audience** – Values differ between audiences. If you are called to minister to the nation of India, their values, cultures, and social customs are very different from those found in the United States. The things that may be important to a man may be different from things important to a woman, and the things that are important to married couples are radically different than things important to youth or teens. You need to know what is important to your audience because values play heavily into the type of needs people have. What is most important to your audience most likely reflects the spiritual needs, issues, and difficulties they have.

- **Be "known" for something** – Most ministers want to be known for the ministry work they run. This is admirable, but in order to be known for ministry work, people first need to know you, the minister. While working in ministry, it's essential that you are known for something that gives an 'edge' or 'kick' to your work. Many display this in a slogan, motto, or a general way of being that helps others to learn more about them. In a more practical vain, what you are "known" for should be something that reveals a side of your personality to your audience. For example, Lucille Ball was known for her red hair. Aimee Semple McPherson was known for being exceedingly dramatic. I am known for wearing fashionable and very high shoes. The things we are "known" for in ministry allow people to know something about us, without having to tell them about it. It helps people to identify our interests with us, and identify those signatures with our ministry work.

- **Plan your steps in ministry** – Every time you get a vision, assignment, idea, or event, plan your steps to bring that specific assignment to fruition. Don't skip planning because you will miss steps, forget important facets, or miss something essential in the vision. Meet with others and take heed in wise counsel. Surround yourself with people who desire to see the work God placed within you succeed, and will work with you to help bring that ministry vision to pass. Plan steps accordingly according to the specific work or assignment. Having plans also helps to encourage in the process, as completing each step is an accomplishment.

- **Identify what is needed on each level of the logistical process to bring the desired product to fruition** – This goes hand-in-hand with planning steps of ministry. Identify the needs of each level, or "step," in a logistics process. For example, if it takes fourteen people to complete a step, make sure you have those fourteen people before you take on the step. Make sure you have all the proper and needed equipment, manpower, and vision to bring each step to pass.

The logistics of self-marketing and identity

The bottom line of marketing any product is the person behind that marketing. In the case of ministry, it is the minister themselves. As we grow up in church hearing about the evils of pride and self-idolization, most ministers are thoroughly unaware of the proper way to market themselves. This is not pride or self-idolization, it is making sure that people connect you to your ministry assignment. You wouldn't want people to confuse your work with that of another minister, and the way you do that is through yourself. On the surface, most ministries today often sound a lot alike. With store-front churches in every strip mall in America, the only difference between what one church offers and another is the assignment and vision of that minister – not to mention the personality driving that ministry.

Ministers need to know that the most effective logistical tool they have is themselves. Within that individual is God's vision and the drive to bring that vision from a divine revelation to each person who needs to partake therein. This means that, while we can't run a ministry on personality alone, the people we are – with all of our God-given talents, anointing, and abilities - is an important part in our logistics process. Ministers need to know themselves and know the ways in which God has anointed them so as to specifically pursue the areas of ministry that will bring forth the anointing in full-force. If you are anointed to preach, you should preach. If you are not anointed to preach, that means you shouldn't market yourself as a preacher, but find the avenue or area of ministry that will bring forth the gifting of God. Whatever you are called to do, that is what you market to the world. The image you want people to have of your work comes from you: your personal presentation, how you dress, how you carry yourself, and how you do the work that you do. This is how you get people to realize that you have a message that can help and empower them. No matter the message or audience you are called thereto, if you don't know yourself and how to market yourself, you can't reach that audience.

Production

One of the basic tenets I learned as a philosophy major was "production precedes existence." There is simple, and yet profound wisdom in that statement. For anything to exist – any stage of a ministry, any purpose of a vision, or any aspect of a ministry assignment to come to pass, it must first be produced. Production is the formation of your product, which is, in the case of ministry, your message. The logistical process for production flows in many different areas and in many different ways. Throughout this book, we talk about both the personal and professional processes as pertain to production for your ministry. Production in the instance we are discussing here relates simply to bringing forth a desired product – whether it is a television show, book, CD or DVD, or even the process of a local outreach ministry. To bring something to pass, you need the four "m's" of production: money, materials, manpower, and motivation.

- **Money** – In order to produce anything, you need to have the money to back up the project. This is where budgeting and research come in very handy. Projects must be budgeted to understand cost and plan other like-projects in the future. This means that the product of every project costs money, and the consumer should be charged for the product accordingly. The Gospel is free, but we still have to buy a Bible. The Word of God we proclaim is free, but we still have to sell the CDs, DVDs, and books because the production therein comes at an expense to the minister. We don't live in a day and age where we can walk in the street and trust someone will take us in, cover our meals and lodging because of a sense of hospitality, and allow us to remain in their home until we are done proclaiming the Gospel to everyone in that city as we visit them in the marketplaces and the streets. Today information is conveyed through media – television, radio, internet – and through the recorded and printed word – CDs, DVDs, books, magazines, and newspapers. Conveying information via these means comes at a cost – and therefore we must have the necessary funds to continue conveying this message.

- **Materials** – If you are going to bring something to pass, you need the materials or items to do so. It's improbable to think you are going to do something without the necessary items. It's also impractical to tackle a project without knowing what you need to have to do it, hoping what you need will just fall into your lap. Know what you need and have those things available to you at the start.

- **Manpower** – Different projects can be accomplished by different numbers of people. If someone is a decent self-starter and has a basic knowledge of a project at hand, they may not need a lot of other people to help them bring it to fruition. Other projects may require more help, assistance, or involvement. Have an idea of the level of help you need, the skills needed to assist in the project, and how many people need to be involved to bring the project to pass.

- **Motivation** – It is essential that those who are involved in a project maintain their motivation. Logistics see things through from start to finish, not from start until they get difficult, uncomfortable, or undesirable. If God has given a vision or assignment, it needs to be seen through by all involved. If people leave along the way, the vision must continue.

The finished product

The finished product needs to be delivered to its audience. The means for delivery pertains to the nature of the product itself. If it's a book, it needs to be available to readers everywhere books are sold, as well as through the ministry itself. If it's a message, it needs to be presented, recorded on CD or DVD, and made available to those who would like to purchase a copy. The finished product must be marketed accordingly, made available where it needs to be made available, and presented in its finished form, completed from start to finish.

CHAPTER TEN

501(C)(3) NON-PROFIT STATUS

At this, the administrators and the satraps tried to find grounds
for charges against Daniel in his conduct of government affairs,
but they were unable to do so. They could find no corruption in him,
because he was trustworthy and neither corrupt nor negligent.
(Daniel 6:4)

MOST governments, both in the United States and abroad (we will discuss about some international countries in the next chapter), grant and recognize certain organizations to have a special status: that of a legal charity. This categorization establishes these organizations as federally exempt from paying corporate income tax to their national governments. In the case of the United States, corporate income tax can be a serious financial blow to a growing ministry or even an established one, at the rate of 30%.

Within the jurisdiction of the United States, a non-profit entity receives their charitable status as recognized through the Internal Revenue Service. Through a standard process, an individual files for charitable non-profit status under the federal 501(c)(3) code. This code is the standard federal guideline for defining a non-profit organization and what being classified as a non-profit entity means.

In understanding the concept behind the federal corporate tax exemption, we must understand two major points of identifying federally recognized charities: being non-profit and being a charity. Being non-profit means that the purpose of the organization is not the personal profit of any partners in the organization, i.e., its purpose is not to generate personal income. This does not prevent non-profit corporations and organizations from paying their executives or staff, but it does prevent them from misusing funds for personal purposes, such as trying to declare personal property as "tax-exempt" or taking salaries beyond a reasonable range. For example, the president of a non-profit organization cannot take a yearly salary comprising millions of dollars without running the risk of losing their tax exemption. Tax-exempt charities must keep careful records of earnings and be clear to separate personal earnings from charitable earnings. The second thing we must understand is the concept of being a "charity." This means that, in order to be deemed non-profit and tax-exempt, the organization must serve a purpose to benefit the greater good. A tax-exempt organization provides a service to the public for the betterment of humanity rather than a corporation seeking to drive a profit.

According to federal statute, being a legally recognized non-profit charity is not a right, but a privilege extended by the government to qualifying agencies. This means that, in order to receive the exemption, the applying organization must meet certain requirements. Some today take great issue with this, but we must admit there must be standards to measure legitimate organizations against false ones. We've all heard stories of people who falsify charitable organizations and run off with people's life savings. Having a governmental status in place helps us to know who is legitimate and who is not, helps the government to prosecute criminals who lie about having charitable status, and also helps to prosecute those who try to misuse the status to simply avoid paying corporate tax. It also helps to raise up those who have legitimate organizations and provide them a way to do their work without having to incur taxation that would be considered excessive to such an organization.

Tax-exempt status is, in a nutshell, a classification given to organizations describing how they intend to use their funds and for what purpose they intend to use those funds. Because the funds are being used for certain purposes, the organization is exempt from paying federal income tax. To many, the laws and regulations surrounding 501(c)(3) status are confusing and convoluted. It doesn't help that many exaggerations and false statements circulate via the internet about what it means to have non-profit status and what organizations can or cannot do.

If you are going to have a ministry that is accepted on a level beyond a local group, desire to receive donations or solicit funding, or receive grants, it is essential you seek out federal non-profit status if your organization meets the criteria as laid out by the IRS. Understanding about this important aspect of tax law is essential to every church and ministry in the United States today.

The big question on the mind of most is, who is eligible for 501(c)(3) status? The following is found on the Internal Revenue Service's website about what is defined as an "exempt purpose:"

"The exempt purposes set forth in section 501(c)(3) are charitable, religious, educational, scientific, literary, testing for public safety, fostering national or international amateur sports competition, and preventing cruelty to children or animals. The term *charitable* is used in its generally accepted legal sense and includes relief of the poor, the distressed, or the underprivileged; advancement of religion; advancement of education or science; erecting or maintaining public buildings, monuments, or works; lessening the burdens of government; lessening neighborhood tensions; eliminating prejudice and discrimination; defending human and civil rights secured by law; and combating community deterioration and juvenile delinquency."[1]

From this definition, the following types of organizations are eligible for tax exemption:

- **Charities** – Organizations giving some sort of aid (financial, material, etc.) to the poor, those affected by natural disasters or some other type of cataclysm; or those giving some sort of support to an individual for their betterment.

- **Religious** – Any organization devoted to the promotion and growth of their spiritual beliefs. This includes those who gather for the expressed purpose of worship, study, or promotion. Also included under this heading is any service or charity work done as part of religious or spiritual beliefs.

- **Educational** – Organizations devoted to educational purposes, such as primary, middle, and high schools; colleges and universities; and the promotion of education without the purpose of generating profit. (Note: accreditation of an educational institution is different from an organization being declared tax-exempt.)

- **Scientific** – Any organization devoted to scientific advancement, study, or understanding.

- **Literary** – Organizations that devote themselves to the promotion of literacy or literary understanding, including the education of reading and distribution of materials for that purpose.

- **Civic** – A civic organization works to better a city or to help a city organization operate better via volunteerism. Civic work includes the care of public buildings, monuments, or "works," such as park maintenance. Civic workers may also work volunteer projects, such as highway adoptions or roadside trash pickup. It can also include a neighborhood watch, as the purpose of such an organization is to assist the city police department.

- **Testing for public safety** – Independent organizations that assess things such as helmets, seat belts, airbags, pesticides, chemicals, or preservatives, or test any other thing or claim to ensure the safety of that product against their independent research.

- **Fostering national or international amateur sports competition** – Such organizations organize events for the promotion of a cause and to foster good will between persons and countries (such as the Special Olympics).

- **Preventing cruelty to children or animals** – Organizations that work to protect both children and animals from abuse or mistreatment, as well as educate on the subjects at hand.

- **Eliminating prejudice and discrimination** – Any organization devoted to promoting human rights and advocating for human rights, either nationally or internationally.

- **Defending human and civil rights as defined by law** – Organizations designed to uphold human and civil rights when there is a question or violation of such. These organizations may work with specified groups of people (such as the poor) or in general. They may do legal representation or give legal advice, or work, within limits, to change legislation on certain issues.

- **Combating community deterioration and juvenile delinquency** – Any organization devoted to community betterment, be it rebuilding after a disaster, working against gang activity, fixing old or historic buildings, restoring a community or historic district, planting trees or flowers, or any community betterment project; or any organization devoted to providing activities for youth or education to prevent them from embracing lives that encourage crime and illegal activity.

Now that we understand more about who is eligible to be exempt, let's look at the requirements for tax exemption. The following is found on the Internal Revenue Service's website about tax exemption requirements:

"To be tax-exempt under section 501(c)(3) of the Internal Revenue Code, an organization must be organized and operated exclusively for exempt purposes set forth in section 501(c)(3), and none of its earnings may inure to any private shareholder or individual. In addition, it may not be an *action organization, i.e.,* it may not attempt to influence legislation as a substantial part of its activities and it may not participate in any campaign activity for or against political candidates.

"Organizations described in section 501(c)(3) are commonly referred to as *charitable organizations*. Organizations described in section 501(c)(3), other than testing for public safety organizations, are eligible to receive tax-deductible contributions in accordance with Code section 170.

"The organization must not be organized or operated for the benefit of private interests, and no part of a section 501(c)(3) organization's net earnings may inure to the benefit of any private shareholder or individual. If the organization engages in an excess benefit transaction with a person having substantial influence over the organization, an excise tax may be imposed on the person and any organization managers agreeing to the transaction.

"Section 501(c)(3) organizations are restricted in how much political and legislative (*lobbying*) activities they may conduct. For a detailed discussion, see Political and Lobbying Activities. For more information about lobbying activities by charities, see the article Lobbying Issues; for more information about political activities of charities, see the FY-2002 CPE topic Election Year Issues."[2]

Within this section of the IRS exemption code are many controversies that cause everything in ministries, ranging from total outrage to fear. Let's break down this to make it more understandable.

- To receive federal status as tax-exempt under 501(c)(3) Internal Revenue Code, an organization must be a corporation, an unincorporated association, community chest, fund, or organization. Most ministries and church organizations file as corporations, incorporated according to the laws of the state where the organization exists. Associations and trusts, although governed a little differently as they serve different purposes, follow a similar filing requirement according to state laws. While the laws vary from state to state, most states require a filing with either the State Attorney General or Secretary of State. This form is downloadable on most state websites, easy to fill out, and contains basic information about the corporation, its locations, main contact people, and bylaws about how the organization will handle board meetings and the governing body of the organization. Being an organization means one major thing: in order to receive status, the work cannot be controlled by one singular individual. A non-profit entity cannot be managed by only one person as to avoid it becoming about a singular person's interests. Incorporation affirms this principle when establishing a non-profit entity. Incorporation costs vary from state to state, but are typically inexpensive.

- Tax-exempt organizations must allocate their funds for their own exempt purposes. The charitable donations received may cover the costs and expenses to run the organization (including salaries) and any events or activities that are a part of its work, but they may not allocate funds for personal gain. Even when an organization dissolves, the remaining assets must go back into another public or charitable organization. This is a statement clarifying that all monies generated for this organization will forever be for non-profit purposes, whether the organization reaches an end or not.

- Organizations that are tax-exempt (with the exemption of public safety testing organizations) are entitled to receive contributions without those contributions being subject to corporate federal taxation. Tax-exempt organizations are required to provide receipt for donations over the amount of $75 to the donor. If there is a disclosure made in the solicitation of such a fund (clarifying its charitable tax-exempt status), the organization is not required to provide a specified receipt.

- Non-profit organizations are not operated for the purpose of private benefit. This is another statement on the way non-profit funds are allocated. In other words, the purpose of a non-profit organization is not to make money or generate financial profit.

- If finances are received for the purposes of benefiting a certain individual or given by the organization to someone who disqualifies from receiving such a benefit, the organization is subject to taxation as well as any members of the organization involved in the financial transaction.

- Non-profit organizations must limit their political and lobbying activity. The reason for this is simple: money for a charitable purpose cannot be used to line the pockets of a political campaign or candidate because political activity and contributions are handled differently under tax law. Political work, contrary to popular belief, is a government function, and not about the betterment of humanity. Money that is otherwise specified for a specific organizational purpose cannot be given to a private individual campaign because that translates to shareholder and personal interest with tax-exempt funds. The law does not prohibit organizations from all participation in lobbying, but it does prohibit using tax-exempt money for campaigns or candidates. The level of lobbying and involvement allowed depends upon the organization's purpose, and what issues are of relevance to the federal standing or funding of that organization. For example, an educational organization would be very interested in laws which pertain to the governing of federal aid, and an organization giving medical care to the poor while receiving federal funding would be very interested in maintaining their level of funding or increasing it. As these decisions are legislators, they are allowed a lobbying privilege. In matters of Christian ministry, lobbying is a sticky subject. It is not prohibited for individuals, but becomes precarious for organizations, especially when the matter is one of a personal belief on a subject that has no legal pertinence to the organization (such as the death penalty or sex education) rather than an issue that pertains directly to the organization (such as funding for a specified community betterment project).

Then there is the matter of understanding public status and private status. A federally recognized tax-exempt organization can be either a public organization or a private organization. Most churches and religious organizations are headed under the category of a public organization. Public organizations are so-called because they receive most of their funding from the public: through donations, public grants, fundraising, and collections. As a result, holdings, reports, and the bookkeeping of an organization is subject to public inspection at any time upon request. Private organizations receive their financial holdings from private individuals, trusts, private grants, or organizations other than the public or those with public interest. Once again, it is a matter of where money comes from and how that money is allocated.

There are many debates about filing with the IRS for non-profit status. Contrary to some beliefs about the process and what the status means, there are benefits to being a federally recognized 501(c)(3).

- **Being a federally recognized non-profit organization gives validity to the organization in the eyes of the public** – I know a lot of Christians don't care about the court of public opinion, but the reality remains: our purpose as a Christian organization is to reach out to people. If the people we work with find a reason to question us, we run the potential of losing our target audience. Having the status gives an automatic credibility to the work as it is recognized for its charitable purpose. It also shows an organization has put in thought and time to its purpose and creation, giving it direction and clarity.

- **It is easier to receive donations** – It is not easy to receive donations for work without non-profit status. People are leery about giving to something with no legitimacy to back it up. It is also impossible to receive donations from corporations or companies (even for local events) such as Wal-Mart or Target without non-profit status. It can be difficult to get community or national endorsement from other non-profit agencies. Now sites such as Paypal.com will not authorize an organization to receive donations without evidence of non-profit status. We all know ministries operate by finances, and if we can do something to help us receive those finances, it is best we take the action to do it.

- **If you have non-profit status, you can apply for grant money** – There are few grant organizations that will give grant money to an organization without tax-exempt status. Even if you can find one that will give you a grant, you will have to pay corporate income tax on that money.

- **God calls us to submit ourselves to government leadership (Romans 13:1)** – None of us likes having to stop at a red light when we are in a hurry, but we stop because it is the law. In order to be recognized as having certain tax-exempt benefits, we must submit ourselves to the law. In keeping with that law, we must agree to do certain things to receive that benefit. Having the attitude that we will just do what we please because we don't like the regulations is not a Christian attitude.

- **God tells us to give to Him what belongs to Him (Matthew 22:21)** – Giving 30% of donations received for God's work is rendering unto Caesar what belongs to God. Just as we must give our personal tax as that is due, we also must make sure we do not cross finances and give to the government what has been reserved for God. As ministries, our donations and funding should be tax-exempt because they are set aside for the sacred work of God's Kingdom.

There are numerous reasons why people think obtaining tax-exempt status is a bad idea. Most of the time, these individuals have only partial information about the status and process. It is almost always received from organizations or individuals who believe tax-exempt status is a threat to the church and to public interest. Some go as far as to say the purpose is to execute a 'gag order' on Christians and ministers, eliminating a spiritual presence from the political scene. These vocal advocates circulate blogs and letters among the internet, creating intense confusion about what it means to have tax exempt status. As a result, many do not receive this important exemption and hurt their own work in the process.

The history of modern Christian movements has been

filled with a love-hate relationship with the federal government. Prior to the 1960s, Evangelicals across the board discouraged Christian involvement with the federal system, believing the government to be a part of the world. It wasn't until Christian Reconstructionism in the 1960s (a harsh movement advocating penal law and Old Testament code should be implemented by the American government) and subsequent cases against Bob Jones University in the 1960s and 1970s (all centering around racism) that Christians felt the need to involve themselves in American politics. Now many Christians understand American history differently, their place in American government in a different way than their ancestors did, and also take extreme issue with any legislation or regulation applied to what they perceive to be their rights.

It is this concept of entitlement without justification that is behind the anti-tax exempt movement. Whether we like it or not, there are laws that govern our right to run certain types of organizations. Not just anyone can claim they run a tax-exempt organization and solicit people for money. We don't like it when people do this to us, but then we don't want to follow the regulations, either. We can't cry religious discrimination because we don't like the rules. It is also worth noting: whether or not a church or ministry has a formal 501(c)(3) filing, they are still subject to IRS laws pertaining to non-profit status. In other words, they still cannot back political candidates and must uphold policies against racism.

I think it would benefit the church to step back and ask ourselves why we're so preoccupied with politics and politicians in the first place. Is it really worth the cost of nullifying tax exemption to we can back a candidate who, in the long run, probably lies about having our interests at heart? Why are we so preoccupied with a kingdom that will pass away when we have a heavenly Kingdom to advance? It is to our benefit to agree not to give organizational devotion to a human being and maintain our status, where everything we receive can benefit God's work.

- **Any religious organization can be tax exempt** – This is a bad argument against tax exemption. Some believe that, because groups such as the Church of Satan and several pagan organizations have tax exemption, Christians shouldn't have it because then they are somehow "on par" with these groups. As was examined above, tax exemption is a wide scope encompassing several types of organizations that meet the criteria as explained in the 501(c)(3) federal tax code. Receiving this status is not a spiritual validation of legitimacy, but an agreement on how the finances and business of an organization will run. Having the status does not in any way change Christian belief or force Christians to change what they believe. If we apply such logic, it also means Christian ministries are "on par" with the Humane Society, organizations that test seat belts for safety, and the ACLU. Nobody ever makes this comparison because it sounds absurd when we do. The same is true when we apply it to varying religious groups with differing beliefs. It's also untrue that any religious organization can be tax exempt. If the organization does not fit the criteria, they are not eligible for tax exemption, no matter their doctrine.

- **The 501(c)(3) tax code threatens religious freedoms** – The purpose of the 501(c)(3) tax code is to identify organizations that qualify for tax-exempt status. It has nothing to do with religious freedom. Anyone can coin themselves a religion of one sort or another and then say they shouldn't have to pay tax, but not everyone can prove they have a legitimately qualifying organization. 501(c)(3) is for those who can prove they are legitimate.

- **Getting the status means the government tells you what you can or can't say, and you can't speak out about a bunch of current topics (New World Order, occult, abortion, etc.)** – Having federal non-profit status does not suddenly mean you are no longer an individual with an opinion, nor does it mean you suddenly have no freedom of speech. A ministry or church does not have to change their beliefs or viewpoints on any topic or current event because they become 501(c)(3). There are entire ministries devoted to last days events, current issues, cult watching, religious commentaries, news stories, and a host of things – and they are all tax-exempt. They do not lose their status for their positions. The only immediate social issues at hand for which an organization can lose its status are racial discrimination and endorsing political candidates.

- **There are rules to follow** – It amazes me that the most rigid, stiff, legalistic people can be the most vocal opponents against federal non-profit status. Their reason? Having the status means you have to follow certain guidelines. It is true that in order to be tax-exempt, you must meet certain criteria. To maintain your status, you must follow the guidelines. If a ministry is in alignment with the criteria, as a rule, making the switch to being a federally recognized 501(c)(3) non-profit isn't that big of a deal.

- **You can't back politicians, tell people who to vote for, or raise money for candidates** – How much control do you need to have over those under your ministry? Who to vote for or which candidate you like best based on a personal preference has no bearing on your ministry leadership or development. Beyond that, if you really think it's worth it to pay 30% corporate tax to back a candidate who you are not ever going to influence no matter what you think of yourself...I think it's better to examine your priorities. Ministry money and purpose are not to back a political candidate. If it's that important to you, you can take as much of your own personal money as you like to back that person – but leave God's money for ministry, not someone's private interests.

Another common issue often raised about non-profit status pertains to the separation of monies. When an organization is tax-exempt, it means just that: the organization is tax-exempt. The organization has the status, not the people working for the organization. The status does not entitle ministry or church employees to stop paying personal income tax on personal income. If you are receiving a salary from a federal non-profit, you are still required to pay income tax on the payment you receive.

Having a tax-exempt organization that sells items through a store, website, or other facet specifically designed to sell items for the non-profit's benefit also requires specific financial separations from royalties and income generated from the same items as sold elsewhere. It is very important that individuals generating income from both for and non-profit sources understand the guidelines for such.

When selling items through your non-profit organization – even if they are items that are the same as those sold elsewhere – there is no personal royalty generated from those items. It is assumed that you have the option to take a salary and are paid through your non-profit in that way. If you sell your materials elsewhere, you are allowed to take a royalty on those items and must pay income tax on that generated income.

Most non-profits today sell items. Some sell many items, and others sell only a few. The way they must handle these finances is the same. When selling a product or service through a non-profit, the item or service is tax-exempt. It is not, however, considered to be a donation. People who purchase or receive these services cannot write these items off as a tax deduction. If an individual purchases or receives these services, paying in full for them, and then offering additional money, anything over the set amount for the service or item is considered to be a donation. That amount can be written off as a tax deduction.

Now that we have a better understanding of tax-exempt status, there is only one question that remains: when should a church or ministry file? Many churches, ministries, and other non-profits are often at a loss as to when they should apply for non-profit status. Some think it is advisable to immediately apply the second one has a vision, and still others wait many years to file for a variety of reasons.

The simplest answer about when to file is answered in the following way: you file when you need to file and when you are able to do so. To help identify this time in your ministry history, let me further explain.

According to federal tax law, there is nothing illegal, nor taxable about small groups meeting for worship or service. Churches are not required to formally file for federal non-profit status, as they are assumed to have such whether they file or not. The same is not true for ministries. If a minister intends to operate ministry beyond a local group, they are required to file to receive that status. It is still strongly recommended that a group files as it becomes necessary because having a determination letter makes many other things easier when it comes to tax write-offs, donations, contributions, and the like. Not filing can damage an organization in the long-term, whether a church or a ministry.

An organization should file for non-profit status as soon as the question of donations and funding starts to arise. Most people suggest a filing should occur when an organization has approximately twenty-five to fifty members. When an organization is very small, the giving of money between two individuals is considered a private payment between people. As finances continue to increase, the question raises about taxes and how to report payments incurred. If fundraising is to occur, the organization needs to have a tax exemption.

In dealing with ministry, the amount of money generated from sales, conferences, donations, tuitions, services, and fees also needs to be considered. It is also relevant how much money can be written off in the course of business expenses if one has incorporation status. The general vision of the ministry should be considered as well. When dealing with foreign entities, it is essential a ministry has legal documentation for their work. It is also essential when soliciting donations for a project, through television or radio, or for any type of assistance or relief.

The next question becomes, "How do I file?" Most organizations today use a professional preparer to apply for tax exempt status. The form involved in applying for tax-exempt status is 1023. Most ministers are notably intimidated by these preparations as the forms are excessively long and written in legal jargon. Being afraid to make a mistake and being rejected for status, most seek out a non-profit tax preparer.

Professional preparers can be lawyers or individuals with training to specify in both incorporation and non-profit paperwork. There are many things to consider when considering a preparer:

- **Are they knowledgeable in the topic at hand?** – There has been a rise in so-called Christian preparers for non-profits over the past five years. People think it's a quick and easy way to make money. This doesn't make them knowledgeable in the subject at hand, and doesn't mean they are good at what they do. Can they answer your questions about 501(c)(3) status? Do they understand the procedure? Do they know the ins and outs of the filing process? Have they ever done work that has been rejected? Can they offer testimonials about their services? All of this functions to select a proper preparer.

- **How much do they charge?** – Some preparers charge thousands upon thousands of dollars for a service that someone else may only charge a few hundred to complete. Just because someone charges a lot of money for their service doesn't mean they are experienced at what they do.

- **What kind of information do they need from you?** – Preparers need basic information to process your filing. Many prepare it via a simple form getting information about address, contact info, board members, purpose, mission statement, and the like.

They may ask some basic questions about your work, as well.

In order to be tax-exempt, all church and ministry organizations must have a board of directors for business directions. The purpose of a board of directors is to balance out the ideals of the organization, ensuring financial and business decisions are not to the benefit of any one individual's gain. In the church setting, the board of directors is usually composed of church elders and in the ministry setting, it is usually consisting of individuals who assist in a bishopric or other ministry leaders.

Selecting a board is usually a challenging task for someone with a new ministry vision. While many may be available, only a few can fit the specific description needed to fulfill the task. The guidelines for board members are typically established within an organization's bylaws. Those bylaws may be written by a preparer (if using one) or by the board itself. Bylaws relate to how often a board will meet, what they will discuss, and how the finances of the organization will function.

- Board meetings are usually held quarterly, or as often as is needed.

- During board meetings, agendas, new projects (such as fundraisers, business arrangements, new bylaws, etc.) are discussed. Matters are voted on by the general body and recorded by a secretary.

- Board members should share the beliefs and ideals of an organization, as well as support the vision. They should be familiar with the leader of the organization and with the work the organization has been established to do. Bylaws must be written so as to not threaten the position of the founder by a coup or board overthrow. There should also be no question or threat to the vision of the organization by any board member. If such an issue arises, board members can be terminated and replaced. It is expected that board members will change over time, for any number of reasons. There is no concern in changing or replacing these individuals, especially as an organization grows and their needs change.

- It is essential that, when selecting a board, board members are not related to the founder of the organization. The government deems boards consisting primarily of family members as 'familial control,' which translates to private interest. Board members can be friends, fellow workers in ministry, associates, or supporters – as long as they are not family members.

- A typical board requires at least five individuals, including the individual establishing the organization. The founder is the President of the board. Other offices required for a board are Secretary and Treasurer. These positions can be combined and held by a singular individual, if necessary.

- Board members need to be available for meetings, whether within the state the organization resides or not, or whether done via telephone, satellite, or internet conferencing. They also need to be able to discuss matters professionally and civilly, with respect and understanding about ministry matters.

Understanding the process to non-profit status is also extremely helpful, given the vast amount of information available on the topic. People often wonder what the next step is and grow concerned when they don't hear from the IRS immediately upon filing. Here are the steps involved in obtaining tax-exempt status:

- **Documentation** – The first step to legal non-profit status is documentation. It is the time to write whatever essential aspects of the work that have not yet been written, and if they have already been written, to gather them up and edit them. A Mission Statement, Vision, and Statement of Purpose are all essential documents describing the organization and are needed to show forth the thought and dedication for the organization. It is also important to provide a statement on activities and operations, different programs and events made available through the organization, and different services you will provide as part of your organization.

- **Gathering information** – To complete the process, an address to receive mail, operational address, telephone number, email address, website, a contact, board members (complete with names and addresses), and basic operational information must be gathered together and organized. Also: if you haven't yet, plan a financial budget for about five years, estimating costs and salaries.

- **Bylaws** – The bylaws must be written, clarifying name, purposes, offices, authority and duties of directors, committees, meetings, officers and employees, books and records, the corporate seal, financial administration, waivers of notice and notices, emergency powers, issuing finances, amendments, and indemnification.

- **Incorporation** – Incorporation is done through the state where the organization will hold its primary base. It is done by filling out a basic form containing the who, what, where, when, and why and is then filed with the secretary of state or attorney general's office. It is a reasonably inexpensive process, typically under $100. Within 27 months of filing for incorporation, an organization must apply for non-profit status.

- **Form 1023** – Form 1023 is a twelve-page, daunting, and complicated form required to receive charitable status under the federal 501(c)(3) code. It is filed out by providing basic information and then again reiterating specifications about the organization and its purpose to the IRS. The answers to these matters help to verify whether or not an organization is applicable for the status, and also how they will use or benefit from having that status. With this form must include purposes, vision, and board members.

- **User fees** – To process Form 1023, there are two established costs. Which one an organization pays depends on the budget they plan to have over the next four years. If a budget is estimated to be under $10,000 for the first four years, the organization pays $400. If the budget is estimated to be over $10,000, the organization pays $850. If an organization is eligible to submit 1023-EZ online, the cost is $275. There is no fee incurred if the organization makes over $10,000; these are just estimations given to determine possible income.

- **EIN** – An EIN is an Employer Identification Number. This number is assigned by the Internal Revenue Service to any corporation, whether for-profit or non-profit. In the case of non-profits, this number identifies your organization as being non-profit when individuals write off donations. When seeking donations, especially from businesses, you provide your EIN number. This number is assigned to you when the IRS receives your application for tax-exempt status and is sent to you via a letter.

- **Waiting** – Once you apply, you wait for several months. In this time frame, you can check updates on your status by calling and providing your EIN or searching at IRS.gov.

- **Determination** – Once a determination has been made, the IRS sends a letter about the determination. An organization's application has either been accepted or rejected. If the organization has been accepted, the determination letter must be kept on file, showing the status of the organization as tax-exempt. If the application has been rejected, the IRS will request further information, clarification, or detailing to process the application. The additional information, once provided, will go back for review. This will continue until the IRS can determine the proper status of the organization. Upon confirmation of status, some states require a non-profit organization to file as a charity through the state. Check your state laws for the regulations on this matter.

- **Annual reporting** – Tax-exempt organizations are required to report annually to the IRS using either Form 990, Form 990-PF, Form 990-N, or Form 990-EZ. When an organization's filings are under $25,000 (or recently increased to $50,000), they fill out Form 990-EZ, a simple postcard form online that declares the amount of money is under that amount and updates contact information. When the amount is over that, non-profit organizations must file Form 990, the long form detailing holdings, donations, and acquired finances. The other forms of 990 are for specific types of non-profit organizations. Some states also require non-profits to report annually to a state organization to maintain their status within the state where they reside.

The last thing we need to keep in mind with non-profit status is that it is a privilege. As with all privileges, it is possible for an organization to lose its non-profit status for certain reasons.

- Failure to comply with annual reporting guidelines
- Misappropriation of funds

- Providing for private interest
- Failure to follow guidelines laid out in the non-profit tax code
- Employing racism in hiring policies or in community work or involvement
- Backing political candidates

If an organization is sincere and holds to its purpose, there is no reason why it should do anything to violate its status. If having non-profit, tax-exempt status is sincerely sought and carefully upheld, there will be no problem in maintaining the status in the long-run.

CHAPTER ELEVEN

———◆———

CHARITABLE STATUS AROUND THE WORLD

He went through Syria and Cilicia,
strengthening the churches.
(Acts 15:41)

W HEN I first authored this book, I included information exclusively about tax exempt/charitable status within the United States. Since first writing this book in 2011, it has come to my attention that there are many ministries operating outreaches, missions, schools, or working with ministries overseas. In doing so, this makes it relevant to learn just what defines a ministry as being a legal, tax exempt organization in other countries. Because different countries have different systems, most ministers don't consider questioning foreign ministries about their legality or the intricacies of the systems they have in regard to charitable status.

If you are going to work with foreign missions, ministries, or schools, it's important you know what you are getting into and how organizations must be run in accordance with the laws of that nation. This shows a true heart of submission to governmental authorities (Romans 13:1) as well as understanding the needs and integrity of the people with whom you are working. By recognizing the legal status of an organization, you are able to tell if a group is politically subversive, somehow threatening, or otherwise in question.

Even though we do not have room to include the requirements from every country in the world in this book, I am outlining the requirements of many countries we frequently hear about in this day and age. With any foreign undertaking, be sure to do your own additional research and be fully informed prior to making any sort of commitment with foreign ministries, ministers, or schools.

Australia[1]

Australia's charitable system operates through the Australian Charities and Not-For-Profits Commission (ACNC). Organizations declared charitable or not-for-profit are governed by the Australian Charities and Not-For-Profits Commission Act 2012 (Cth), Australian Charities and Not-for-profits Commission (Consequential and Transitional) Act 2012 (Cth), Australian Charities and Not-for-profits Commission Regulation 2013 (Cth), Charities Act 2013 (Cth), and Charities (Consequential Amendments and Transitional Provisions) Act 2013 (Cth). Charities and Not-For-Profits are defined as organizations that do not benefit any specific people associated with its operations. Such must be clearly stated in their clauses and documentation. Approval grants an organization the right to operate without having to pay the government certain taxes and also allows donations to that organization to qualify for tax exemptions as tax write-offs. In order to receive these tax benefits, the organization in question must register, be approved, and then register with the Australian Taxation Office (ATO) and their state, territory and local governments.

Brazil[2]

Charities in Brazil are governed by the Brazilian Non-Governmental Organization Association (ABONG). Organizations that sought to educate the public or operate for political purposes began to form in the 1970s, while Brazil was still under the rule of a dictator state. In the

1990s, such organizations began to work with the state and with various businesses to bring about sustainable economy. The model for Brazilian non-governmental organizations was the non-profit system established within the United States, thus making the two systems similar. NGOs in Brazil are governed by the Third Sector Law of 1999, requiring them to form relationships and connections with both the government and private businesses. Ministries, however, are not a part of the NGO classification within Brazilian law. Brazil has not recognized a state church since 1891 and it is, therefore, very easy to start churches and have them recognized by necessary government authorities within Brazil under their codes of law.

Cambodia[3]

Becoming a Non-Governmental Organization (NGO) in Cambodia is a complicated task due to system abuses (while the actual process itself is reasonably easy). NGOs are a newer entity to Cambodian government, emerging only in the 1990s after many decades of political turmoil. About one-quarter to one-third of the population of Cambodia receive aid or assistance from an NGO, which run from the spectrum of housing, to humanitarian aid, to religious and educational work. Charitable organizations apply through the Cambodian government's division ConCERT (Connecting Communities, Environment & Responsible Tourism), providing the basics of organizational members, structure, and policies. Within the structure of Cambodian government, there is little formal structure or reporting required of NGOs and the organizations do operate exempt from corporate taxation. This has led to widespread abuse of the system, including scams and schemes among NGO organizations. While legislation has been in the works since 2008 to try and curb these issues, the needed legislation to structure the system has yet to pass through governmental system.

Canada[4]

In Canada, charities are governed under the Income Tax Act. Non-profit organizations are considered social entities that serve the common good and welfare of humanity. No one in a non-profit Canadian organization is allowed to personally profit from funds generated in a non-profit organization. These, however, are different from charities, which exist exclusively for charitable purposes. The major difference is how donations are registered, and that non-profit Canadian organization donations are not considered tax deductible. Non-profit Canadian organizations that are not charities may also have to pay out tax on their capital gains, whereas charities do not. According to the definitions of the two, ministries are eligible for charitable status under the Canadian government. Much like application in the United States, the Canadian government requires applying organizations to be incorporated, having a board, a necessary set of business plan documents, and governing authority within the organization to maintain the necessary order over it. Canadian charities are required to file Form T301 once per year, within six months of the end of each fiscal year.

China[5]

The history of non-profit and charitable organizations in China is considerably younger than in most other nations. The laws governing charities in China go back to the 1950s, when organizations known as government-organized nongovernmental organizations (GONGOs) were first implemented. The first nonprofit in China did not emerge until 1994. While there are many different types of groups in China that operate under these laws – labor groups, nature preservation groups, educational groups, etc. – churches are not among them. In China, mainline churches that exist do so as entities of the Chinese government, and there are only two official Protestant groups recognized in China. These groups are known as the Three-Self Patriotic Movement of the Protestant Churches in China and the China Christian

84

Council.[6] Ministries that exist are classified as "underground," meaning members meet in secret, in homes, basements, and secure locations, to avoid governmental attention and scrutiny. Evangelism and Bible distribution is prohibited according to Chinese law, but information and literature is disseminated via these underground church networks. Churches that are not underground tend to face persecution and harassment from government officials. As a result, Chinese churches tend to be isolated outside of their own nation and seldom to never do they have government approval for their operations.

Ghana[7]

Registering as a non-governmental organization (NGO) in Ghana is a relatively simple process. Ghana charities are governed by The Companies Code of 1963, registering them as incorporated businesses in the country. One must purchase the required NGO registration form from a post office to apply for the first steps of status: a Certificate to Commence Business and a Certificate of Incorporation. The government of Ghana requires basic information about the organization, including name, address, officers, and objectives. Paperwork is submitted to the Registrar General's Department and processed within approximately a month to six weeks' time. After the paperwork is processed and certificates are issued, the applicant can then go on to apply for NGO status through the Department of Social Welfare. The applicant provides further information on the organization, especially letters of recommendation from regional welfare offices and governmental offices and proof of the organization's actions in their purpose.

Guatemala[8]

The Republic of Guatemala recognizes three types of Non-Profit Organizations (NPOs): Civil associations, foundations, and non-governmental organizations for development (NGOs). Religious, educational, and social welfare organizations are eligible for tax-exempt status as an NPO in Guatemala as they are registered with Superintendencia de Administración Tributaria (SAT), and as their profits do not benefit private owners or corporate members of the organization. Guatemalan NPOs are governed by a series of documents and codes, including the Political Constitution of the Republic of Guatemala (1985), Civil Code (1963), Law of Non-Governmental Organizations for Development (2003), and Municipal Code (2002).

Haiti[9]

It is not a big secret that the government of Haiti is plagued by corruption and bad management. Even though the nation itself should, in theory, be easy to help, excessive corruption, false agencies and charities, and years of mismanagement have created a situation whereby it is nearly impossible to tell a true charity in Haiti from a false one. While the government does require charities to file with them, they are not closely monitored, and there are more NGOs in Haiti than in any other country in the world, and many are operating under false pretenses.

Hong Kong[10]

In Hong Kong, charities are distinguished from other non-profit organizations as being specifically for relieving from poverty, advancing religion or education, or another charitable purpose that relates to the three already mentioned. Charities must be for public benefit, and must be registered with and recognized by the government of Hong Kong for operation therein. This means the registration process, done through the government, must be completed for recognized and acknowledged status. It is a reasonably simple process, providing basic information subject to governmental approval. Charities in Hong Kong must be governed as societies, trusts, companies under specific ordinance, or a group established by the legislature of Hong Kong. They are tax exempt agencies and eligible for donations.

India[11]

In India, all religious groups are under a common heading of Non-Governmental Organizations, commonly abbreviated as NGO. They are the third classification found under this heading, commonly called non-profit organizations or "section 25 companies." There are several laws by which non-profits are governed in India, namely Constitution of India Articles 19(1)(c) and 30, the Income Tax Act of 1961, Public Trusts Acts, Societies Registration Act of 1860; Indian Companies Act of 1956, section 25, and Foreign Contribution (Regulation) Act of 1976. They are tax-exempt as governed under the Income Tax Act of 1961, and there is no economic restriction of any sort on their activities (although charities are prohibited from political activity or backing political candidates). All financial contributions to a section 25 company must go exclusively to the promotion of the work, and never to private individuals within the organization.

Indonesia[12]

Indonesian charities are classified one of two ways: as foundations or associations. Associations function under Dutch laws dating back to the late 1800s from the era when Indonesia was under Dutch occupation. Foundations operate via modern Indonesian law, and the regulations are much more involved than that of an association. Foundations are forbidden from receiving any financial benefit from the organization, both directly and indirectly. When a foundation dissolves, all its assets must be submitted to another organization with the same focus and interests. Financial interests with associations are not governed as strictly, and upon dissolution, operating officers can retain and disburse their holdings among themselves. Approval for a charitable status comes through the Ministry of Law and Human Rights. Charities are not required to operate for the public benefit, and organizations can have their license revoked if they are in any way violating the laws of Indonesia or perceived to be a threat somehow to the good of the people. Charitable organizations are tax exempt as long as no relationship exists between the donators and the organization. Contributions of $70 or more must be made public, and no limits exist on the amount of a tax deduction.

Jamaica[13]

Jamaican charities are governed through the Department of Co-operatives and Friendly Societies (DCFS) and are ruled by the New Charities Act of 2013. Organizations file through this department with the Jamaican government and must provide adequate documentation to prove they do not exist for private benefit and serve a common good to the community. Charities in Jamaica may be charitable trusts, incorporated, or unincorporated agencies. They are required to fill extensive reporting obligations and keep financial records of all activities and donations. In a unique point, individuals who are board members of a charity in Jamaica have to prove themselves as "fit and sound" individuals, proving they are mentally capable and adequate to serve their duties for the charity.

Japan[14]

Non-taxable status for charities in Japan is virtually non-existent. Non-Profit Organizations (NPOs, as they are called) must file hundreds of pages worth of paperwork in order to be eligible for basic status, and the process in and of itself is long, cumbersome, and burdening. 70% of donations must be spent within five years, thus making it impossible to build up stores of income for large projects. Donations also only rate a 10% tax break (although there is currently legislation pending for a 50% tax break on donations). Japanese lawmakers are also trying to make the process for non-profit status less difficult to obtain.

Kenya[15]

Kenyan charities are governed by the Non-Governmental Organisations Co-Ordination Act of 1990. As in many foreign countries, charities in Kenya are classified as non-governmental organizations. Submissions for an NGO must be made to the Non-Governmental Organisations Co-Ordination Board in Nairobi, Kenya. Kenyan charities must include at least one out of three Kenyan citizens on its board of officers and members of the organization must be cleared as not having any ties or affiliation to terrorist organizations. When an international organization is taking over an existing organization or establishing a branch in Kenya, the process is more involved and requires extensive verification as to the organization, involvement and funding of the organization in Kenya. Beyond these specifications, the process of registering an organization (including their name) is similar to that of other countries: name, location, governing body, governing guidelines, and general financial operations.

Mexico[16]

Mexican charities recognize four different types of non-profit organizations: civil associations, private assistance institutions, civil societies, and trusts. Any of these organizations have the option to file for tax exemption and register under the Income Tax Law/Law for Promotion of Civil Society Organizations. Once an organization files, they are able to receive donations. Charities in Mexico are governed under Article 97 of the Mexican Income Tax Law. The United States and Mexico adhere to what is known as a bilateral tax treaty, which gives United States taxpayers the option to make tax deductible donations to certain registered Mexican charities.

Nigeria[17]

It's not a secret that the government of Nigeria has faced severe instabilities, corruptions, and issues spanning the past several decades. Corruption has caused inefficiencies in governmental function and has led to severe corruption among the citizens of Nigeria, as well. Nigeria is known for scams of all sorts, which are untamed by the government due to its own corruptions and inefficiencies. As a result, dealing with Nigerian ministries or doing ministry in Nigeria requires research and disciplines to ensure everything done is legal and above board. In Nigeria, charities operate as public trusts. This means a trustee or trustees must oversee the finances and personal property – in other words, the person or people involved need to be trustworthy. Charities are governed by the preamble of the Statute of Uses Act, 1601 and Companies Income Tax Act (CITA), and there is no specific limitation as to define what can or cannot be a charity in the nation of Nigeria (although charities are prohibited from doing or engaging in anything that is defined as illegal according to law). Registered, charitable organizations are allowed to receive donations but are still subject to a value added tax (VAT) under the Value Added Tax Act (1993), the VAT Amendment Act (2007) and the Federal Inland Revenue Service (Establishment) Act 2007 (a consumption tax based on purchase prices).

Pakistan[18]

Much like India, Pakistani ministries are constantly contacting ministers in the United States through email and internet social networks. What American ministers seldom know is how to tell a legitimate Pakistani ministry from a counterfeit one. Non-profit organizations (NPO) in Pakistan are governed by Income Tax Ordinance 2001 and Income Tax Rules 2002, Companies Ordinance 1984, Trusts Act 1882, Societies registration Act 1860, and Voluntary Social Welfare Organizations Ordinance 1961. Pakistani non-profits take one of four forms: society, trust, nonprofit company with limited liability, and social welfare agencies. Non-profit agencies are approved by the Commissioner of Income Tax and are exempt from the minimum tax levy of 50%. Donations given are counted as a tax rebate to the donor against tax liability. Pakistani non-profits are required to report the success of their activities and their financial interworking every three years to the government.

Poland[19]

Non-profit organizations in Poland are classified as associations or foundations. Associations consist of several people who all agree with and receive the directives of that organizational system. These organizations are governed by supervising agencies who ensure the organization will function properly and rightly, according to its established, registered guidelines. Foundations have no membership to pursue their non-profit agendas, and are governed by sponsors. Organizations are registered through the Register of Polish Foundations, located in the capital city, Warsaw. Charities in Poland receive full tax benefits and donations are not taxable.

The Philippines[20]

Non-profit organizations in the Philippines are classified as foundations, and are exempt from tax according to the governing laws of the Tax Reform Act of 1997. Foundations are non-stock corporations operating with the goal of charitable work, serving the common good. They are registered with the Philippine Securities and Exchange Commission (SEC). Following typical forms of non-profit requirements, the government requires basic information as relates to name, governance, structure, and finances. Unique facets to the Philippines process are two requirements: a notarized certified bank note of no less than one million pesos and a statement agreeing to an SEC audit. Depending on the nature of the organization, further endorsement from governmental agencies (such as the department of education or the department of health) may also be required. NGOs in the Philippines have the option to receive an accreditation from the government through the Philippine Council for NGO Certification (PCNC), but will not be accredited without proper government office verification.

Russia[21]

In the Russian Federation, charities are classified as non-governmental, non-commercial organizations (NCOs). Given the structure and complexity to the Russian government, applying for status is an involved process. While donations, items sold through a charity, and grants are not taxable when given to NCOs, NCOs still must pay tax to the Russian Federation on their economic activities. Federal reporting is not required for NCOs when annual profits are under three million rubles. Regions in Russia may provide benefits not covered in the federal tax code to NCOs. The governing of Russian Charities falls under the Tax Code Act, Constitution of the Russian Federation of 1993, and the Civil Code of the Russian Federation, among many others.

Rwanda[22]

Rwanda has a long and difficult history that has left its citizens dire and in severe need. Plagued by a severe genocide in 1994, the nation of Rwanda has struggled to pull itself together, often very unsuccessfully. In response to the genocide, organizations known as Civil Service Organizations (CSOs) began to emerge to help the people in their serious state of need. In 2008 and 2011, new laws were put in place within the Rwandan government to help govern Non-Governmental Organizations (NGOs) and CSOs (Organic Law no. 55/2008 of 10/09/2008 governing Non-Governmental Organizations (O.G. no. 23 of 01/12/2008), but these guidelines have done little to help the structure and supervision of these organizations. Due to limited communication with the government, low funding, many of these local and grassroots organizations are unsupervised. In a nation with nearly 40,000 NGOs, less than 400 are registered with the government.

Singapore[23]

Charities in Singapore are either societies registered under the Societies Act, a public company registered with the Accounting and Regulatory Authority of Singapore under the Companies Act, or a trust under a trust deed, in compliance with the Trustees Act. Most charities are required to register with the Commissioner of Charities; however, universities and educational institutions, hospitals, and religious bodies established by an Act of Parliament are exempt from such registration.

Thailand[24]

Charities in Thailand are registered with the government as foundations. Applications are submitted through registrars of the district wherein an organization will function. Along with an application, the organization's members must provide extensive documentation about the organization, its purposes, its finances and allocations, and provide extensive proof of individuals who will work for the organization, including government and household identification. Foundations are required to have 500,000 baht, with at least 250,000 baht in cash. Once the process is completed, the district offices forward all paperwork to the Ministry of the Interior, wherein the organization will be legally governed.

United Kingdom[25]

The United Kingdom's process for charitable establishment is similar to that of other nations. Filing requires at least three trustees, a name and structure for the organization, a governing document (providing typical information on purpose, governing body, and financial procedures), and register as either a charity (if your earnings are over £5,000; you will have to prove financial assets) or as a Charitable Incorporated Organisation (CIO). Having registered status exempts organizations from most tax and also allows donations to be tax deductible.

General guidelines for dealing with international merger requests or inquiries to assume a ministry

- **Demand honesty...and proof** – I do not question people lie everywhere in the world. We cannot deny, however, that it is a lot harder to prove what someone is saying when they aren't right around the block or governed under the same laws as you are because it is easier for people to sneak around. Just because someone sends you a bunch of pictures doesn't mean the pictures are theirs, nor does it mean what you are being told they are doing is accurate. Websites and social networks can be deceiving. If you are going to make such a large commitment, putting your ministry, name, reputation, and yes, finances on the line, you need proof that these people are exactly who they say they are. Given guidelines for nonprofits, charities, and NGOs exist in every country worldwide, you need to be aware of the rules and guidelines for working with or assuming an organization. Ask for paperwork, for proof of filings, for financial statements, copies of certifications and licenses, and any other documentation that is essential to operate such an organization in that nation.

- **Consider a mission trip/operation to that nation before making a formal commitment** – Yes, travelling is expensive...but so is losing your own charitable status because you have unknowingly merged with a terrorist organization or a group somehow classified as politically subversive. It is also a lot cheaper than losing all the resources you have financially due to a scheme or scam. If the organization is really serious about connecting with you, they will wait pending your investigation into them. Take some time, look into them, and organize a team for a missions trip.

- **Receive legal advice** – There are lawyers specifically trained in international law, taxes, and charities.

Before you draft anything on paper, it's best to consult with an attorney who specializes in this to make sure everything is right on both ends of the spectrum.

- **Familiarize yourself with the language, culture, government, and social customs of that nation** – The Gospel is universal, but the ways in which it is conveyed may be very different depending on cultural norms. It is best to make sure that, due to the ethics and issues at hand in a nation, you are prepared for the obstacles, difficulties, and problems you may encounter by endeavoring in such a complicated venture.

- **Set extremely clear parameters** – If you are assuming or merging with an organization, you need to call the terms, document them via contract or somehow in writing, and make sure everyone understands them. Issues such as not accepting financial membership kickbacks from denominations or other organizations, controlling the materials disseminated and taught within the organization must be addressed, and guiding through ordination and acceptability policies.

- **Examine other options before officially taking on a merger or assuming an organization as your own** – Assuming or merging with an organization that you cannot see every day, cannot control the day-to-day function thereof, and can pretty much be doing anything they desire with your name and status means you have to deeply trust those who are operating the organization. Supervision is an important facet to properly functioning ministry, and if you are not able to provide people to train (in-person, not over the internet) and govern the project directly, assuming or merging organizations may not be your best bet for effective function. Covering is always an option, whereby you are able to train from a distance, implement programs from headquarters, with the foreign organization maintaining their own identity, governmental guidelines, reporting, and policies.

- **Never forget about the vast amount of work that needs to be done in your own backyard** – I know that becoming a charity is easy in many countries, and it is tempting to think it's easy to make an impact in nations that have so much need...but the reality of such is simple: it's easier to get status in nations that deal with government corruption and political upheaval. That means it's harder to get the people the specific aid they need. There is plenty of work that needs to be done right where you are, plenty of people who are in need, and never ignore nor negate what can be done as you put your hands to the Gospel plow in your own communities, states, and nations.

CHAPTER TWELVE

DOCUMENTS EVERY MINISTER MUST HAVE

This is what the LORD ALMIGHTY, the God of Israel, says:
Take these documents, both the sealed and unsealed copies
of the deed of purchase, and put them in a clay jar
so they will last a long time.
(Jeremiah 32:14)

IF ministry is to be professional, ministers must have certain documentation to go along with their ministry offices and titles. I recognize the power of anointing, but we cannot deny the fact that ministry is done in real time, in a real world full of counterfeits and deceivers who claim to have power, but have nothing behind it. On a professional level, ministers must be able to validate their claims to their office and hold legal and professional claim to their titles and ministry operations. For our ceremonies, certificates, and work to hold legal validation, we must recognize the power of paperwork, identity, and citizenship documents. If we are going to minister to the nations, we cannot do that without the proper paperwork. Let's stop the temptation to over-spiritualize what we do in ministry. No government is going to allow you entry into their country without passport documents and government-issued identification. As a result, we need to establish what is necessary for a professional minister.

Valid minister's license (with one's current office)

Let's stop the "we don't need licensing and ordination" game. Some people insist on it, other people think it's optional. Then we complain when someone operates in ministry and they turn out to be false, because we feel deceived. A minister's license is the legal remedy by which you, as a minister, have the right to do whatever it is you do as a minister. It also serves to verify you have undergone training and have not made up a call for yourself in this life. If you are operating without a valid minister's license, you are technically working under illegal premises. You will also find many organizations will disregard the validity of your work and will not regard you as a legitimate minister.

It is vitally important a minister understands the terms of their specific license and the different things that license entitles them to do. Minister's licenses should clarify the office to which a minister is to function and where this license is issued from, and why (review of doctrinal beliefs, completion of training, etc.). Today, organizations can be funny about issuing licenses, and may include all sorts of random terms or tags within them in order to limit the work of a minister.

So, for the sake of understanding, let's clarify what makes a minister's license valid:

- Current title/office (if you're not a pastor any longer, your license as a pastor is no longer valid and cannot be applied to your work in the apostolic; the exception to this rule are licenses for general works, such as a minister, that have no expiration date).

- The document is signed by at least two officers of the valid organization issuing the certificate of license with a date and contains a raised seal.

- The date on the license has not yet expired (some licenses do contain an expiration date; if there is no expiration date, it is presumed to be unexpired, if it has not been revoked).

- If the license must be filed with a county or state authority, such has been done.

Valid ordination (with one's current office)

Ordination and license go hand-in-hand. Some organizations will incorporate the two into one document as a result. This does not mean, however, that you can have one without the other. While a minister's license provides legal means to operate as a minister in your office, ordination provides the legal establishment of the duties and responsibilities you will be performing as a Christian leader.

All offices of the five-fold require ordination by a validly licensed and ordained Christian minister of the apostolic or prophetic office. Once again, it is vitally important a minister understands the terms of their specific ordination and the different things they are allowed to do as part of that license. Each minister's license should include the right to perform weddings and funerals, administer Holy Communion and baptism, and preach, as the opportunity arises. Apostles and prophets should also contain a clause in their ordination specifications about ordaining and licensing other leaders and establishing appointments (bishops, elders, and deacons) in churches, with evangelists, pastors, and teachers specified to assist at such events. As with a minister's license, the same guidelines apply: ordination must be to the specific office in which you are functioning, and not an earlier one or one in which you do not serve; it must be in valid and good standing, not revoked or expired for any reason; must be signed, with a raised seal, and must be filed with a county or state authority, if such is required.

Employer Identification Number (EIN)

Discussed in brief in the previous chapter, an Employer Identification Number (EIN) is assigned by the Internal

Revenue Service to identify your organization as legally recognized, valid, and in connection with the necessary governing laws for your type of organization. It is required for a number of professional deals, including donations, grants, banking, contracts, tax filings and issues, annual IRS charity reporting, and property acquisitions.

State incorporation filings

Already discussed in the previous chapter, the first step to charitable status is incorporating as a corporation in the state in which you live. State incorporation consists of separate paperwork verifying your organization as having corporate structure in its non-profit purpose. This verifies familial control and profit are not the forefront purpose of your organization. These documents are often required along with 501(c)(3) verifications for business purposes.

Valid state or government-issued driver's license

It's a fact: ministers today need to drive. Gone are the days of horse and buggy, and it is generally understood that when you hang out your ministry shingle, you are expected to travel within a certain radius from your residential location. If you are going to operate professional ministry, it is impractical to hope someone will always be available to drive you where you need to go. As a sign of practical independence, ministers need to be prepared to drive.

Driver's licenses are also needed for identification purposes. As a stepping stone for numerous other government or state-issued identification documents, a driver's license is about far more than just driving. They are also required for all business operations, from opening a bank account to obtaining property or being added to a lease.

Valid passport and passport card

If you have any intention of preaching the Gospel or operating in ministry beyond the bounds of your native country, you will need a government-issued passport for identification. A passport is a legal document issued by a federal government authorizing an individual to travel beyond the borders of their country of origin or citizenship. A passport authorizes you to travel in any country, unless there is a restriction on travel to that nation. A passport card authorizes travel to "border nations" or more immediate nations. In the case of the United States, this includes Canada, Mexico, and the Caribbean. In the case of other nations, a passport card or an "enhanced driver's license" (as they are sometimes called) allow access to nations within a certain region.

To obtain a passport, one fills out a form that is accessible online and takes it to a passport office or completes the process through the mail. It is a reasonably inexpensive process, usually less than two hundred dollars. An individual needs to provide documentation that proves they are who they say they are, they have legal right to dwell in the nation where they are living, and that they have the legal ability to leave the nation in which they live. Once the process is approved, a passport is issued. Most are good for ten years, at which time they can be renewed.

Visa

Unlike the other documents mentioned here, a visa is not a document someone has on hand at all times. A visa is a document authorizing an individual's entry, movement, and departure from a nation, all within a set period of time. In order to work, minister, or even visit certain nations, a visa is sometimes required. Some nations have what is known as a "reciprocity" program, by which visiting a foreign nation does not require a visa as long as the stay is within a certain period of time (usually three months or less). If you are a United States citizen, reciprocity countries include the European Union, Russia, and Brazil. Other nations will require a visa for any period of work or visit.

There are a number of different visas one can apply for, and it is prudent to investigate the type of visa required to match the type of trip and duration therein. There are also different requirements that must be met to obtain a visa. If one is going to certain countries, vaccines or health exams may be required. Some nations may require interrogation prior, during, or upon departure. Visas also cost money, and require processing time – usually a minimum of eight weeks prior to trip departure. In addition, you must be able to prove you will have somewhere to stay or adequate means to remain in the country for the period of time in which you will be staying there.

There are a number of reasons why a visa may be denied. Some of these reasons include:

- Dishonesty in the application
- Criminal record
- Threatening to the security of the nation in some way
- No good reason for the trip
- Has not met with necessary health or documentary requirements
- Illness
- Passport will expire while you are abroad
- No proper proof for travel plans or way to stay while in the other country
- Not enough notice in the application

For these reasons, it is very important that trips outside of your immediate country are adequately planned, proper documentation is in place, and that any and all procedures are handled properly before ever attempting to travel outside of your native country.

CHAPTER THIRTEEN

NECESSARY BUSINESS SKILLS

But remember the LORD your God, for it is He
Who gives you the ability to produce wealth,
and so confirms His covenant,
which He swore to your forefathers,
as it is today.
(Deuteronomy 8:18)

IT'S been said that anyone born after a certain year has certain technical skills simply because of the age in which they live. I used to believe this until I went into ministry. It amazes me the vast number of ministers who lack skills necessary for communication and ministry today.

In days gone by, all one needed to be a good minister of the Gospel was a Bible and a loud voice. If you travelled, you needed a tent. Sound equipment wasn't an issue, computers didn't exist, and if you wanted to write, you picked up a feather pen and a piece of paper. Nowadays, being a good minister of the Gospel is somewhat more involved. You still need a copy of the Scriptures, a loud voice is still somewhat more beneficial than a very soft one, and from there, you need a host of other skills that will help you to be a better minister. Gone are the days when computers are for technicians or scientists!

There are a lot of people who think you need to do a lot of different things in order to be successful in the business of ministry. It is true that ministry is a lot On the contrary, there are a few things we need to know how to do, and know how to do them well. If we master these skills, we will be professional in business and successful in whatever ministry God has assigned to us.

- **Computer skills** – Ministers today can't get by with a fear of computers like they could in past generations. Ministry today is more hands-on than ever and it is essential for a minister to have basic computer skills for things such as writing, blogging, and using the internet for ministry promotion. A minister needs to know the basics of word processing (through a program such as Word), a spreadsheet program (such as Excel), email (such as Outlook or a common email provider such as Yahoo! or Gmail), a slideshow program (such as PowerPoint), and a publishing program (such as Publisher, Adobe InDesign, or Serif PagePlus). Ministers also need to know how to use the internet, basic browsers such as Microsoft Edge, Google Chrome, or Mozilla Firefox.

- **Office skills** – Some office skills never go out of style. Typing, phone skills, filing, alphabetical order, use of a calculator, and ability to sort and organize paperwork are all essential skills that no matter what technology comes along, will forever be needed.

- **Presentation skills** – It's been said that it's all in how you present it. There is some truth to this. Ministers need to be able to create presenter notes for their sermons, speak well, look the part, dress the part, and carry themselves with dignity. We need to be able to talk to people, talk in front of people, talk to people on the phone and online, and handle the work we must to do be able to present to other people.

- **Customer service skills** – As public non-profits, the bulk of ministry funds will often come from the public. Many of these funds will come from ministry-related sales. When dealing with sales, it's important to be courteous, friendly, accommodating, and to have a can-do attitude rather than an I-don't-care attitude. Our policies about returns, exchanges, shipping, and courtesy should be clearly presented wherever we do business (whether online or in a store or shop). We likewise should expect our customers to display proper courtesy, and maintain any right to refuse service to those who behave badly.

- **Marketing skills** – Marketing is probably one of the most difficult things for ministers because it's not something we learn in training for ministry. Instead, we just assume everyone will flock to the message because of what it is. If we look at some of the styling of Jesus – on the Sermon on the Mount, for example – or during the feast of Pentecost when the Apostle Peter spoke up to educate on repentance – both were using ancient marketing techniques to convey the message to a large group of people. There are things to consider when creating flyers, book covers, advertising events, promoting events, writing, styles, and other matters of presentation that we must consider and learn about if we desire to draw people to the work we are doing.

- **Perseverance** – Numerous stories abound about various famous people who failed at numerous business ventures before they were successful in their work. The same is true of ministers. Ministry does not create itself; successful ministries come about by years of perseverance and endurance. It comes as a minister learns every aspect necessary to make a ministry work and embracing the necessary spiritual knowledge and business knowledge to bring the two together in the empowerment of Kingdom business.

The business side of ministry reminds us of the essence of good foundations to everything we undertake that applies to the Kingdom. We use the term "Kingdom of God" frequently, but we forget that as part of every Kingdom we will find necessary structure and government. When we walk in the business skills necessary for ministry, we will come to a greater appreciation for Kingdom government, order, and structure. In the long-term, Kingdom business makes us better ministers.

CHAPTER FOURTEEN

BUSINESS ARRANGEMENTS

Do you see a man skilled in his work?
He will serve before kings;
he will not serve before obscure men.
(Proverbs 22:29)

IF ministry is classified as Kingdom business, that means a minister of God will be faced with decisions pertaining to business arrangements. Many ministers are notably intimidated by business agreements. Others find business arrangements offensive and contrary to ministry. If we understand the foundation of our faith to be based on a covenant, which is, in its essence, a spiritual contract, business arrangements are in no way threatening or contrary to the foundations of ministry. The use of business documents, arrangements, and negotiations is essential to good Kingdom business, especially as one's ministry grows and various financial arrangements are involved.

Whether entering into a lease to rent office space or outlining requirements for travel, business arrangements are now necessary on the church scene. We must prepare ourselves by understanding basic business procedure and why it's important to have these documents in our ministries.

Most ministers ask, "Why do we need these things?" Some believe contracts, honorariums, negotiations, and the like are worldly, and rob the local church of resources. The reality, however, is that the church today needs these things for ministry structure and discipline. These things are a part of wise business arrangement and dealing. Ministers cannot afford to be out thousands of dollars due to bad lease or mortgage agreements, loans, credit cards, churches who know they can't afford a leader but take advantage by inviting them anyway, or by clever and slick business deals. If a minister intends to write professionally, they need to understand the contracts they sign in those deals. When dealing with media, a minister must sign agreements and, likewise, understand what they are signing. Having a good head about such documents leads to better business sense overall, and a better handle on utilizing ministerial financial resources.

Leases and mortgages

Many ministries and other non-profits start out in the founder's home. When a group reaches a point where more space is required than can be afforded in a home or apartment, finding a space to rent or buy becomes the next logical step. The options that exist should be considered carefully and considered in connection with prayer and efficient budgeting, as was discussed earlier. The conditions of leases and mortgages vary depending on one's state, city, credit score, economic circumstances, and the agency or individual granting a lease or mortgage. Even though the specifics are often different, the principle behind a lease and a mortgage are the same: signing a lease or mortgage commits an organization or individual to pay a certain amount of money every for a specified period of time in order to reside in an office, space, or building. In the case of a mortgage, the signer owns the property, while paying back the borrowing agency whatever has been borrowed to cover its cost. Leases and mortgages should never, ever be considered if there is question of ability to pay because of lack of funds. Additional costs should also be considered, such as requirements for maintenance, fees, and furnishings.

One very important thing to consider with a mortgage is

interest and with a lease, increases and fees. Interest rates are calculated based on credit rating and the length of a mortgage. On a lease, the amount of fees one pays is also related to their interest rate, as well as the scale of fees required by the company or landlord holding the property.

It is very, very important to understand a lease or mortgage before it is signed. If there are terms you are unfamiliar with or criteria you find confusing, it is important you strive to understand them. Educate yourself about your lease and mortgage before you sign. Defaulting on leases and mortgages can be very harmful to credit, both personal and professional. It is good to consult with an attorney or a financial professional if any confusion exists about a lease or mortgage before signing.

Loans

A loan is an amount of money granted from a loaning institution, such as a bank or lender, with the loaning agency charging a set rate of interest and fees to make the loan as lucrative as possible to their interests. Loans are sought out as an answer to financial assistance. Unlike a mortgage, which is a type of loan, a loan is not typically specified in its purpose or extended as long as a mortgage. Loan money can be used to purchase a vehicle, equipment, pay off debts, or any other assortment of purposes.

Loans can be easy to get into, and difficult to get out of. A loan is another incident where it is essential to read the fine print, and understand both interest rates and credit. When considering loans, it is best to consider a few points:

- Can the loan be paid back?

- Is there another option that can be considered, such as waiting to make purchases or obtaining finances from another source?

- Is a better loan option available?

Loans often have varying interest rates and fees, making paying off a loan as quickly as possible a feasible and purposed option. One should not default on a loan because doing so can severely hurt credit and affect one's ability to borrow money in the future.

Contracts

A contract is a legally-binding agreement reached between parties for a specified purpose. Contracts are used for an assortment of business deals, ranging from services to acquisitions and mergers. Contracts are excellent points of reference as they specify what all parties involved are to do as part of the agreement. In order for a contract to be legally valid, four things must be present:

- **A meeting of the minds between parties**[1] – In other words, all parties involved must understand the conditions of the contract and agree upon the terms.

- **Consideration**[2] – The purpose for the contract: i.e., an exchange of some sort (services, money, goods, etc.).

- **An agreement to enter into the contract**[3] - Typically displayed via the signature of all parties, whether live or electronic (done when an individual types in their name).

- **The legal competence of each party**[4] - In order to enter into a contract, one must be over the age of eighteen, of right mind (cannot be impaired by drugs or alcohol, mental illness, or mental retardation), and has the legal authority to enter into a contract (either as an individual or as a proxy representative).

Once a party signs a contract, that party is bound to uphold their end of the contract by law. When any one party fails to uphold their end of the agreement, they are guilty of breach of contract. When a breach of contract occurs, the contract is, according to law, null and void and none of the remaining parties are required to uphold their part of the agreement.

Contracts are required for book publication, facility and room rentals, hotel rentals, car rentals, records, recording, and promotion, an advertising agent or representative services, radio and television negotiations, and other aspects of public arena ministry. Whenever we are using the space, services, facilities, or work of another, contracts will always be involved.

When signing a contract, it's important to ensure all four points are present and that you understand the terms of the agreement. Contracts tend to be written in legal jargon, and can be complex in their description of things. This should not be intimidating to any of the parties as it is just how contracts tend to be written. If one doesn't understand something, ask about it for clarity or receive legal advice on the contract before it is signed. If terms are unacceptable, in some circumstances, the contract can be reworked to accommodate all parties involved. At other times, this is not an option, which is why it is so important to understand the contract prior to signing it.

Warning signs of a bad contract

Because contracts are legally enforceable documents, it's important nothing is ever signed if you do not understand the terms of the document or if you are not comfortable with the document. I have met one too many ministers who entered into an agreement on blind faith, not properly understanding the terms of the agreement, who suffered for it greatly after the fact.

It's an unfortunate reality that many people who operate business – or even ministry – are not in it for the right reasons. There are many individuals out there who hold positions and titles and are in it for nothing more than selfish gain. They will sell their point under the guise of faith or assistance, only to get a minister in a legally binding position of extortion. Because signatures indicate agreement, it is vital a minister recognizes the signs of a bad contract:

- **They refuse to give you a copy of the agreement before you have paid them any money** – It is not professional business conduct to exchange money prior to discussion of lease terms and contract agreements. As part of contract negotiations, you have the right to see the agreement prior to any financial exchange. Businesses frequently do this to compare and sort out agreement terms prior to finalization and to make sure those who engage in the agreement understand the entirety of the agreement in full, in case there are any questions. If someone refuses to let you see a copy of the agreement before you have paid them, you need to pass up their offer. Monetary value or property exchange is never due prior to a legally binding, officially signed agreement.

- **They refuse to furnish you with a copy of the agreement after you have signed it** – As part of an agreement, both parties are to be furnished with copies of said agreement upon signing. If someone refuses to give you copies of something you've agreed to, they are already in contract violation.

- **Terminology is extensively vague and leading** – Contracts, leases, honorariums, and other business documents are very technical and wordy in order to be as specific and clear as possible. This creates a situation where as far as the legal profession is concerned, there is no question as to what everyone's rights and agreements are in the given situation. If something seems vague, leaves out details, or just doesn't seem very clear – the agreement in question is designed to cause problems for one of the parties.

- **The terms of the agreement are not clear** – Contracts and agreements should be very specific, clarifying what is expected of both parties. If details seem to be missing or terms seem to be vague, the contract will be fuzzy legally and can cause extensive legal issues.

- **There are no names, addresses, dates, times, locations, or specifications mentioned in the agreement** – Contracts should specify the names of all who are signing for their respective organizations, the names of the organizations, the stipulations of the agreement, the duration the agreement will be in place for, the amount of times an organization is able to engage in the agreement, and specific locations and other stipulations that will be required as part of the agreement. If a contract does not mention these factors, it becomes legally questionable.

- **The agreement makes vague and unspecific threats as to action that will be taken if the agreement is not upheld** – The words "take action" can mean a lot of things – everything from "we will throw you out of our facility if you do not pay" to "we will reprimand you sternly" to "we will have a meeting about what to do" to "we will take you to court." "We will take action" is not really specific enough for proper understanding of the terms of the agreement, and it should be clearly stated about what will happen if for any reason the agreement is broken or violated prior to its conclusion.

- **There is no clarification about what will happen if the agreement is somehow violated due to circumstances beyond one or both of the parties' control** – Some contracts call this an 'act of God clause.' It includes all the things that happen that are beyond the control of either party – inclement weather, power failure, natural disaster, equipment failure, or other things that can affect the details of an agreement. Every agreement should include the details of what happens in such a situation, and how both parties can seek and discover remedy therein.

- **There is no early termination clause** – Things happen in life that are unforeseen: people die, people move, ministries and other organizations unfortunately go under, and general circumstances in people's lives can change which force other things in their lives to change. There should be a clearly specified clause in every contract that details what will happen if the agreement is broken before its fixed time frame.

- **The language used in the agreement is not professionally written** – Amateurs who attempt to write legal documents and pass them off as valid, legally-enforceable documents will try to use terminology that sounds excessively "spiritual" or "churchy," using various words and terms that make an agreement sound valid to someone who doesn't understand business agreements. In this case...run!!!

Honorariums

An honorarium is a specific type of contract that specifies the condition or conditions of payment for a service or services on the premise that certain agreements will be met in exchange for that service or services, either prior to or upon delivery. Honorariums pertain to invitations to minister or work with a minister versus travel, visits, or work a minister may cover at their own free will and volition.

In the ministry arena, honorariums have become very popular over the past ten years. Years ago, ministers covered their own travel expenses and hotel accommodations in exchange for a very large offering of $1,000 or more. As things within the church started to change and ministers started receiving less and less for preaching, appearances, and services, honorariums requiring certain conditions to be present for preaching started becoming very popular.

There is a lot of controversy over honorariums in the modern church. The reason for the controversy is simple: there are ministers who use the honorarium system to recover excessively large sums of money and excessive accommodations for the services they provide. Some believe the honorarium is a ploy to destroy the local church. As a result, people disagree about the validity of honorariums among ministers.

Both sides of the debate bring valid points. I agree it is wrong for ministers to ask for excessive amounts of money for appearances. On the other hand, I also think it is wrong for churches to invite speakers they can't really bless in the offering and expect the minister to just deal with whatever they are given. The church as the Body of Christ is far larger than just the local church, and the local church can't expect those representing that larger Body to consider what they do to be financially substandard. The answer to the honorarium debate is simple: the church will not have to deal with honorariums if inviting ministries and conference hosts will abide by principles of hospitality (we will discuss more about this principle later). Since that is a basic issue present in the church today, we need to understand more about honorariums.

The honorarium works to protect a minister and their ministry from unnecessary financial expense and burden via contractual agreement. An honorarium outlines the criteria required for a minister or ministry to visit another ministry, organization, conference, or event. In the case of a minister, it typically outlines who will handle travel expenses when a minister must go beyond a certain mileage (i.e., plane tickets, fuel costs, etc.), hotel accommodations when a minister must spend the night away from home due to an event, and the matter of offering and ministry sales (such as providing a table to sell items). Sometimes an honorarium requires a certain offering total a minimum amount, and other times it is a certain portion of something, such as a nightly collection. Some honorariums just require a love offering of any amount or a specified amount, requesting it to help cover expenses. Other things that may be included within an honorarium are required forms of transportation or types of accommodations.

Whether or not a minister calls it an 'honorarium,' most ministers do have and use the honorarium system in their ministries. This manifests through the necessary requirements established by that minister to have them speak at, preach at, or minister at an event. Ministers should figure out their honorarium requests taking three major things into consideration: what would be required for travel, what would be required in accommodations (or hotels), and what to request in offering and opportunity for sales.

It is good business to state travel and accommodation are non-negotiable given the circumstances dictated within honorarium statement. Offering can be negotiable, sometimes stated as a "love offering." It should be expected, however, that a minister is not given $20 and wished well. Love offering indicates the inviting ministry does their best by their guest minister to bless the work of God upon their lives and uphold God's vision within them.

The issue of ministry tables and sales as part of an honorarium is controversial among some because Jesus drove the moneychangers and sellers out of the temple (Matthew 21:12, Mark 11:15, John 2:15). Refusing to allow a minister sell ministry-related and Kingdom-related items in a foyer or hallway is a misappropriation of Jesus' teaching present in that passage. In the temple, those individuals sold things that were mandatory for temple offerings at exceedingly high prices, gouging the people of God financially to make a profit. Ministries who sell Kingdom-themed items at reasonable prices make such sales optional, rather than mandatory. Anyone is free to walk away from a ministry table and never buy a thing, as such purchase is available, but not required. An upright minister should never be refused from a table to sell Kingdom items. If, for some reason a minister prohibits this, they have the double responsibility to give rightly and appropriately in the offering, doubly blessing the minister of God.

There are two types of honorariums: verbal and written. Both are binding agreements and can uphold in a court of law, although it is more difficult to prove a verbal agreement. A verbal honorarium is established when a minister outlines the conditions necessary for them to speak at another's event and, even though nothing is made in writing, the inviting party agrees to meet those requirements as they uphold the invitation. A written honorarium is established when both parties sign a written agreement stating the necessary conditions. Whether an honorarium is verbal or written, Christians must remember their command to keep their word and be bound by their agreements. In the eyes of God, it does not matter if an arrangement is verbal or written: it must be kept.

Honorariums are calculated according to basic facts about the minister and the ministerial relationship in the projected event. The basic facts to calculate honorarium are as follows:

- **The amount of revenue and celebrity a church, ministry, or event will receive because of the guest minister's involvement with an event** – This is the business end of ministry: guest ministers should be well-matched with their event. Putting the picture of a minister on a flyer is a strategic move – one designed to bring people in for the event. If a minister's notoriety, gifting, or anointing is being utilized for an event, it needs to be compensated in kind.

- **The nature of the event** – An event specifically designed for a church group is different than an advertised event designed to draw in a crowd. If a minister is speaking specifically for a group and no one else, that is to be considered in honorarium amounts. It is also relevant how many days the event is for, how many times the minister will be expected to speak or minister, and the quality of ministry service.

- **The specialty of the event** – If a minister is being called in to an event because they are known for a specific expertise, area, or ability, that expertise must be compensated.

- **The amount of inconvenience for the guest minister vs. the amount of inconvenience for the host** – It's common knowledge that most ministries refuse to cover travel if a guest minister is considered within "driving distance." This kind of attitude, however, is incorrect – especially if a minister is driving an hour or more for an event. The reason the attitude is incorrect is simple: the guest minister is put at a higher inconvenience than the host ministry. They have to prepare themselves, drive there, do their own setup for tables and sales, and then clean up, drive home, often when they are done, because the attitude displayed toward them is that they are "close enough" to drive themselves home. If a ministry is covering travel and hotel, that should be calculated in an honorarium. If a ministry is not...at least part of the cost of such should be given to the guest minister.

- **Other factors include:** How many people travel with the guest minister (technical support, taping crews, assistance – not fifteen armor bearers but someone to assist the minister), cost of transport for sale items or props, and what the minister has to cover in order to come and minister for you. These costs should be kept in perspective, and are a part of the inconvenience and expense mentioned above: obviously if a minister is on television, that is their choice; if they travel with an excess of people, that is also their choice. These are peripheral costs that should be considered, but not overriding costs within an honorarium.

As a final note on honorariums, I want to remind everyone reading this that what I have written above represents the best and ideal circumstance as pertains to offering, honorariums, and what we, as ministers, can and should be able to expect when involved in a conference, meeting, or are asked to speak. At times, we may need to be flexible about some of our guidelines, work with the host, or adjust some things in order to participate in an event. When such is involved, follow the guidance of the Spirit. Consider what is offered in the light of other options, as well as the relationship you have with the minister hosting or presenting the event. Above all, pray and ask for God's guidance when a non-ideal circumstance arises as pertains to events and honorariums.

Covering expenses without an honorarium

As we discussed above, the circumstances which surround honorariums do vary. There are instances where people do not pay honorariums, and when people come without expecting to receive one. No matter what the prior arrangements are before an event, if you are not covering expenses up front, it is proper etiquette to cover those events through the offering an individual receives after the event. If that is not possible, the minister should receive as high compensation as possible to cover the various expenses they were out in order to participate in an event.

Instances where honorariums are inappropriate

Honorariums are not appropriate when people come to travel for every occasion. Some instances where honorariums are inappropriate are:

- **Convocation** – If you are covered by or part of an organization and you are attending or speaking at convocation or another event sponsored by your own organization, the organization you are a part of is not required to cover your expenses because it is understood you are coming as part of your membership with the organization. If you are a guest speaker for such an event and you are not part of the organization, traditional honorarium rules should apply, but depending on the circumstances of your organization, should be discussed and worked out with your leaders.

- **If you are being ordained or celebrated in an event that directly relates to you** – If you are being ordained or somehow commissioned as part of an event that is taking place in another city (and not in your own church or location), you are responsible for your own expenses to attend that event. If your leader is coming to do the service in your locale, you are responsible to cover their expenses.

- **You are attending an out-of-town event as an attendee, and not a speaker** – No matter who is holding the event, if you are attending and not speaking, no one is responsible for your expenses.

- **Retreats/cruises** – If an organization has the money and offers to cover your fare for a retreat or a cruise, that's a great thing, but technically, due to the nature of these events (they tend to be more recreational than conventional) and the fact that they tend to extend for five days or more, a host organization is not responsible for covering fare, travel, or lodging for such events.

- **You are a leader (even though you are not the founder) of an organization that is holding a conference** – If you are a part of an organization as a leader (such as a women's ministry, men's ministry, etc.) and they are holding an event, it is more or less in the category above: it's great if they are able to cover it, but because you are a recognized leader with position in the organization, your participation is part of the requirement of your work with that organization. The reason for this is simple: organizational events often encompass many people from many areas, and it is often not feasible for the organization to cover the expense of so many people attending who are going to attend no matter what they do in the event each time.

Insurance

Most Christian meetings and events are "held at your own

risk." This is never printed on flyers, but is an implied aspect of attending public Christian events. "Held at your own risk" means patrons and attendees are responsible for whatever risk may come from being present in the event – whether it is injury, accident, or incident, without any liability to the ministry or minister hosting the event.

The problem with this is simple: unless every person who attends a service signs a liability waiver each time, people attending still can sue if they feel a circumstance arises serious enough to warrant litigation. If someone falls down a flight of unmarked church stairs, for example, or someone is injured due to mishandling of the individual during the laying on of hands, they do have the right to sue the minister in question. Ministers must also be wary of medical claims: while we certainly acknowledge we are called of God and do receive words from God about certain conditions a person may have, we need to be clear that we do not dispense medical advice for any situation, nor do we stand as diagnosticians.

Obviously, seeking waivers from every person who attends a meeting is unfeasible and also insulting to an audience. Ministry operates by trust, and we can't violate the whole because there are a few people who go overboard as troublemakers. Insurance may not be a necessary facet for a small ministry or even a developing ministry. If God wills for a ministry to grow beyond a certain limit, however, insurance consideration becomes essential. When planning large events, some facilities require a ministry carry insurance to protect any workers from suing the facility in the process of business or volunteer work, and most facilities, loans, and mortgages also require insurance on the loaned property. Whether insuring an event, a minister, workers, a facility, a rental property, a vehicle, or equipment, a solid insurance provider can assist in the process. When dealing with insurance providers, be very clear in what is needed and be wary of schemes or scams to raise a policy's rates for something unnecessary.

Equipment

Ministries need equipment to function. A small house ministry may need less equipment than a larger one, but in a technological age, a ministry of any size must use technology as a means to grow and develop the work. All ministries need a functioning computer (and understanding of how to use that computer for ministry development), a printer, and programs that can help assist in the spread of information within a ministry. If a ministry desires to use live music and has an audience large enough to require acoustics, the ministry must take into consideration costs for musical instruments and an adequate sound system. Children's ministries and nurseries require furniture and toys. Sanctuaries require seating, lectionaries, decoration, and design. With each project and advance of the vision, ministers must sit down and calculate needed equipment and the finances needed to get good equipment. Equipment should be in good condition and should be designed to last. There is an old expression, "You get what you pay for." When it comes to equipment, this is certainly true. Even though something may be cheap, that doesn't mean it is good. Weigh options including consumer reviews, recommendations, and the standard of name brands before making purchases. In addition, some items, such as computers and printers, should never, ever be bought used.

Lawsuits

When in business, lawsuits and arbitrations are an unfortunate aspect of professional life. Even though the Bible encourages believers to resolve disputes among themselves (Matthew 5:25, 1 Corinthians 6:1-8), we know this does not always happen. While we live in the world, we must prepare ourselves to deal with and encounter worldly systems and situations. In that vein, we are going to look at lawsuits and arbitrations.

A lawsuit is a legal situation in which a person or organization brings a legal suit of action against another person or organization. There are several different types of lawsuits, all of which relate to the laws, distribution of winnings, governance, and type of suit involved. Lawsuits involve the courts of a nation in a dispute between parties to determine the rights of the parties involved and how those rights may have been violated. It is up to the court system to determine how the violated party can receive restitution in their situation; some parties receive a service, financial compensation, or some other type of reparation. The case is argued before a judge and sometimes a jury, and the decision is reached based on the evidence presented. Both sides must prove their arguments in the case, providing as much evidence as possible to prove their perspectives. For many types of lawsuits, a lawyer is paid to represent a party. A lawyer is a person trained to argue a legal case according to their understanding of the law and the evidence presented. Just as there are different types of lawsuits, there are also different types of lawyers who specialize in certain areas of law. Lawyers are noted for being very expensive, and wisdom should be used when selecting a lawyer. One should also watch for conditions that could cause a lawsuit to drag on and become more of an expense than is necessary.

Sometimes parties are able to reach what is known as a settlement either during the process or own their own prior to the lawsuit reaching a courtroom. A settlement is an agreement reached by both parties satisfactory enough to both of them to end the lawsuit. Settlements may involve an exchange of money, services, or other binding agreement that is as legal as if the case were to have a verdict from a judge or jury.

Arbitration

Arbitration is a legal remedy designed to avoid lengthy lawsuits. When a case goes up for arbitration, it goes into the hands of an arbitrator. An arbitrator reviews the issue in question (such as a contract dispute) and both parties agree to abide by the judgment, viewing it as legally binding. Arbitration resolves a pending legal dispute without having to appear in court or pay for representation.

It is my recommendation that we do what we can to protect ourselves from legal action and avoid pursuing legal action when situations arise. Most contracts contain different elements about lawsuits or arbitration, and we can avoid such legal action to the best of our ability by abiding by our agreements and understanding what we agree to sign. When someone else is in violation of an agreement, we should make our best effort to see the dispute resolved without legal intervention, if it is at all possible. If legal intervention becomes necessary, it is important we understand what we are allowed to dispute, how we are allowed to do so, and receive adequate and thorough legal advice in such situations.

Why Christians are advised against seeking legal remedy

Most believers know the Biblical commands to avoid secular lawsuits and relying on our various secular governments to execute justice for us. Looking at believers today, however, you would never know the Bible speaks on such matters. Every time I turn around, I hear about believers suing one another, pursuing legal means to resolve issues that affect Kingdom believers. While I do encourage believers to be prepared if something of that nature happens, I think as professional ministers it benefits us to look at the various reasons why God has given believers the admonishment to avoid the secular court systems. While there are obvious reasons why things such as divorce, annulment, child custody, and child support must be sorted out from a secular, legal perspective, there are reasons why, when it comes to business matters, believers should strive to handle things in-house.

- **We should be able to work out our differences, one to another** – Believers who come into agreements or business partnerships should be mature enough to resolve their differences with one another. If you were mature enough to enter into the agreement, you should be mature enough to get together, talk things over, and come to fair and just resolutions. I know this does not always happen, but if everyone involved claims to be a Christian, everyone involved should be able to grow up long enough to confront issues with the parties directly involved.

- **Owe nobody debt, save love** – The Bible tells us: *Let no debt remain outstanding, except the continuing debt to love one another, for he who loves his fellowman has fulfilled the law.* (Romans 13:8) If we enter into agreements, we should do all we can to fulfill them, not break them. Agreements are not taken lightly by God – after all, His entire relationship with us is based on an agreement! Entering into debt and thereby breaking agreements and good faith between other believers is morally and spiritually wrong.

- **It is not for the secular world to see or handle church matters** – Going into the court system of any nation whereby both parties are believers gives the secular world a keen insight into behavior that goes on within church circles that simply should not be. I don't deny it exists, but just like it's improper for us to air out all the dirty laundry we may have in our families, it is just as improper to do the same with church matters. The world already suspects – and laughs at – the disagreements and hypocrisies in the church. There is no reason to give them evidence what they suspect is true, and damage Kingdom reputation in the process.

- **Money is not an emotional nor spiritual remedy for sin** – It's nice to think that whatever financial or property restitution is sought will make everything better and instigate the healing process, but time and time again, history has proven it does not. If you really believe money will make you feel better for the offense someone committed, you are mistaken.

- **Legal remedies are not as easily sought as one might hope** – I have been to court, more than once. There have been times when I thought I had a very clear-cut, easily resolved case, only to find out that my case was not so legally cut and dry as I believed it to be. Even if someone wins their case, all that has been established is an individual has been wronged and has the legal right to recover whatever remedy is necessary. It does not mean the other party will remit restitution, and often means more time, money, and expense will be required if that remedy is sought. It's a nice idea to think going to court will solve all your immediate problems, but it brings a host of new ones into the forefront.

- **Forgiveness is more than a four-letter word** – We either believe in forgiveness or we do not. This means we either move on from wrongs, or we do not. Sometimes we have to put our spiritual money where our mouths are and literally live our concepts, even in the face of a financial or agreement-based loss.

- **Have no confidence in this world** – It fascinates me that we jump up and down about how we, as believers, should have nothing to do with the world – right up until the second we feel we've been wronged and can seek legal remedy. Using the legal system indicates you believe this world can right your wrongs. If you don't have confidence in the world, you aren't going to find what you seek from the legal system, either.

- **Establishing "courts" within the church** – In 1 Corinthians 6:1-8, the Apostle Paul clarifies that if the saints are to one day judge the world, they should also be competent to handle the various trivial matters that sometimes arise among them. When disputes arise between saints, the leaders of the church should be able to dispute the matter between them. Listening fairly to each side and assessing each case based on evidence and witnesses, church leaders should be able to guide the dispute to a fair – and Kingdom-based – resolution. By being involved, church leaders should guide disputing saints to handle and resolve the issue peaceably among themselves.

CHAPTER FIFTEEN

DECIDING BETWEEN FULL AND PART-TIME MINISTRY

The spiritual man makes judgments about all things,
but he himself is not subject to any man's judgment:
"For who has known the mind of the Lord that He may instruct him?"
But we have the mind of Christ.
(1 Corinthians 2:15-16)

DECISIONS, decisions, decisions! Most people are very taken aback by the number of decisions, both personal and professional, that follow a ministry call. Ministers of God are faced with a host of choices, some daily, some on a large scale, some immediate, and some long-term. Some ministers try to avoid these decisions or circumvent the importance of them, not realizing just how important the decisions they make are. The decisions we make as pertain to several major choices can affect the direction of our ministries, their long-term impact and success, and our own success and well-being as ministers of God.

Starting out

When most people are called into ministry or called to change their ministry circumstances, they are not expecting to receive such a call. Most have jobs, lives, families, obligations, and situations that either need seeing through or cleaning up. They have commitments, duties, and things that demand attention and time. As a result, most people in ministry start out in their work part-time.

Part-time ministry is defined as an individual working a non-ministry full-time job a minimum of forty hours per week, while maintaining smaller ministry work on the side. When one is a part-time minister, this means that ministry (however they are called) is not their primary job. It may be their heart, where they get their main fulfillment in life, but it is not what could be classified as a full-time career employment.

When working part-time in ministry, it indicates the minister does not expect to receive their livelihood from their ministry work. They may simply preach on occasion or as the opportunity arises, and may do a little evangelism or writing here and there. There is no initial pressure, as there is no expectation – it is simply the beginning of a ministry call.

The benefits to part-time ministry

When working in ministry part-time, a minister has an excellent opportunity to work toward vision and organization. They receive their calling from God and pursue it between working hours and family commitments. Depending on the specific ministry call, they may preach on weekends, operate ministry work in spare time, work in development of another ministry as an assistant of sorts, or pursue ministry education for a while.

The primary reason why most maintain part-time ministry is usually financial. When a ministry vision is first in development, ministers often fund part, if not all, the vision themselves. The need to finance the vision pushes many ministers to work full or part time jobs. This also becomes a means for networking and connection for the vision, as many people are met and maintained through the immediate environment of the visionary.

Some ministers are content to remain in part-time ministry for a number of reasons. If a minister is facing illness or some sort of physical difficulty, full-time ministry may not be an immediate option. Some ministers are not called to a life on the road or to deal with large, complicated ministries. Sometimes having young children or an active and contented family life keeps a minister from desiring more of ministry than they can handle. If a ministry vision is not to grow beyond a small community level, there may be no reason to pursue ministry full-time. Another reason may be because a minister finds an important outlet on their full-time job that somehow relates to their ministry work. For example, some people who are in ministry find a job, such as nursing or social work, to be an extension of their calling and feel no reason to quit their main job. Still, some people do not want to deal with the complications of operating their own business through ministry, and prefer to keep things as basic and simple as possible.

Switching to full-time

Full-time ministry is defined as an individual working in ministry a minimum of forty hours per week. When one is a full-time minister, this means that ministry (however they are called) is their primary "job." A full-time minister may operate in a part-time job to help supplement income or operate a secondary for-profit business or company, but ministry is the primary work for a full-time minister. When in full-time ministry, a minister operates the ministry as a full-time professional business.

Many ministers desire full-time ministry work. Some desire it because they are called to it, and others desire it because they think it's what they should do based on what others are doing. The decision to move from part-time ministry to full-time ministry is not an easy one. One must be truly called and led by the Spirit in that direction. It is often a difficult transition from part-time to full-time ministry, for a number of reasons many don't consider.

It is not uncommon for ministers to approach full-time ministry as the answer to many different things without seeing the intense responsibility it also is. They see the endless opportunities to witness to other people, counsel others, and imagine their ministry growing beyond its current boundaries. What they do not consider is the commitment full-time ministry requires. Full-time ministry is full-time work, whether one operates out of their home or an office. Full-time ministry work demands a minister spends extensive hours either learning skills or applying skills to make ministry work. It can be difficult to fight distractions, opposition, and various difficulties that arise as one pursues full-time ministry work. As with any business, these issues must be overcome rather than become overcome by them. With time and patience, a ministry grows into what it is to become, but it doesn't get there without many hours of labor and hard work. A minister in full-time ministry can't spend two hours a day on ministry and six hours attending to housework or watching television. Finding the necessary balance and fighting distractions are key to success in full-time ministry.

Profit vs. survival

Even though full-time ministry may be the desire of many, it is an end with new complications and challenges. The reason for this is simple: people believe ministers should not be in ministry for the "profit," or financial gain, of the work. As a result, the expectation of many is that ministry work should be free, even if it is a full-time endeavor for the minister. This puts the minister in a highly complicated and often difficult circumstance. To be in ministry today, one must be truly called – and know they are called – to take on the work full-time. No matter how much we are working to restore professional ministry, every full-time minister will face the following issues:

- Not getting paid for an event or offering, even if the event came at a substantial cost to you.

- People who want you for their events, but expect you will "understand" their circumstances if they do not compensate you like they should.

- A highly competitive atmosphere that is often unfair, demanding, and not always based on who is right for a job or engagement.

- Lack of opportunities to excel and make ministry work, even after many years.

- People who take issue with your consideration of ministry as a "job" or a "professional endeavor."

- Constantly being reminded that ministers who have worked for-profit are damaging to all ministers, and therefore, people aren't going to give to you because they assume you are for-profit.

There's one really simple precept ignored here: the fact that most ministers are not looking to profit – they are looking to survive. Being in ministry not only comes frequently with contracted or work-for-hire pay (in other words, you get paid for preaching or for engagements – but you do not receive a regular salary), it is also extremely expensive. In our "do-it-yourself" world where it is expected you will either do things yourself or pay others to do them, ministry comes at a high cost to the minister, all the while dealing with diminishing offerings and crowds. Therefore, when going into ministry full-time, everything must be considered. The major consideration? How a minister will provide for survival if they are spending forty-plus hours a week taking care of ministry duties.

We are taught in the church that God provides for the needs of His ministers, but we don't tend to go beyond that statement in our understanding. It is true that God does provide for His ministers; however, the Bible also explains that God provides for His ministers through the offerings of others (Leviticus 27:30-32, Numbers 18:21, Proverbs 11:24, Luke 6:38, 2 Corinthians 9:7, Philippians 4:14-16). This doesn't always happen easily in modern society, where the general church body thinks God provides for ministers by some sort of ethereal, mystical plan. Full-time ministry often requires financial adjustments, changes in personal spending habits, and other financial struggles that can become disappointing if one is not prepared for them. Just because ministry is full-time work does not mean that it is always financially profitable.

Financial changes also often require those in our immediate surroundings to change as well, which can lead to conflict. When transitioning from part-time ministry to full-time ministry, finances must be a consideration, especially if one has a family. It may mean that everyone in a family is required to make certain sacrifices and luxuries in pursuit of a ministry call. For this reason, it's important that the matter is discussed and others understand the changes that may result from switching to full-time ministry. It can also be challenging to work toward meeting many needs and serving many different purposes for the work of God as one tries to cut financial costs and gain ministry exposure at the same time.

Other considerations for full-time ministry

Full-time ministry is more than just a financial change. The minister also finds themselves with more time to attend to the needs of those they minister to and many more hours for study, focus, and discipline. It also gives the "do-it-yourself" minister more time to focus on the extensive needs a growing ministry has, even if a minister deals with lack of help or a very small office staff. These are great and good, but they also come with other realities:

- **Don't expect full-time ministry to leave you more time for you or your family** – I meet a lot of ministers who think the answer to having more leisure or family time lies in being a full-time minister. Just as with any job, working in it full-time means it's full-time – it's not something you do for one or two hours and then spend the rest of the day relaxing. Full-time ministers put in far more ministry hours than part-time ministers, and the temptation exists to go beyond normal working hours in pursuits. Because preaching engagements don't often pay the bills, full-time ministers often pursue other avenues that relate to ministry, such as writing books, articles, or blogging, to make up the difference in expenses. Some teach, work as counselors, or operate schools. These activities are done in addition to normal ministry endeavors which may be more of the same or totally different works. The full-time minister is going to have even less personal and family time, especially if the ministry grows.

- **Your entire position on your faith will change** – Doing ministry full-time means it becomes more than just a Sunday morning outing or an occasional musing by which you think about and relate to God. Full-time ministry gives your faith a different edge and perspective about your beliefs that you never had prior. The level of revelation you receive is different, and the way you feel about others, the things they do, your interactions with God, and how you perceive what you believe will all change.

- **Isolation** – The majority of ministers I meet who are in full-time ministry today tend to be very isolated individuals. As one moves closer to a calling, they move further away from other people and activities in life. If one is called to pursue full-time ministry away from a former job or former denominational position, that can cause further isolation as one moves away from the old and into what is new. In our modern society, work is a common pool for social interaction. Moving to full-time ministry – often without a full staff – can be socially isolating, whether ministry is conducted through a household or a small office space.

- **Avoid the temptation to get all your social needs online** – More and more ministers are moving toward the internet as a means to minister to others. As is addressed in this book, there is nothing wrong with having a presence online, but don't think the world of ministry is a virtual one. Escaping into the internet is not the answer to developing a solid full-time ministry. Make sure your life is balanced with offline presences as well as those you find online.

- **Don't use full-time ministry as an excuse to be unprofessional** – Even if you are working out of a home office, you still must meet ministerial professional ethics and conduct. It's not the fault of other leaders that you have a young child, a husband or wife who doesn't believe in your vision, or that you can't keep up with your housework and do ministry. Make sure you keep appointments, even those that are online or through the phone; return phone calls made as pertain to ministry inquiries or orders; and always present yourself in an appropriate manner: neat, clean, and orderly.

Biblical examples

We see examples of both full and part-time ministry in the Bible. The Apostle Paul worked in a secular job for part of his ministry, as did Aquila and Priscilla (Acts 18:2-3). Lydia was also a businesswoman in addition to serving as a pastor (Acts 16:14,40). It would appear that, at some point, the Apostle Paul worked full-time in ministry, and the Apostle Peter always appears to have been in full-time ministry after the resurrection of Jesus Christ, and encouraged others to remain focused on that pursuit. The matter of full or part-time ministry remains one between God and His servant, and no one else. While it is unadvisable to leave ministry to serve church disputes (Acts 6:1-4), the way a ministry holds its provision is between that minister and God.

CHAPTER SIXTEEN

THE THINGS WE'RE NOT SUPPOSED TO SAY ABOUT BEING IN MINISTRY

What do you prefer? Shall I come to you with a whip,
or in love and with a gentle spirit?
(1 Corinthians 4:21)

IT'S been said that "The truth will set you free, but first it will make you miserable." This statement could definitely apply to the modern "fantasy bond" people have with the romantic notions of ministry and ministers that...quite honestly...don't really exist. I believe we need to be honest and real about ministry in today's day and age. In the years since I have become a Christian (over fifteen), I have seen a great dishonesty exist within the ministerial offices. The concept exists that ministers are not human beings and are held to impossible-to-meet standards of need, want, and conduct throughout their lives. I believe the pressures of ministry coupled with often impossible standards creates difficulty, confusion, and isolation for ministers who feel guilty for their thoughts and feelings that appear to the outside world to less than "measure up."

There is truth in honesty. I believe part of the reason why the leaders of today's church are in such a negative state, falling apart at the seams, is from too many years of "playing church minister." Too often we feel the pressure to become a certain image or meet with a certain concept of ministry (that is often a kickback from religion and denominationalism) that, in the long run, hurts ministers. It causes them to feel desperation and discouragement, and, over time, break up ministry into a wildly long list of "dos and don'ts" that becomes intimidating and legalistic.

As a minister of God for a number of years, I want to see the church break through this nonsense so we can get back to Kingdom building and stop play acting as preachers. So, as usual, I'll break the silence and run the risk of being unpopular for airing out the things we all know are true, but remain the great unspoken truths of ministry. It is my hope that, through writing this, many of us will be able to step up and be comfortable with how we feel - not because we are wrong, but because it is a realistic truth that ministry today is hard. We are all human. Let's stop pretending we're not. That having been said...

- **Minister's personal relationships are not always brimming with meaning** - Today's church puts a lot of pressure on ministers to be married and have that picture-perfect ministry life...even if it is a total lie. There is a reason the Apostle Paul encouraged people to remain single if they were able to do so, not putting down marriage or eliminating it as an option, but encouraging those who were able and duly called to remain single to do so without stigma or shame. Even in the first century, the cultural standard was marriage, much like it is today, for all sorts of reasons: from political alliances to social standing to child-bearing and companionship. There is one simple reason why the Apostle gave his advice on relationships: married life, dating life, courting life, engaged life, etc. all bring unique challenges which can bring difficulties for ministers and can complicate their calling without the right help and support. I have yet to meet people who are married in ministry and do not experience the challenges of the two lives of ministry and marriage colliding or clashing at some point in time. If anything, I have found that the majority of minister's relationships are very difficult.

While I am sure this is not the case for everybody, being a minister of any variety in the five-fold bears with it its own unique challenges. We understand this in application to other professions: if you're married to a cop, there are certain issues that come along with choosing a mate with that profession, being married to a CEO or business executive also brings with it certain issues. The same is true with ministry. A powerful call on one's life can easily cause misunderstanding, especially when a mate's call is different. It can be a challenge to live with someone who walks in the power of God and, as we all know we live in a world that still dominates with the flesh, ministers can experience the sting of lack of support, encouragement, challenge, debate, and role stereotyping from their mates. It's not a matter of "not trying hard enough." Never assume that the pictures, images, or concepts you see of couples in ministry are always an accurate portrayal of what goes on behind-the-scenes in their relationship dynamics. Ministers can have difficulties in their private lives, just like everyone else.

- **We too wonder about what our lives would have been like had we done something else** - This doesn't mean ministers despise ministry or don't want to be in ministry any more than it does when other people wonder about it. The number of stigmas and taboos that surround ministry - it's something we're supposed to want to do, all the time, and feel good about, all the time, because it's God's work - deeply hurt ministers and prevent honesty within the calling. Most ministers do not despise their calling, but deal with the challenges of that calling. I know every minister out there has thought about what it would have been like had they taken that high-paying job, didn't have financial struggles and choices to make, or what would have happened if they went on the road as something other than a minister. It's not a desire to change directions or despise God, it's just a curiosity of how things would have been different had circumstances been different. It doesn't make ministers vain or evil, it makes them human!

- **We are not always happy or in a good mood** - I don't know why we think ministers need to be people who are constantly upbeat, smiling, and happy 24/7. In the Bible, the majority of people who walked in a calling were deeply serious, melancholy, authoritative, and contemplative people. They were grieved by the sins that surrounded them and wanted to establish the order of God in the midst of chaos. This led them to not always be the picture-perfect crowd dressed in white, walking around on a cloud, and singing the *Hallelujah Chorus* all day. Ministers get disgusted with people who walk in disobedience and with unresolved issues that seem to arise time after time after time. By the tenth counseling session of the day, filled with marital problems, suicidal children, people who come back time and time again with the same issues, and the total lack of order, doctrine, and responsibility displayed in people's lives, we're most likely not in a good mood, not feeling like talking to anyone, and not feeling like meeting any more needs, seeing any more people, or hearing about another person...possibly for as long as we live. Then the sun sets and rises again and we start all over again. While normal jobs operate on a five-day workweek with an eight-to-nine hour workday, ministers often spend extensive hours working behind the scenes in counseling, study, research, and then spend additional hours in the pulpit, on the internet, or working on the road in preaching, Bible study, teaching, covering...and then there are the many peripheral things ministers may do, such as writing, sermon preparation, prayer, and sometimes, a secular job to help supplement income. We get tired. We get moody. We sometimes cry and sometimes face exhaustion. Ministry can be overwhelming. We are not always in a good mood. Please, don't hold it against us. Are you always in a good mood? I didn't think so. We forgive you. Now extend that courtesy back to us.

- **We get tired of other people "needing" us all the time -** A former friend of mine, who is also in ministry, once described ministerial covering as going from being all about money to becoming garbage cans...where people back up and dump their garbage in and all over us. It is exhausting to constantly be expected to always listen to everyone, support everyone, talk to everyone, hear everyone else's problems (sometimes over and over again), pray for people at all hours of the day and night, receive phone calls at all hours, anoint people for everything they need, listen to whining and complaining, build people up, pray for them, lay hands on everyone...and do all this with the expectation that everything is being done for free only to have to do it again the next day. The needs of the people we serve often leave little time to expand the vision, especially when those needs seem excessive. Most ministers highly appreciate those in ministry who are not exceedingly needy, because it is a sign of fruitage. The goal of ministry is not for people to live dependent upon their leaders, but to grow and mature to the point where people don't always have to run to their leaders for every little problem. We like it when you reach a point to where you don't call us every ten minutes to ask our opinion or "bounce" things off of us. We are here for what you need...but you should reach a point where you don't need us constantly.

- **We need "pouring in" from time to time -** Once I was talking to someone about finances and spiritual needs. This individual felt that he was under no obligation to be covered by this ministry and tithe to it or support it in any way. When I addressed the issue that financial matters and support come from the people we work with - and I asked where he thought it would come from, his answer to me was, "Well you're the leader, so I just assumed God dealt with you directly." I responded, "By doing what? Planting a money tree in my backyard?" Some people today, in an effort to be lazy and irresponsible, dump a lot on their leaders. We're supposed to be happy all the time, never complain, never have a bad day, never get tired, and always be ready to do something for someone even if they should be doing it for themselves. It is assumed ministers get everything they need from God, and that those leaders who we work with or cover owe nothing to their leaders because "God will take care of them." I am the first one who believes God takes care of us - and in all instances, I know God provides. However - God provides through others. Ministers need financial help, a word of encouragement, prayer, edification, and signs of appreciation for what they do.

- **We are very aware we often don't make enough money** - I get tired of being asked to do things for free, at my own cost, or give to other people's causes because when the tables are turned, I've found the majority of them have no interest or desire to give back to God's Kingdom on this side of this vision. It is deeply offensive to me when a minister gets in the pulpit and starts bullying other ministers to "fund their vision" and give a certain amount of money (usually $50 or higher) when we all know they have no intention to shell out that same amount of money when in one of our events...if they even attend one of our events. Every day of my life I get the bank update letting me know exactly how much money I have – or, sometimes, do not have. Ministry is expensive. Visions are expensive. Please don't tell me to "step out in obedience" and give you a certain amount of money or to bankrupt myself to help "your vision." Jesus is well aware of how much money I have in my bank account and the way things go some days, consider yourself highly fortunate that I gave in the offering at all.

- **We know we don't spend enough time with everyone who wants our time...because there aren't enough hours in the day to go around** - Most of the time when you come to us and say, "Do you have a minute?," the truth is no, we don't have a minute...we are too busy preparing the Bible study you are going to attend...or writing the blog that you are going to read...or writing the book that you don't want to buy because you think we should give you a free copy...or writing the sermon you are going to hear at the service or conference...or planning the next event you are waiting for, but don't tell anyone about and do not attend...especially to hear you complain because you want a new car and God told you that you have a car and to live with what you have because you can't afford a new one without being evicted from your apartment...but we'll give you our time...anyway. Ministers face constant pressures in ministry, at home, among friends, and among those who are our spiritual responsibility. We are supposed to be all things to everyone in our life and wear multiple hats of apostle, prophet, evangelist, pastor, teacher, minister, friend, lover, girlfriend, boyfriend, husband, wife, sex kitten, stud, housekeeper, mother, father, student, disciple, author, counselor, chef, chauffeur, internet connoisseur, IT personnel...did I forget anything? I am well aware there are plenty of days when I don't spend enough time with someone, don't get back to someone fast enough, don't spend enough time attending to issues with family, or don't do what would make someone else happy in an endless cycle of instant gratification. If you want to step up and become my assistant and take some of the work off my back, then I'll appreciate it. In the meantime, I am tired of sermons, speeches, lectures, and opinions telling me to extend myself further than I am able. We can't be lighting fast people who flip on and off at the move of a switch. I'm sick of sermons that place additional pressure on ministers to have more sex with their spouses, spend more time with their children, establish "date nights" (you want me to enjoy "date night?" Stop calling me twelve times to pay attention to you!), have family Bible study more nights a week on top of church responsibilities, keep the house immaculate, and never let the "check oil" light come on in the car. Ministers need a break!

- **We get tired of the scrutiny and sting of "double standards"** - I haven't yet met a minister who is not disgusted with the fact that big-time preachers can get away with stealing people's money and having sex with underage children, yet we're not allowed to have an opposite sex friend for fear of "enticing lust." When it's a famous person, we aren't allowed to "judge" and if we say anything negative about their conduct, we aren't even allowed to have an opinion! When it's us, all we hear is about higher moral standards and face gossip...even when we've done nothing morally or spiritually questionable. We don't have to answer everyone's intrusive questions about our private lives or subject ourselves to torture for things that "they just don't agree with" because we're not a television personality. I believe it's a good practice for the church to mind its own business. In guarding that, if you ask me something and I feel you are going in a certain way with that question, I'm not answering it. If you're mind runs wild, it was going to run that way anyway. That's going to be your problem. In Jesus' Name, go and pray.

- **Ministry is hard** - We get through ministry with God's help, but that doesn't always make it easy. I believe ministry is a little bit of everything: counseling, public speaking, writing, study, personnel, business and finance, spirituality, image, and persona alike. Wearing multiple hats in one area of profession is a challenge. It is often difficult to get help, and even harder to get good help. Many people today want to be compensated and don't readily volunteer, even if they know God has called them to do so. What ministers see breaks their hearts, as they watch nations, cultures, and most of all, people fall into disrepair in their lives, into idolatry and all sorts of sin, and far away from God. Ministry is a gift from God and often a burden with the people. Don't demean your ministers by ever thinking the call on their lives (which costs personally as well as publicly) is an "easy" walk.

- **We don't always like the people we deal with (covering and work)** - With the heavy emphasis on spiritual parenthood popular in today's church, the expectation of the relationship between minister and covering is compared to parents and children. This means the great unspoken thing we are never to think, speak, or dwell upon with natural parenthood is also the major thing prevalent in many covering situations: ministers don't always like the people they cover (just like parents don't always like their natural children). As God works many things out in an individual – both those who are covering and those who are covered – the people we cover are not always brought to us to have an infinitely loving, caring relationship - they are there to work patience and discipline within us as we develop what is necessary in them. The same is true with other ministers with whom we work: sometimes the relationships are awkward or strained. They are there for a purpose, but the purpose is not to run off into the Kingdom of God and live happily ever after. I am very blessed to truly love the people I work with - both in covering and in ministerial relationships - but that has not always been the case, and I know it will not always be the case. In ministry, we deal with people. This means we don't always like everything about everyone, and we don't always agree with the course someone may take or the decisions they pursue. You may never know it from the way we behave, but like everyone else, we have opinions, likes, and dislikes about the people we work with, deal with, and cover.

- **We do not need any more responsibilities** - Ministers are generally overworked, underpaid, intensely stressed, and trying to find the balance between ministry and their private lives. Most of the time, we figure something out. This doesn't mean what we figure out is great or the best answer, but we find ways to get through and keep going. We don't need suggestions that involve taking on additional weekly activities. If one more person tells me to start taking on something else, whether it's a weekly prayer line, another weekly broadcast, or another job, I fear I will truly say something to that person that will not be very nice. I understand that people may be well-meaning, but there is also a larger-than-life expectation that ministers should all be doing whatever everyone else in ministry is doing. If we are doing what God has asked of us to do, we are doing enough.

- **We get lonely** - Ministry tends to be a very lonely walk. We think ministers are surrounded by people all the time and, therefore, that they should have every need met. What people don't often consider is that the majority of people around ministers are not their friends - they are either ministerial associates or people they cover. This means there's a lot of people around us all the time who need us for one thing or another, have a question, or just generally want something from us. We are ministers, not rock stars. The people around us are not groupies, wanting to buy us stuff or throw their underwear at us. Living with people who constantly need all the time and who don't always care about us as people or our own needs can cause us to feel isolated and lonely. This is why it's very important ministers have other friends who are also ministers to talk and share with about their walk and what they are going through - and to share in mutual support when things are difficult or discouraging.

- **We get tired of people touching our stuff** - One of my biggest pet peeves is watching people take a minister's personal belongings - and either manhandling them, moving them - or both. I recognize you accept the anointing on my life and are taken with what God is doing through me and through my ministry. That does not mean that every item I own becomes communal property. I'm glad you like my handkerchief. I'm glad you like my prayer shawl. Ask me where I got my things; don't pick them up and play with them. It's just rude to assume it's OK to touch a minister's things, whether it's their Bible, their personal items, or their teaching syllabuses, because they are there to be of service. You could be a perfectly lovely person. You could also be a witch. Don't touch our stuff!

Chapter Seventeen

<figure>✦</figure>

Assistance and Support

This service that you perform is not only supplying the needs of God's people but is also overflowing in many expressions of thanks to God.
(2 Corinthians 9:12)

SOME ministers are blessed to have people who support a vision from the beginning. In these circumstances, a leader has assistance as ministry work grows beyond its beginnings and is able to start easily. In our modern times, such assistance is often rare and, if it exists, may have complications. What is more common today is finding a rotation of people who support a work for a period of time but eventually move on to something else, for whatever that reason may be. As a result of this modern trend, it can be challenging for a full-time minister to find the assistance needed to productively grow a ministry. Most ministers today become a little bit of everything: their own educators, production crews, designers, producers, promoters, agents, and beyond. There are two sides to this balance: on one hand, it's great to be able to promote one's work; on the other hand, it means other aspects of ministry development may fall by the wayside. It also means a minister must work many long and lengthy hours to complete tasks. As a ministry grows and more promotional work is needed, it is a sign to turn to God for the right assistance and people to help with the work.

In an earlier chapter, we discussed the selection process

involved in picking board members. Board members are a part of the assistance and support we receive as ministers. For more information on what to look for in board members, review Chapter 10.

The first position we should seek to fill in a ministry (aside from board members) is an assistant or administrator. An assistant/administrator works in assistance to the ministry in office work, arrangements, planning, mailings, telephone conferences and calls, and event hosting. Having an administrator is an important role to fill because the administrator works closely with the one they assist. The administrator comes to know exactly what a leader needs and expects and is able to work well with that leader for that reason. Administrators should be carefully selected and screened, trustworthy and maintaining confidentiality and integrity in their position.

We fill additional positions as they arise to be filled and as the ability to bless comes forth. It is important that, as we are able, we are a blessing to our employees. Employees should be paid well, offered insurance plans as necessary, duly compensated for their work, and on a legitimate payroll. Christian leaders should be kind to their employees, treating all with respect, all the time maintaining the necessary balance of respect due to a leader. We should offer what our employees need and seek to be relevant in how we operate our Kingdom business just as much as be relevant in how we preach or teach!

Most in ministry understand the relevance of having a leader for teaching and support, as well as having followers who also support and share in the vision. What we don't often hear about is how important it is for ministers to have friends and support in ministry aside from those who follow the ministry or cover the minister. Every minister needs to have people to discuss various issues, dilemmas, and aspects of the ministry life with, without judgment, criticism, or misunderstanding. This calls for wisdom, as we must move with caution when selecting those who shall become a part of our inner circle. We don't need thousands of people; just a few solid, mature ministers who we can support and they too can support us as God calls, leads, and guides.

There are certain traits we should seek when having people around us for support. People should be trustworthy; efficient in their ministries; non-judgmental; able to keep a confidence; understandable; and believable. The person who is always looking for famous connections is not the right person to befriend because they will flip you as fast as look at you. Someone who is all about advancing their ministry through their connections is also someone who cannot be trusted. Also, never forget about how important it is to be a supportive person to the people who love, care about, and support you both as a person and minister of the Gospel!

CHAPTER EIGHTEEN

＜◆＞

TIME MANAGEMENT

There is a time for everything,
and a season for every activity under heaven.
(Ecclesiastes 3:1)

IN Luke 10:2, Jesus tells us: *The harvest is plentiful, but the workers are few. Ask the Lord of the harvest, therefore, to send out workers into His harvest field.* In many ways, we don't consider just how true a statement this is when it comes to a minister's time. Perhaps time is the biggest dilemma for a minister with a growing ministry. Without a lot of assistance – and sometimes, even with it – a minister's life and call is always strapped for time. It takes many, many hours to bring the various components of a ministry and its vision together. Ministry is also complicated in that the hours which go into ministry work are not always conventional. Even though a minister puts out a shingle with hours listed from 9 AM – 5 PM, ministers often work weekends, nights, mornings, afternoons, and evenings, depending on circumstances and needs. The people we need to talk or confer with aren't always available during normal business hours, and that can mean chats, calls, and discussions early or late in the day. We may deal with driving times, commutes, travel stresses, and exhaustion. To try and stick ministry within a box of time can be difficult, and it can also be difficult to balance that time with personal or family life.

No matter how hard a minister tries, there will always be times when time seems short and not every aspect of life is balanced because there is too much to do and not enough time to do it. Not everyone in a minister's life will understand because not everyone in a minister's life has the same calling. This can lead to conflict that may, in some ways, seem to never end or be resolved. Just giving in and not attending to the work of the ministry is not the answer. Following the guiding of the Holy Spirit and being directed about the division and allowance of time comes through application and purpose is the best way this can be accomplished.

Scheduling time is a good option when dealing with appointments, clients, and phone consultations. It is very important time spent with those learning, training, or being taught of the ministry in some way are scheduled in their time, as this establishes a boundary. In today's church, most people believe a leader should be accessible anytime, anywhere, for any length of time. Leaders who allow those under them or benefiting from the work (whether directly covered by them or not) to run their time establish a pattern of disrespect and disregard for themselves. Limits and boundaries are essential, especially when it comes to time. Phone consultations should follow the same line of regulation as in-person appointments: limited to a certain length of time and for a certain purpose.

Scheduling others also helps the minister to manage their own time better, recognizing what needs to be done in a day and manage the various projects that are at hand. If a minister is writing a book, for example, and heavily into the process, visits and phone calls will be kept to a minimum. If it is more of a day for academic, financial, or spiritual direction, the day is planned accordingly. Obviously not every day will be easily scheduled or fall into a typical plan, so flexibility is needed (especially in emergency situations). Ministers should also know their own limitations and abilities, and work with those in a weekly or daily plan.

Scheduling also applies to a ministry's annual, monthly, and weekly events. Every year, starting in September and running through to about December, a ministry should sit down and seek to plan the events they will be hosting for the following year. Anything – from services, to revivals, conferences, meetings, gatherings, etc. – should be included in the calendar schedule so advertising and planning can operate as smoothly as possible. Ministers should also monitor a personal calendar which includes every event to which they are invited to minister, to balance various events and keep track of things to come.

When it comes to invitations to minister, the inviting ministry should give the minister plenty of time to plan to attend the event. Invitations for major trips (that involve extensive travel) should be given at least four-to-six weeks advanced notice and invitations for shorter distances at least two-to-four weeks advanced notice. If a minister has backed out at the last minute and a minister is invited at the last minute, they should be blessed for their last-minute rearrangement to help in the situation.

Ministry is an intense work. I do not believe anyone ever really retires from their ministry calling, nor fully takes a vacation from it. A minister may never retire or fully go on vacation, but ministers still need times for refreshment, spiritual perspective, vacation, and rest. If possible, ministers should schedule at least one period of time off per week as needed (afternoon, morning, day, etc.) and at least two one-week periods of time off per year – one time for retreat and sabbatical with the Lord, and the other time for relaxation. As a part of a yearly schedule, these events should be documented and planned for all involved to know about, and prepare accordingly.

CHAPTER NINETEEN

———◆———

EVENTS AND EVENT PLANNING

Commit to the LORD whatever you do,
and your plans will succeed.
(Proverbs 16:3)

MOST ministries hold events. An event is a gathering of some sort for a specific purpose. Everything from a church service to an international five day conference counts as an event. No matter how big or small an event may be, events all have one thing in common: planning.

There are six major components to planning a good event: a set date, a set theme, a good location, good advertising, organization, and order.

- **A set date** – It is amazing how many events are planned either at the last minute or where a date change occurs several times due to various poorly-planned circumstances. Events should have a fixed date, one that is set and planned for a minimum of four to six months in advance for advertising purposes. A date can change one time for a venue accommodation with plenty of advanced notice, but should not change more than that. Set dates give the ministry, the ministers, and the attendees plenty of time to plan and structure for the event.

- **A set theme** – Events today don't often have a lot of structure to them, which is part of why they fail. A theme helps to unify the event and also unify the participants in the common theme. In making conference preparations, deciding how to advertise an event, and beyond, a theme helps to guide and direct those preparations. A theme for an annual event can change from year to year, but a conference theme should remain consistent within the scope of its yearly specific event advertising.

- **A good location** – Matching your event to a location is key to event success. Just because you have access to a church doesn't mean a church is the best location for whatever it is you are doing. It also doesn't mean that where you live is the right locale for what you may be doing. If you are looking to do an inner-city outreach, a rural country church is the wrong place for that event. When considering location, accessibility must be considered (is there a local airport for travelers from out of state? How far do people have to go to reach the event?), audience must be considered (Is this just a local event? A regional one? Where is our audience? How can we reach them?), and purpose must be considered (What are you going to be doing in that event?). The right location can make an event – while the wrong one can break it.

- **Good advertising** – Good advertising for an event doesn't start two weeks before an event; it starts months in advance. To advertise an event, you need to have good 'staying power.' Staying power recognizes that not everyone will be drawn to an event, and that perseverance is needed to continue for the event's success rather than just giving up because things get too difficult. Events must have a flyer that can be distributed both in paper format and digitally online; a website or webpage (if one already has a website) for the event; an announcement through social networking websites; and word-of-mouth relay through friends and associates. If possible, commercials can also be designed through basic video-making computer programs and distributed via YouTube, TikTok, and other sites online. If possible, podcast announcements and radio and cable access advertising can also be inexpensive options to spread the word. Event flyers, sites, and announcements should contain the essentials: location, dates, times, relevant personalities within the event, registration information, a contact phone number or information, and should display the general theme of the event.

- **Organization** – Before sending out the flyers and the event invitation on Facebook, take the necessary steps to host a well-organized event. Who will help with things such as registration and planning? Who will be the contact person for the event? How will this event operate? What are some commonly asked questions, and how can we answer them? Who can assist attendees during the event? Good events operate with good function and good organization. Take the time to make sure the event is organized, well-thought out, and not haphazard.

- **Order** – The Word of God tells us that God is a God of decency and order (1 Corinthians 14:40). No matter what your type of event, order functions the same way, although its execution may be different: things are purposed to flow in the Spirit while accomplishing the goal of the God-given event. Beware people who interrupt when preachers are speaking, who are hasty to exercise gifts when you cannot vouch for or verify their ministries, or having speakers, guests, or ministers who are not in alignment with the conference theme or vision. Order begins when an event starts in unity: the speakers walk in unity, the workers of the event walk in unity, and all are able to come together in the theme and vision of God's purpose for that event.

How good events come together

Events come together through great participation, work, unity, and prayer. All who are helping with an event, speaking for an event, or participating with an event need to be on the same page and share the vision of the event, as well as endorse the event's visionary. Just as with any other vision, writing the vision, purpose, and mission of an event is essential to its success and to convey its order and organization.

Great events don't just happen. The steps above truly prove that having a great event is about much more than just having a great idea. Mega ministries spend thousands of dollars on event planners and other staff to make sure their events have a certain feel to them. Everything from the setup and decoration to sound and music are carefully executed in a certain order and with a certain purpose, to inspire a certain sense when the event begins.

Just because you don't have the money for an event planner or the extensive amount of staff larger ministries do does not mean you cannot hold a great event! I personally know many ministers who are tired of the expansive and extensive orchestration some mega ministries use in order to produce the feel present in their events. Many people in the church are looking for more than just a big show for a large audience. This means that smaller ministries should seriously consider the relevance and impact a conference can have upon their regions or the area where God commissions an event to take place.

Event planning is about walking in the Spirit of God unto teamwork. Too many conferences fall apart or never materialize because people are unwilling to assist and participate Above all things aside from the Spirit of God's work in an event is the principle of teamwork. Too many conferences fall apart because people are unwilling to help and unwilling to stand with a leader or aside a leader to help it come together. Finances also tend to be an issue, as do some other matters in the church today. Below we are going to deal with some of these issues – and learn the correct ways in which to handle them so every event you host can be a lasting success.

Registration

Registration fees seem to be a controversial issue today. Even though many will not balk at the idea of a mega church leader charging registration fees that may range in the hundreds to thousands of dollars, when smaller leaders take on an event, people try to find ways to get around them. I've hosted events where people will boldly show up at the door and think they are just going to walk in past the registration table without paying. Some such as this leave, others throw a fit or behave unseemly because they don't want to pay. Some think that registration fees are a sign a leader doesn't trust God, while others think they are a must for every event. Who is right?

I am inclined to agree that registration fees in the high hundreds and thousands of dollars are out of control. I do not, however, believe that registration fees are a sign a leader doesn't have adequate faith, nor that they are inappropriate. I think the registration fee should fit the event, and I encourage registration fees as part of conference events. The reality is that most leaders do not have the space, nor the ability, to host a conference event in their immediate surroundings. This forces the leader to find an alternate location for the event and often requires payment up front. Having to find an alternate location requires the leader to know how many are coming and plan for things such as seating, food, materials, and space usage.

- **When to charge registration fees, and why** – If a church or ministry is holding a conference designed to reach people outside of their immediate church or ministry (in other words, if the event is designed to draw people in from other churches and ministries as well as others in and beyond the area), the event should have a registration fee. When people are coming to that event who are not part of the immediate ministry, they need to understand the planning involved and show proper respect to that ministry by helping to fund its inception. It is wrong to assume those who are part of that immediate ministry should cover the entire cost of the event that is mainly held for other people. This is especially true if the event must be held in a different venue from the normal church location. If an event is simply for those under a local ministry in their normal setting, registration should not be charged, because those people are already contributing financially to that ministry. If the event for that ministry is held at a retreat center or other special-themed location, registration in accord with the cost of that event should be charged to each participant.

- **Consideration** – Event planning requires an approximation of guests attending the event. Those who are attending should see fit, without complaint, to register for the event in their payment of required fees and in providing registration information in advance. Registration fees force people to make a decision about attending and those who register are more likely to attend than those who wait until the last minute to decide about an event.

- **Creates a storehouse** – In Malachi 3:10, the Lord speaks: *Bring the whole tithe into the storehouse, that there may be food in my house. Test me in this, says the LORD Almighty, and see if I will not throw open the floodgates of heaven and pour out so much blessing that you will not have room enough for it.* Tithing is a controversial subject today, with many on different sides of the fence about it. The bottom line about tithing, however, is it is a systematic principle of giving that creates a storehouse so the needs of

God's Kingdom can be met. The Kingdom of God, as it functions in this world, cannot function without the financial support and gifts from those who are a part of it. In the case of a conference, a registration fee represents the "tithe" of the event. A conference registration fee should be set at approximately ten percent of the conference budget (and can be adjusted to a round and workable number, up or down, as necessary). These fees enable a host to cover the cost of a location, food for the participants, conference materials, and take care of speakers. Everything else that comes forth financially from a conference is the offering, which helps supply additional costs that arise after the registration fees are collected.

- **Food and materials** – Most people expect to walk away from a conference or event with something in hand. They forget gift bags, conference materials and booklets, CDs, T-shirts, and souvenirs all cost money. If as part of an event lunch or dinner is provided, that creates a high expense for the conference host. It is unreasonable to believe such should be provided with no financial participation from those attending the event.

- **"But I can't afford it!"** – It amazes me that people have money for eating out, movies, pornography, cigarettes, beer, new clothes, manicures, shoes, and other things, but suddenly have no money and want a free ride when it comes to registration fees. If you have the money to get to an event, then you have the money for the registration fees. It is wrong to expect the leaders to fund things out of their pockets so someone else can have a free ride. Some ministries establish scholarship funds for those who can't afford to attend a conference – but in establishing such, operate with caution. Make sure there are guidelines in place and that those guidelines are upheld rather than giving everyone who wants a handout access for free.

- **Vendors must always be charged a vendor registration fee** – Whether your event is just for your ministry or for everyone involved, vendors must always be charged a separate registration fee for the event. As vendors are specifically coming not to participate but to sell items, vendors must pay for their access to those who will be attending your conference. Vendor fees should cover their access to the event, set-up, and any other costs a vendor may create. When calculating this cost, a vendor's expense should be approximately two to three times the cost of a regular attendee. Vendors should also be pre-screened and only allowed to sell items that are considered appropriate for a Christian event.

Using another church/welcoming another ministry for an event: an all-around etiquette

It is quite common for conference hosts to use other churches and ministry buildings for events. This may be due to a number of factors, including the size and location of a building, hosting a conference event out of town, or due to economic reasons. This sharing or renting of church buildings belonging to other ministries has caused new issues in required etiquette among ministers and members. There are two different sets of etiquette required among the different ministries. The first we shall address is the etiquette of those renting or using the facility. The second is the etiquette of the ministry who owns the building.

When you are using or renting another space:

- **The space must be maintained in the condition it was presented in** – If people can't control their behavior, they should not be at an event to begin with. Many churches today have high-tech equipment, expensive furniture, fixtures, and materials that are able to rip, tear, break, or be destroyed in the wrong hands. It should be understood that using the facility means taking care of and respecting the items present in the facility when you arrive.

- **If items are destroyed, it is the responsibility of the guest ministry to replace, fix, or pay for damages** – There is a legal clause known as indemnity which makes a renter responsible for damages to property while renting a building for an event, even if it was not the renter themselves who did the damage. This is because by renting the facility, the renter makes themselves responsible for the care of the facility while it is on their watch. If you want someone to reimburse you for their damages, it is your job to obtain it from them – but you are still required to pay for or replace damages to a facility, regardless of whether or not that individual repays you. Indemnity clauses are often included in rental agreements, and it is important to read them carefully and pay careful, close attention to the wording.

- **The conference attendees should be courteous and polite to ministry leadership and staff at all times** – Remember, you are guests in a facility and correct protocol requires correct behavior. Leadership issues should be handled by leadership – not by members. Courtesy, good manners, and good etiquette are all in order.

- **Make sure the terms of agreement are clear** – It should be clear what times you will need the facility, what you will need in the facility, and what you will pay or exchange for use at the facility.

When you are providing the space for rent:

- **Have the building in presentable order** – Don't provide a building for an event that is sub-par. Make sure the building is in good working order and everything within that building is functional. Also, do not pass off pre-existing outages, breaks, or malfunctions as being the responsibility of the renter – be upfront about it. Don't try to get someone else to pay for things you know are not working correctly.

- **Expect your staff to be courteous** – Just because the people hosting and attending the event are not people who are part of your regular ministry does not mean they should be treated any differently than those who are a part of the regular ministry. Leaders are leaders, and should be treated as such – with respect and courtesy. Make sure the staff provided matches the event – whether it is for security, sound, opening and closing the building, or any other need which may arise during the event.

- **Make it known that those who attend the conference from the church are expected to register for it** – If you have guests in your facility who are having an event, you are giving a seal of approval and interest to what they are doing. As part of renting out your facility, it is important your members know they are able to attend the event and should attend. It is important for them to understand, however, that doing so means they must follow the same guidelines as everyone else attending – they are not exempt from registration fees and offerings because the organization is using their facility. Being in the facility means someone is paying to be there – and it is inconsiderate to expect a conference host to accommodate people who attend the facility regularly for free. Work out a deal for a group registration fee with the conference host (where members of the church who register with the church group are able to get a discount) and present the entire registration list and fees to the ministry hosting the event. It promotes good morale and shows respect.

- **Encourage and expect your members to attend the event out of support** – If you aren't comfortable with someone using your facility, then don't allow them to use it – but don't have someone use the facility and not help promote the event. Part of the appeal of using a church facility versus a hotel or secular conventional center is having the support and promotion of a church family. This becomes especially relevant when an event is held outside of one's own city or region.

Hospitality

When hosting an event, we cannot ever forget the host's call to hospitality (Romans 12:13, Romans 16:23, 1 Peter 4:9, 3 John 1:8). Hosts are responsible to cover travel (when over a certain amount of miles) and hotel accommodations, unless the guest speaker insists on paying for those things. Even then, host ministries should always provide an offering for their speakers. The offering should reflect the best a ministry can offer for the service provided.

Host ministries have the obligation to communicate well with those they invite as guest ministers. It is understandable that not all events come off well, nor does every event wind up happening in real time. Host ministries must recognize they do not have the right to pass off such inconvenience to guest ministers. When a minister accepts a speaking engagement, that means they are excluding themselves from accepting other speaking engagements during that time. Such needs to be acknowledged by the host ministry in more than just agreeing to honor an honorarium or certain conditions if the event takes place in real time. This is an acknowledgement that preaching, speaking, and ministering is about more than just what happens in the pulpit of an event. Ministers spend weeks preparing for events, planning sermons and notes, in prayer before the Lord, and seeking God about how to be His most effective servant and messenger for that event.

If an event is cancelled within three weeks or more of its

scheduled date, the host ministry should act with courtesy, thanking and acknowledging the minister for their time, effort, and it should be made clear that if the event is to be rescheduled, they will be notified within at least four weeks of the reschedule to minister for the event. If an event is cancelled two weeks or less prior to its date, the host ministry is responsible to notify the guest minister and pay them an offering for their time and exclusion of dates to attend the event. This is an honorable and hospitable move, recognizing their time is valuable and valued, and leaves the host ministry and guest minister on good terms. Dumping a minister at the last minute without pay and without explanation is both a sign of disrespect and a move that is, at best, inhospitable.

When invited to an event, it is expected that guest ministers will make appropriate preparations. This includes asking questions, getting essential information, understanding about the theme, if any, and taking the time to prepare for the event through prayer, study, and sermon or ministering preparation. Doing these things shows respect for the host ministry, and just as they are expected to show respect to guest ministers, so too the guest minister needs to show respect to the host in adequately preparing – both practically and spiritually – for the event at hand.

If an invited party becomes exceedingly demanding, requesting things unreasonable or unfeasible, or starts displaying an attitude contrary to the vision of an event, the inviting host has every right to recant the invitation. Some people do this verbally, some by email, and some by formal letter. I recommend either email or formal letter, as such establishes a record and the reason for such a dismissal. When working in ministry, we must be discerning about who we invite and why we invite them. Not every speaker is appropriate for every event and it is important to match the anointing with the event. Invitations should be clear about the intent and purpose of the event and should reflect the values of the event, so a potential speaker can make an appropriate choice and decision about whether or not to accept the invitation. Invitations should come no less than three to six months in advance and should be accepted within that time frame. It is also important that event hosts make it clear who to contact with questions and that they maintain a steady and purposed communication with those speaking or helping with their event as much as possible.

If an invited party attends an event and causes disruption, disorder, and chaos when the intent of an event has been clarified, the host is under no obligation to offer financial compensation or allow the individual to remain in the event if they are scheduled to speak or participate further in the event.

Virtual events

With the advance of the internet has come the virtual conference, an event by which the entire conference structure is held online or via conference line, on the telephone. As this is a new medium for conference hosting, many undertake this as a cheaper alternative to traditional event hosting. Given there are no extreme overhead costs (such as building rental or travel and accommodations for speakers), some are turning to the virtual conference as an answered prayer for event hosting.

This has left a severe gap in conference etiquette, planning, and protocol, as virtual hosting may solve a host's overhead issues, but opens the door to a whole new area of questions. Whether considering hosting a virtual event or participating in one, here are some things to keep in mind.

- **Virtual conferences are not the same as having an in-person conference** – I understand that the Spirit connects us wherever we are, but as I have stated before – it's fine to have a presence online, but it is not fine to try and use the internet to avoid doing ministry in real-time. As a conference host myself for a number of years, I completely understand the expense involved in real-time conferences. I understand that registration and enrollment are down unless you are a Christian celebrity with a big-name ministry, and that expenses are up, especially if you are a minister without a regular church building or other meeting place. That having been said, the virtual conference is not the same as having a conference in person where you can see the people you are ministering to, can lay hands on them and pray for them, and can enjoy the fellowship of the speakers and attendees. The spiritual atmosphere is different because the believers are not gathered together in the same physical location. Many people still do not regard the internet with any level of severity when it comes to ministry and do not consider the time or effort that may go into preparing a virtual event, and even if they knew it, there are those who would scoff at it. Do not expect a virtual event to feel the same, look the same, or be regarded the same as a conference held in real-time.

- **Virtual events still require planning, good hosting, and good advertising** – Just because you are not hosting a conference that people will have to travel to and meet in person does not mean that it should be poorly planned. Virtual conferences still need a set date, a speaker line-up, a flyer, and good advertising. As a host, it is improper to pass your overhead or expenses to your speakers or expect them to cover your fees, the expenses for your flyer, or to have "professional" items, such as professional headshots or specific technical equipment to meet with your expectations. It is also good faith to give your speakers an offering, even if it is something smaller than normal, for their time and trouble.

- **Don't expect to receive offerings or high registration fees for virtual events** – I know all too well that it costs us money to keep our electricity on, to buy equipment (such as a webcam or have a cell phone) to do a virtual conference, and to maintain internet and phone access, but the reality is that those are things anyone who is online already has in their possession, and they are not things seen as a burden to someone hosting or preaching for a virtual conference. Because a virtual conference is, in reality, nothing more than someone teaching or preaching while sitting in front of a webcam or on the phone, it is seen as something with no overhead and as more of a hobby than a professional endeavor. As a result, offerings are seen as an inconvenience for a virtual event and few – if any – people see fit to give for them. People see it like this: they can go sit on Youtube or Facebook and watch people preach, for free – so there is no reason to pay for a conference on the internet. It doesn't matter how innovative or different you may feel your conference is. To your audience, it's just something else they can find elsewhere on the web.

- **Registration is only appropriate in certain situations** – If a conference host has an overhead for doing a conference, such as joining a specific site or using a specific service, or something specific comes with the conference – such as instruction, school credit, or materials – registration is fine. It must be reminded, however, that registration must be considerably low, even in these circumstances. Unless it is a formal tuition-based class through a school website and not just a conference, registration for an internet event should not exceed ten dollars per person. If there will be no provided materials and the site you are using for the virtual event is free to you, as the host, registration should not be charged. Remember, overall, the internet is still a largely free resource for people and they can easily find what you claim to offer with someone else. Expecting people to register for a conference that is coming from their computer is unrealistic if nothing else accompanies it.

- **You still must consider and take care of your speakers, unless alternate arrangements are made** – If you clarify that everyone is offering their time for a virtual conference, then your speakers agree to do so voluntarily, at their own time. In this instance, no offering should be taken and no registration should be set for the event. Speakers should under no circumstances be asked for money to pay for behind-the-scenes costs (such as the flyer or host's equipment). If the speakers are expected to offer their time, than everyone involved in the event should be doing the same, not some compensated and some not. That having been said, if there is no such arrangement as pertains to offering, you should be giving your speakers something for their time and preparation. Even though the event is not in real-time, having a virtual conference with no prior arrangement as pertains to the event's offering means your speakers are expecting to study, plan, and prepare for this event like it is anything else. While speaker's fees and offerings for a virtual event should never be as high as a real-time event, speakers should receive something in the ballpark of $25 to $100, depending on the nature, size, and situation of the event.

Chapter Twenty

Signs a Conference is Worth Your Time

As a prisoner for the Lord, then,
I urge you to live a life worthy of the calling you have received.
(Ephesians 4:1)

EARLIER I spoke of the relevance in order when one plans events. Now we are going to take some time to look at signs for selecting an event. If you are a preacher, teacher, five-fold minister, minister, leader, or other public figure, the odds are good you're going to be invited to speak at an event, conference, workshop, church service, or convention.

I've been on an active conference circuit since 2007. Prior to that, I took sporadic events and even planned a few small events on my own dating all the way back to 1999. In my years as both a conference host, speaker, and yes, even one where I attend events, I have seen conferences ranging from the good, to the bad, to the very, very unspeakably unimaginable. I have also been a part of non-church events that were, at times, often better planned and prepared than church events. I've seen people literally break into arguments and fights in the church sanctuary, threats and intimidations made at the altar, people being waited on hand-and-foot in the sanctuary under the guise of "altar service," total disrespect to leaders, and numerous events where I walked away without an offering or with an insulting offering. There's the infamous story where someone gave me $24 and a raw chicken to take home as my offering - and then wanted to know what "spirit" I saw over him - it was all-too-tempting to say, "I see the spirit of cheap!" There's been the conferences where the hosts have put up all their speakers in cockroach-infested motels, left me at the airport for three hours in a strange city, or expected me to pay for my own accommodations when the conference budget didn't "quite measure up to expectations."

In the church, everyone wants to hear or be acknowledged as "doing their best." We see conference hosts as doing a favor to their speakers – and, therefore, it's considered extremely "ungrateful" for leaders to complain about unacceptable offerings, accommodations, or treatment. It is commonplace for conference hosts to expect their speakers to meet conference budget, make up for lack of funds, or put up with all sorts of unprofessional nonsense, just to make the conference come to a reality. My general disgust with the way so-called leaders treat other leaders in today's church has caused me to step back and think long and hard before accepting most invitations I receive. As a speaker, I do not make unreasonable demands or ask for unreasonably high sums of money. On the other hand, I do expect that those who seek me out for their events are doing so because they recognize the anointing and intend to do their very best to honor that anointing as they seek out it in their events. It is truly an offensive thing when people seek to cheapen God's anointing for their own successes or gains. We forget that how we honor God also reflects in how we treat others, especially how we treat those who are called of God. While there is no question that some people in the church today have a prima donna complex and think the world is their oyster of servitude, leaders who are solid, mature, and seek to find balance and success for building the Kingdom of God can lose their voice if they are accused, manipulated, or degraded for believing they should be treated better in an event than people see fit to treat them.

I don't believe every conference leader deliberately seeks to misuse God's people. At the same time, I think that becomes inevitable when an event is poorly planned or when one is relying too heavily on the event to take care of itself, which is sometimes the case. Planning events is work. Being a conference host takes more than just an anointing; it also takes good planning. Worldly events sell out every day while church events are many times virtually empty. Why? Worldly events are better planned.

God clearly tells us He is a God of "decency and order" (1 Corinthians 14:30). This means God does not do things haphazardly. He used order and precision when creating the world, and that tells us there is an order to creating things. Visions don't just happen; they are created. Here are some ways to determine whether or not a conference vision is created...or just "happening."

- **A set conference date** - Most ministry events change dates multiple times before they settle on one to have the event. It's not uncommon for speakers to be told to reserve one set of dates, then told to reserve another, and then sometimes, yet another set...not to mention the multiple dates which may be advertised for the event. This causes confusion in those seeking to attend something, and it's a major turnoff when an event is constantly rescheduled before it has even happened yet. It's perfectly understandable if weather or extreme circumstances cause a postponement, but even then, an event should not be rescheduled multiple times. If a conference date or dates are not established, then the event isn't worth making a commitment to attend. Leave the suggested dates open for a fixed, well-advertised event rather than an invisible one that may or may not materialize.

- **Advanced event notice** - Sometimes people back out at the last minute and we are called in their place. That is completely understandable, and a circumstance to which I am not speaking of here. It takes time to put together a solid event that will both be a blessing and will come together as smoothly as possible. In planning an event, conference hosts must take special spiritual and practical care to match speakers with their event. Out of respect for their time, ministries, and anointing, speakers must be notified with as much advanced notice as possible.

- **A reality event** - We'd be amazed if we stepped back and thought about the vast number of conferences that are largely hypothetical. A hypothetical event is one with no name, no date, no content, no plans, and no structure - but someone wants to ask you about this hypothetical event to see if you'd be interested to speak for it. A hypothetical event is just that - it's someone's general idea for something they'd like to do but have taken no steps to bring that event into reality. Hypothetical events have this creepy way of becoming figments of people's imagination - and tend, more often than not, to never materialize into a conference. If someone can't give you the name of the event, some content about it, and a date for the event - even if the date is far in the future - politely decline or tell them to contact you again when they have more information about the event.

- **Keeping speakers informed** - Conference hosts are a varied group. Some update speakers daily - to the point of informing about problems, personal issues, and things that are nobody's business - to those who never tell anyone anything until the second they arrive. Speakers need to be informed about conference developments, when they are scheduled to speak, a daily itinerary of conference events, and anything else that may be relevant to their presence at the event. Too much information is not necessary; at the same time, too little information shows poor planning and lack of courtesy for speakers who are in a strange city and location.

- **Advertising** - In order for people to attend an event, people need to know about said event. It's not uncommon for conference hosts to schedule an event and then only tell their immediate church or friends about the event. While I recognize conferences tend to have budgets, every conference can and should utilize any and all means available them to get the word out about an event. Flyers, free websites, Facebook, twitter, blogs, emails, mailings, visiting local church events and talking about it, and getting as many people involved in the word-of-mouth promotion as possible let a large scale audience know about an event and indicate a much higher probability for a great turnout.

- **Use the word "blessing"...correctly** - I once spoke to a man who sought me out, invited me to come to his conference events in another state (and, in one case, in another country), and then announced to me I would receive no offering and would have to pay for my own travel. When I told him I would be unable to accept his invitation because this isn't what I require to speak at an event, he turned around and told me that he pays for himself to go to things all the time because he's going seeking "the blessing." I won't repeat what I said to him after that. As a leader I once knew (who is also a pastor overseas) said to me - when we preach somewhere, we are God's gift to them. They must honor God enough to respect that gift and be a blessing. It's unreasonable - not to mention offensive - to ask someone to come and preach somewhere at their own cost and without offering of some sort so the host minister can abuse and exploit the anointing of that individual. I believe in coming to be a blessing; but I believe blessing is a mutual process and experience that goes both ways. We're not going to find a blessing somewhere if we spend hundreds or thousands of dollars to get somewhere and then someone gives us no offering or

177

a low offering because they expect us to be a blessing - and then wishes us well. Don't tell someone to come and be a blessing if you don't expect to be one yourself!

- **Acknowledge your ministry** - I've been contacted on Facebook on two different occasions by people who have known of me and my ministry going back to 2007 and they have never once - at any point in time - spoken to me prior. It's not that I never spoke to them - they just never responded to me, so I figured I either was irrelevant to them or they didn't really know who I was. Imagine my surprise when I was contacted and they started saying all these things to me to try and get me to participate in something or help them! My first response was, "So you did know who I was." Amazingly enough, neither one ever responded to this statement. One went on to dump me from her event for very unethical reasons and the second one acted as if she never said she was considering me as a speaker for her event. If someone has known of you and your ministry for an extended period of time and they have never reached out or shown interest, odds are good that, consideration or not, you probably won't be picked as a speaker for their events. Why is this? Because they've never even shown the courtesy to talk to you and acknowledge your work.

- **Disclaiming their offer** - In one of the incidents I just mentioned above, I was contacted by the individual in question to let me know she was considering me as a speaker for her 2011 event. She was "praying about it" and wanted a CD or something of me teaching. I provided this and she told me she would be in contact. I heard from her about two months later, telling me what a good teacher I was and letting me know that if I was not to speak, they still wanted me to come and be in "their midst." I knew when I got that message they weren't going to have me speak - I mean, come on, really. Talk about obvious and tacky. However, this woman never confirmed or denied me as a speaker for the event - she just kept telling me, over and over again, that they were still "praying about it." For months following she failed to update or establish any information and just put off dates. She never confirmed or denied anything. After modifying the dates for the event, she sent me a message, wanting me to come and be "in their midst and fellowship." To be quite honest, she was dishonest about her presentation to me. She knew she didn't want me to speak, but wanted me to believe speaking was still an option, so I would attend her event, even if I was not on the program. Speakers need to beware conferences where people don't confirm or deny your place as an invited speaker - but they still want to keep the option open for you to attend even if they don't want you to speak. Even the world doesn't ask this of people. It would be like going for a job interview and not getting the job but being told instead, "We're not going to give you the job, but we want you to come to the workplace every day to hang out with us all!" If I'm not right to speak, why would I be right to just be in the midst of everyone and fellowship at my own expense? Ministers, there are plenty of places where we can go and fellowship and be in the spiritual midst of God right where we live and it doesn't cost an outrageous amount of money. We do not need to be manipulated into being downgraded in events to be in God's presence.

- **Offering** - There can be a lot of ways offerings manifest. I am not going to say everything is necessarily monetarily based, depending on the circumstances. I have attended events where I speak or teach in exchange for something else connected with the event; and that worked out fine, because of the circumstances involved. If someone is asking you to attend an event and they are offering you nothing outright - not even something in exchange for your speaking - then it's a bad event. Time to move on.

- **Honorarium** - Whether or not we want to call it that, most ministers have some sort of honorarium. When I have to travel a long distance, I require the host cover my travel arrangements, my hotel accommodations, and provide a love offering, often of a specified amount. When I don't ask for a specific amount of the offering, I do expect those in question do their very best...and I do know when they don't. If I am not travelling as far, I adjust what is needed to the specific circumstances. How responsive a host is to these not-so-unreasonable requests determines whether or not I even want to talk to the individual further. In today's church, there are those who expect everything to be done not just for free but at our own cost, all the time, and without any regard to the fact that ministry is supposed to be a mutual blessing. We don't want to hear about money, talk about money, requests for money, or anything that has to do with money - we just want to pretend ministry gets here by angels' wings and good wishes. It doesn't. If you want to be honored as a speaker, it's important to make sure the honorarium is practical without being excessively demanding and that those who consider you as a speaker do not try to evade what you ask for as a minister of God.

SECTION III

COMMUNICATING THE VISION

CHAPTER TWENTY-ONE

MINISTRY AS A FORM OF COMMUNICATION

How, then, can they call on the one they have not believed in?
And how can they believe in the one of whom they have not heard?
And how can they hear without someone preaching to them?
And how can they preach unless they are sent?
As it is written, "How beautiful are the feet of those who bring good news!"
(Romans 10:14-15)

MINISTRY is a purposed communication. The purpose of ministry is to communicate the Gospel through whatever means the Lord has gifted an individual to do so. Even though it may seem obvious, those who communicate the Gospel need to be able to communicate. They need to be able to see that the message they have to convey is clear, understandable to their audience, and relayed through as many different mediums as possible.

Many ministers just don't know how to do this. A basic trip to Bible College doesn't educate the minister in means of vision communication. Most ministers don't know the basics of sermon presentation, use social networking for ministry expansion, or how to talk to others about their work. Promotions and advertising are confusing...not to mention the ever-expanding world of internet promotions, websites, and internet marketing.

Some aspects of communication we discover as we venture out and work in ministry. We learn how to best deliver our message based on our audience responses. We grow in our own styles of ministering and communication as we discover our own unique ministry personality. We learn about the best ways to relay information via word of mouth and as we start to learn the appropriate channels for networking. We know how to work what is necessary in our immediate circles and among those we know. What we don't know is how to spread the word beyond those we know, work with, or have already reached.

We don't know because we simply are not taught. Most Christian educational systems have found their collision with modern technology. Some go as far as to say the worlds can never collide. Every excuse in the book is used against learning the various technological systems to improve communication beyond an immediate circle. I thank God that the printing press did not meet such opposition! We know from history how important the advance of printing technology was to the Reformation and every Christian movement since. Instead of regarding technological advances as evil, we need to see how these various means can be used to help us advance the Kingdom. Any means we can use to convey the Gospel is good and should be acknowledged. As means to communicate the vision expand, we must expand ourselves to meet with these new avenues for Gospel proclamation while learning what avenues are worth our time, and what avenues are not.

In this section, we are going to look at modern means by which we communicate the Gospel. While some may seem confusing at first, if we will all apply ourselves to learning, it will become an essential aspect of modern-day ministry life and witness.

CHAPTER TWENTY-TWO

THE INTERNET AND MINISTRY

As you go, preach this message:
"The Kingdom of heaven is near."
(Matthew 10:7)

WHEN the internet craze first started, I remember only one attitude most had in relationship to it: fear. We were told we should never post photos, our real names, or give out any personal information. We were discouraged from talking to people privately. Fast-forward a number of years, people post everything online: personal pictures, information, details about their private lives and jobs, contact information, and everything else. Nowadays divulging too much online is commonplace. People will give every detail of their day, talk to people about exceedingly private matters, post relationship details for the entire world to see, and don't even shy away from posting provocative pictures. We went from hiding everything to exposing everything. We have grown so used to seeing extremes online, we don't often recognize the balance needed to have a ministry presence online.

About eight to ten years ago, a move started pushing for what is now called "internet ministry." Prior to this time, only mega-ministries or major ministries with a wide-standing scope had an internet presence, using websites and email distribution lists. With the advance of social networks such as ning, MySpace, YouTube, Periscope, and Facebook, a growing presence of less popular ministers (most could be classified as "unheard of") flooded the internet. For most of these ministries, their purpose in having an internet ministry is to be discovered. They either have a small following in real time or no following at all. Much of their time is spent "praying" with or "giving a word" to people or posting on these social networks, and they often speak of the importance of networking. Many are self-published using various internet resources and may be recognizable among a small group of devoted internet followers.

The catch with most internet ministers is they do not have much of a reality ministry, or a ministry in real-time. Many have not been in ministry long and see the internet as an easy and quick way to spread a message so they can be discovered. What they do not realize is, due to the changes in technology and the internet, popular internet hot-spots are constantly changing and it is an education all in itself to keep up with the changing technologies. Many also think it requires less work than traditional ministry methods which seem to fail in modern society.

To date, there have been no mega break-out ministries due to internet discovery. Despite this fact, the internet seems packed with ministers trying to be noticed for their teaching, message, or content. Most internet ministries are very much alike, with similar teachings copied from one another to try and achieve a stable following with "what works." As a result, ministry online is a competitive and tough game. It seems easy to break into, but is difficult to maintain.

The internet can be deceptive when it comes to ministry because a minister can appear to be something beyond what they are. A cleverly disguised website can make someone look far more famous, relevant, and solid in doctrine than what they may actually be. There is no way to tell, upon inspection, whether or not a ministry has valid 501(c)(3) status in good standing with the federal government. There is no way to tell how finances are spent unless a website contains a financial report. Just because someone wants to give someone else a word online or because they give themselves a title does not mean someone has any gifting or right to do so.

Most Christians have a love-hate relationship with the internet. Some see it as an endless source of temptation, evils, and sinister lusts, sent from the devil himself. Others see it as a perfect place to spread the Gospel and do ministry work. The truth about the internet, as with all things, lies somewhere in between. The internet does bear with it temptations, lusts, evils, and problems that someone can easily get entrapped within if they do not have enough of the right spiritual balance in their lives. There are lots of websites catering to pornography, buying and selling goods to steal from others, drugs, and dating sites designed to facilitate wrong relationships among people. We also must be fair in admitting these different issues are present offline as well as online, and have manifested in various forms of temptation throughout the ages. One could just as easily be drawn into the temptations found online in reality time. If one is not cautious, being sucked into a vortex of dangerous internet temptations, false teachings, and yes, even false teachers is inevitable. It is also easy for a minister of God to get so caught up in the internet and internet work they forget all about the ministry work they are supposed to be working to promote online. On the other hand, the internet has numerous avenues to promote ministry work at a low-to-no cost opportunity, with ways to connect to solid believers, ministers, and reach those who are lost or seeking more with God's Word. It is also offers a number of excellent tools for conferencing, distance education, and distance communication.

I prefer to use the term "ministry presence online" rather than call something I do or encourage others to do as an internet ministry. The reason for this is simple: What I am encouraging here is for ministries to have a presence online, not devote their entire ministry work to the internet. Because we live in a technological age, ministries need to have a presence, rather than an internet devotion. Even though there are many ministries that do not want to hear this, we can't replace reality, real-time ministry with internet ministry and think it is as legitimate or the same thing. Ministry is about service – real-time service – and reaching people with that service. Yes, I believe we can touch people's lives and minister to them online. No, I don't believe that is enough to maintain ministry or facilitate necessary ministry connection. Facebook, while it can be a ministry tool, is not a ministry, nor are any of the other sites. God has told us to go into all the world and proclaim the Gospel (Mark 16:15); not sit at home and talk to a handful of people on the internet. If there is some sort of physical incapacitation causing a minister to be unable to do ministry outside of their immediate environment, the internet does provide them a means to do supplementary ministry and continue their work while incapacitated. In that instance, internet ministry is understandable. In the case of people who just find working service too difficult to get noticed, it is not understandable. Here we will examine how to use various technological and modern tools to be recognized for our work, all the while learning how to use these tools to further reality ministry rather than hiding behind the internet.

CHAPTER TWENTY-THREE

MINISTRY WEBSITES

*But He Who sent Me is reliable,
and what I have heard from Him I tell the world.
(John 8:26)*

WEBSITES are virtual spaces designed around a common theme. Websites are created using two things: a domain name and web hosting. A domain name is the link one puts in a browser bar to bring up a web address. It typically starts with www and ends with .com, .org, or .net (among other possibilities). Domain names must be registered in the Whois Database upon reserve and must be renewed, either yearly, bi-yearly, tri-yearly, or beyond, anywhere up to ten years. They tend to be relatively inexpensive. Web hosting is the "space" where a website's files are stored for internet viewing. Hosting is usually sold in gigabytes and should be bought according to what one needs. If a website is to be interactive, with groups and discussions, it will most likely require a lot of hosting. If it will not be so elaborate, not as much hosting is needed. When purchasing a website, hosting is where the expense is. It is either sold monthly or in a yearly package and is usually based on a monthly rate. Basic hosting typically costs anywhere between $100 and $200 per year.

Every viable ministry should have a website. Websites serve as a professional presence of ministry online. It is, in our modern culture, usually a first impression for many of what a ministry does, stands for, and is about. Websites may be complex or simple, but all ministry-based websites should contain the following:

- **A homepage**, welcoming all to the website and giving a brief overview of what they will find in exploring the website.

- **An "about us" page**, giving information on the foundational principles of a ministry: statement of faith or belief, mission statement, and vision statement.

- **A "contact us" page**, where people visiting the site can either fill out a form mailer for more information or can send an email via link for more information. The 'contact us" page should also contain a mailing address and telephone number where the ministry can be reached, as well as other links to contact or 'like' a ministry around the internet.

- **A donations page**, where people can donate to the work via PayPal or Google checkout (or through a merchant service, if that is an option). Note: PayPal requires ministries to be non-profit in order to receive donations. If you do not have one of these options available, provide a mailing address for donations. This page should specify whether or not the organization is recognized as a 501(c)(3) (i.e., whether or not donations are tax deductible).

- **An online catalog**, where people can purchase ministry items via PayPal or Google checkout (or through a merchant service, if that is an option).

- **Other pages of interest** may be:

  o A minister's schedule/itinerary or a church's schedule of events

- Ministry staff with bios and photos
- A testimony or bio on the founder/visionary of the organization
- A page detailing the different ministries of the organization
- A live webcam or video camera for services or events
- Links to podcasts or downloads of sermons
- A page for recommended links

Websites should truly display the beliefs, passions, and intentions of a ministry. They should be ascetically pleasing. A good website is a balance between text and images. Websites should never have too many photos, too much glitz, or too much text. When using a template, the template used should be consistent (i.e., not switching templates between pages). Most domain hosting services have templates with a domain/hosting package in the event you do not have access to a web designer to create a site for you. A template is a pre-designed, pre-coded website that allows you to add text and then upload it to your hosting as needed. With some websites, you do not even need to upload it; it automatically works with your domain name. Templates are a great blessing to those who don't have web development skills, don't have time to learn them, or can't hire someone to learn it for them. When working with a template, keep in mind that templates usually come with a page limit and you cannot easily copy and paste text from other sites into a template (unless it specifies such).

Websites can also be developed through coding for various effects. To do this, one must run a "what you see is what you get" (WYSIWUG) software design program, such as Dreamweaver or CoffeeCup. These programs require technical skill and knowledge of basic website programming. It does allow for greater freedom with what you can do with your site, coding, pasting text, and the like. It also requires hours of basic knowledge and study.

Some ministries will have the option to use a professional web designer. A professional web designer is an individual who has the skills necessary to design a website for your organization. As a rule, web designers are not cheap. It can cost anywhere from a few hundred dollars to several thousand dollars to get a website up and running, with additional technical support, editing, and consultation costing additional fees. Communication with a web designer is essential. The designer should have the basics of your website and the information you want on it along with the vision for the site. Most designers bring forth at least one web option for approval and will modify or change the design to fit the wishes of the client. Honesty is important! Be upfront! Also, make sure you match the designer with what you seek to do with your site. Some excel in certain areas of code and technology over others and, for God's work, always seek the best.

CHAPTER TWENTY-FOUR

INTERNET SCAMS

So be on your guard;
I have told you everything ahead of time.
(Mark 13:23)

O NE of the biggest drawbacks to working online is the endless world of scamming. From the very beginning, the internet has been used to try and scam money from others. Christian ministers are particularly susceptible to receive scams as scammers generate our email addresses and sell them to other scammers via database. Email scams come under numerous headings but all contain certain elements:

- **The scammer tries to establish some sort of trust with you** by presenting a fictitious story about their circumstances. It is usually because of a dead or dying individual – either a family member of yours or their own physical demise. Sometimes it is under the guise of a "romance scam," that someone overseas is interested, in love with you, and desires to be with you.

- **A large sum of money is often involved**. They either want to give it to you or they want you to somehow get it to them. Sometimes it is disguised as a winning, inheritance, donation, or lottery drawing. Sometimes they are seeking school fees or other items.

- **In order to receive whatever it is they say they want to give to you, they require extensive information** that you should never, ever give out: full name (including middle and mother's maiden name), banking information, personal addresses, phone numbers, age, birth date, etc.

- **If you try to contact them by replying to the email, it usually bounces or comes back** as saying the email does not exist anymore, usually because the emails are taken out to spam several accounts, and then closed. If you contact them via the information they provide, you receive another story or additional details of the story, which continue to grow and become more complicated.

- **Extensive contact continues and then continues again, whereas the scammer continually finds reasons not to forward** whatever it is they have offered: they cite you need to forward 'taxes,' fees, and a host of other things via Western Union or bank transfer. They will do this even when the individual has run out of money, threatening all sorts of things if the person tries not to pay.

The majority of the scams that fit this description scams are out of African nations, sometimes Nigeria (they are called 411 scams as this is the dial-up code for Nigeria), or India, and some now even come out of Russia, Romania, Latin America, or parts of eastern Europe. When confronted with one of these emails, it is best to delete and ignore them. As it is very difficult, due to government corruption, to control and prosecute 411 scammers, it is best not to get involved with them to begin with.

Directory and listing scams

It is not uncommon to receive emails – often claiming to be from the Netherlands – inviting an individual to 'update' a listing in the World Business Directory (or other type of directory). Often people fill out the information not realizing this is a prime email scam, as nobody is listed because the suggested directory does not exist. People who submit their information subject themselves to endless harassment for money, false collection agencies, and problems with their business branding. This is another email to delete and disregard.

Domain name dispute emails

Another email scam is the domain name dispute. An organization, company, or individual will receive an email message stating that the domain name holder owns a domain that a Chinese, Taiwanese, or Hong Kong company wants to use as their own brand – and is prepared to take the legal domain name holder to court if they do not hear from them within a specified period of time. People answer these emails only to receive another email reply, and then another one eventually trying to sell the 'questionable domains' at rates triple the cost of a normal domain name sale. Just ignore and delete these emails, no matter how intimidating they may seem.

Delivery scams

Another newer set of emails designed to scam are the delivery scams. These cleverly-designed emails look as if they are legitimately sent from UPS, FedEx, the Post Office, or DHL, saying you have received a package that they have either tried to deliver or for some reason has not been delivered. They instruct you to download the attached file (always a .zip file) to process a claim or to get the tracking number. If you fall for this scam and open the file, you will infect your computer with a nasty virus. It is also wise to refrain from clicking on any links as these too can cause a computer to be infected with a virus.

UPS, FedEx, and DHL never send tracking numbers or other information by attachment via email. If you receive one of these emails (especially if you are not expecting such a package), do not open or download the attachment! If you have question about receiving a package, contact UPS, FedEx, DHL, or the post office directly.

Government email scams

Also popular have become government email scams. These take the nature of notifying an individual that they are in some sort of trouble with the federal government (such as the IRS) and that they should review the attached documents as soon as possible. Some request certain information is returned to them promptly to process the claim. Downloading the attachment will infect a computer with a serious virus, and submitting any personal information to the sender will also land the person in serious trouble. Do not click on any links, download any attachments, or reply to the email in any way.

Federal agencies, specifically the Internal Revenue Service, do not notify about back taxes or financial problems via email; they contact people by regular mail. There is no reason to be concerned if you receive such an email. Forward the email to the appropriate government agency as a phishing email. The address to send phishing emails to can be found on all major government websites.

E-card and friend scams

Although not seen nearly as much as in years past, the e-card and friend scams do still circulate from time to time. The emails look something like this: You get a subject line that says: "Your friend has sent you an e-card!" They want you to click on the link to view it. Clicking on the link connects you to an IP address that will cause you to download a virus. When someone sends you an e-card, it is either sent with the sender's name or their email address in the "from" section of an email. Any other similar emails should be discarded and unopened if possible.

The "friend" scams are along the same lines of the 411 scams, only sent to entice an individual into a friendship or relationship. They are usually sent naming an individual with their interest in getting to know you better. Some cite viewing a profile or seeing something about you. They list their interests and things about themselves. Ignore these emails and delete them.

False return email addresses

A newer development in the world of email technology is the ability to falsify a sender's email address. Many spam emails appear to be sent from the receiver's email (with the literal email address in the sent box and sometimes appearing in the sender listing in the closed email), even though they have not actually been sent from their account. This is a common spamming technique that serves to get you to open the emails because you are curious or concerned about your account and the email's contents. There is no reason to be concerned or to fear your account has been hacked; just refrain from clicking on links in the emails and delete them. At current, there is no way to stop people from falsifying email addresses.

Phishing emails

Phishing emails serve one exclusive purpose: get your information into the hands of hackers. Hackers want to access your data; phishing emails give them that opportunity. A phishing email is one that specifically seeks to steal your information. Phishing emails may come disguised as bank notices, social networking site logins or friend requests, professional notifications, and other disguising avenues to try and get you to click on their links or respond in some way to the email so they can get the information they desire. Most professional agencies emphasize the importance of ensuring you check notifications carefully and only login to approved sites. The best way to avoid a phishing scam is not to become victim to one. If you receive a notification and you are unsure about it, contact the organization in question outside of that email and check things out rather than responding directly to or through it.

Church requests for funding/money

The internet is an awesome way to communicate events and needs. It's also a great way to falsify a work and request needs for a non-existent program or project. A common foreign scam is to present a situation which, without a doubt, sounds dire and needy and request either financial assistance or items to assist with those needs. It is designed to tug at Christian heartstrings, causing the minister or believer to respond emotionally and send whatever is requested. Denials meet with harsh words or branding the individual as uncharitable; however, such is still better than giving what is requested, because the never-ending cycle of scamming begins. Be very wary when sending money overseas. There are many organizations within the United States with verified legal, tax-exempt standing that contribute to causes and do extensive work overseas. When in question, contribute to a United States organization doing viable work overseas.

Engagement scams

Scammers also disguise themselves as conference hosts. Increasing in popularity is the scam in which someone invites you for an overseas event (usually in Europe), saying you are the perfect minister based on what they've seen on your website and they give you the dates, a location, and even a contact person and phone number. They either ask for your information (often very detailed) or they ask for you to contact them so they can get your information. When accepting invitations from people you don't know and cannot verify, proceed with extreme caution. Also check out the information you are provided carefully. If you cannot verify an event, never accept it. Delete these emails and never give them a second thought.

Ponzi schemes/pyramid schemes

One of the most common forms of scam is the Ponzi scheme. While this scam has crept into the lives of people dating back long before the internet even existed, Ponzi schemes are now perpetrated online at an alarming rate. A Ponzi scheme operates as an individual is tricked into believing they can make a large sum of money if they will only put up so much money in order to do so. In other words, an individual is going to make their own money back. They may be required to do multiple pay-outs over a period of time, all with the same theme – they will get a windfall back if they continue to pay.

Any time you are promised a windfall of income if you will only pay so much toward it needs to be treated with suspicion. Be very cautious about those who approach you in regards to investments, payments or other things where they guarantee a return on your investment. When it comes to matters of investments, whether stocks, bonds, mutual funds, or some type of business venture, it is never possible to promise a return. Even when it seems likely, there is still never a guarantee of windfall or success. That is why it is essential to read the fine print and understand a contract before signing it.

Akin to a Ponzi scheme is the pyramid scheme. A pyramid scheme functions from the top down: a few key people at the top make the profit for what many people down below are doing, but make little to no profit from. The many workers on the bottom push products, aggressively market, and often also do so at much of their own expense, but do not see much of the profit from what they make (as it is often only a commission). As you go up the "pyramid," you see different positions and different profits, mostly based on sales, until you see the very top of the sales chain, where the bulk of profit goes.

The internet is a haven for pyramid schemes that offer different start-up packages and promise unlimited income, benefits, and profits if you sell their products and recruit others to sell them, as well. Whether it's beauty products, vitamins, roadside assistance, phone service, or technological products, there are more pyramid schemes out there than I care to recall. As with the Ponzi scheme, be very wary of promises to bring forth endless wealth and prosperity just from selling a product...and read the fine print on contracts, agreements, and other things that require upfront "investments."

Dealing with spam

One of the biggest mistakes we make is inadvertently responding to spammers. Our first impulse is to open up a spam email and try to get off the mailing list. All this does is confirm to a spam list that an email address is valid and even though they may remove us from one list, they sell or share our information to other lists. In the process, we get more spam than is imaginable. The best way to handle spam is to delete it. Eventually the amount of spam received will decrease.

CHAPTER TWENTY-FIVE

SOCIAL NETWORKING AND INSTANT MESSAGING

But if we walk in the light, as He is in the light,
we have fellowship with one another,
and the blood of Jesus, His Son, purifies us from all sin.
(1 John 1:7)

SOCIAL networking is exactly what it sounds like: it is making certain friends, meeting new people, and exchanging information for the purpose of networking online. Social networking is accomplished through a website known as a social networking site. Social networking sites vary in what they allow and in their themes, but all contain similar elements:

- **Users have a profile** – A profile usually contains a picture and any relevant information someone would like to share with others. Most social networking sites include information about current location, likes, dislikes, interests, education, current or past employment, favorite entertainments (television shows, books, movies), and the type of person someone is interested to meet. Most social networks give the option to fill out a lot of information or only a little. Some networks make certain information required.

- **Users are able to 'friend' other people** – Social networks serve to connect people. This means they are able to add people to their available contacts on the network, commonly called 'adding as a friend.' People can add or remove friends as they so desire, for any reason. When someone is a friend, they have access to the personal profile, postings, and information conveyed by you. Some social networks have limits on the number of friends one can have; for example, Facebook (perhaps the most famous social networking site in the world) has a 5,000 friends limit for personal pages.

- **Users have the freedom to post things on their own page and on the page of their friends** – Facebook calls it a 'wall,' MySpace calls it a 'page." Whatever it is called, a user is able to post things on their unique page: status updates, comments, notes or blogs, photos, and often links from other pages and sites to share with their friends on the network.

- **Businesses, celebrities, organizations, and professionals can have "fan" pages** – Other people can follow or like these pages and receive updates from those pages.

- **Users can participate in "groups," which are groupings of people interested in a common topic, interest, or theme** – Groups are founded by a person and moderated by either that individual or a group of individuals. They are a smaller version of the larger website, centering around that one commonality, where individuals are gathered to comment, post, meet one another, share, and talk on their specific interest. The postings of the group may be visible to everyone on the social networking site or only visible to those in the group.

- **Users can promote their events on the site and invite friends to the event** – This special feature offers a ministry free promotion for their events and gets the word out on the internet, which I have often called the "telephone pole of the world."

- **People can be blocked or banned from most social networks** – There are a variety of reasons why people would want to 'unfriend' someone on a social network: they don't gain anything from the connection, they haven't spoken with the person for a long time, they don't like someone's content, etc. Some go a step further to decide they do not want to even see a trace of that individual online and go through the process to 'block' them. Blocking is like unfriending, with the exception that, whenever a person blocks another, a report is made on the blocked individual. A person is blocked for only a few options: spam, abuse or harassment, a false profile, or a double profile of someone who can't log in to their original account anymore. Reporting someone as spamming or being abusive online can cause their content to be blocked, prohibit them from posting in groups or on the pages of others, or sharing their content. Blocking should not be done because someone is angry at someone else, but only when a situation truly warrants and justifies the process and marking involved.

- **On most sites, users can play games or install applications ("apps")** – The games played on these sites usually are just an interactive application. By installing the application, the user allows the app to pull information from its profile page. Some games and applications are reasonably harmless, but some can be spam or contain viruses.

- **Accounts can be removed or disabled** – Nobody has to remain on a site they do not want to, and not every social networking site works well for everyone. Anytime you desire to leave a social networking site, the option is there. Most allow for the option to temporarily disable a site in case a user will be unable to check it or keep up with it temporarily.

Popular social networks

There are numerous social networks in existence – more than can fit here in this book. Below are listed the top social networking sites where having a ministry presence can benefit, and why.

- **Facebook** – Facebook is the number one social networking site worldwide. There are currently over 1.28 billion people on Facebook.[1] Facebook is a good ministry tool because it is relatively simple to use and a minister can connect to whomever they feel led to connect: other ministers, the saved, the unsaved, special groups of people, etc. On Facebook, a person can connect to as few or as many people as they want, in a city, a state, a region, a country, or the whole world. With an instant messaging feature built in the site, a minister can talk 'live' to any person they need to in a more private setting than having to display commentary all over the internet. The social forum allows a minister to write and post notes, share videos, teaching, and the like with anyone on their friends list. They also have the option to post in groups or start their own. As great as a forum is for ministry, Facebook also has some major pitfalls. Facebook is increasing its level of control over its users in order to prevent spamming and abuse (both of which can be common on the site). It is easy to be labeled as abusive by an angry person and have rights suspended or temporarily restricted for no justifiable reason, and also easy to be misjudged as a spammer within the system due to multiple posts. Facebook is still a great resource, despite the increased levels of security.

- **Twitter** – A very, very popular site, Twitter allows its users to post short statements, called "tweets" which are in turn read by followers. A tweet cannot be longer than two hundred eighty total characters (including spaces). Twitter is good for event invitations, notifications for blogs or things happening around the net, and are also good ways to keep in touch with others and keep others updated in a short and brief way. The very thing that makes Twitter what it is, is its drawback: statements have to be short and kept to a minimum.

- **MySpace** – Once upon a time, MySpace was the most popular social network in the world. Fast-forward a few years and MySpace has been sold multiple times and rumors have flown around the net of its eventual demise. As Facebook has, in many ways, replaced MySpace as the most popular social network in existence, MySpace has many features now to compete with Facebook: event invitations, instant messaging, private messaging, games, applications, and a semblance of groups (a little different in nature; mostly a labeling of a group of people). There are the options to blog, share photos, and share information. MySpace is more complicated to use than Facebook, and a number of changes to it over the years have contributed to its decreasing popularity. MySpace is more frequently used today for music groups or emerging artists.

- **Ning** – Ning was another extremely popular social network at one time. In the years between 2007 and 2010, Ning (from the Chinese word for "peace) was a major social forum because it offered full, private social networking for free. Ning sites allowed all the perks of larger social networks: blogging, forums, photos, music, adding friends, private messaging, instant messaging, and other features for smaller groups that desired to discuss matters on a common theme. Some Ning networks (such as Black Preaching Network) grew to hold over 25,000 members. Most networks, however, didn't generate that much traffic. After a buyout, Ning networks started charging their network creators to have any size network and began limiting available features as well. Due to this change, many Ning users left the networks in 2010. There are still a few ministries around that are paying for Ning services, so it is possible to find a ministry with either a main Ning site or a secondary Ning site.

- **LinkedIn** – LinkedIn is a professional networking site designed to help people with job and skill promotion. LinkedIn is a little different from other social networking sites in that it does not have as many features and is not very interpersonal in nature. A user's profile contains educational, employment, and skill histories. People "connect" to one another and are added to one another's networks (circle of friends) via request. In ministry, LinkedIn can be a great way to promote one's self on a professional level and to find other ministers to work with who excel in various areas of ministry.

- **Snapchat** – While not a social network in the same way that many others are on our list, Snapchat is a messaging app used to send text messages, pictures, and short videos to individuals one adds on their account. All features, including personal correspondences, are only available for a short time before disappearing. For this reason, Snapchat is considered a champion of internet privacy. Though a private service, it does have public features, including a "story" feature by which everyone on one's list can see whatever is going on, pop culture stories, pop culture videos, and celebrity gossip. Snapchat is also well-known for its photo filters, emojis known as bitmojis, and optional maps to help friends find one another.

- **Goodreads** – A growing site that is all about sharing books, Goodreads is a great social networking site for authors or those who just love to know what's both up and coming and what might be a great read, but you would not hear of it otherwise. Through Goodreads, a member of the site can write reviews, reserve or catalog books, and create library lists. The group also features book groups and online discussions about books.

- **Pinterest** – A photo-themed site, Pinterest is all about "pinning" or posting various pictures on a page (called a board) which can be grouped or themed. Others are able to see, like, and re-pin these photos onto their own boards, thus generating a quick turnover for an event or something to be promoted. Others on Pinterest can follow your board, and you can do the same with theirs.

- **TikTok** – A video-focused social media site, TikTok focuses specifically on short videos created by members. These videos range from the silly and sublime to more serious conversations and discussions, all done from around fifteen seconds to three minutes. People can follow users, like videos, and leave comments. It is, at the current update of this book, the fastest growing social media network in the world.

- **Instagram** – An all-photo platform owned by Facebook, Instagram allows its users to share photos and videos (up to fifteen seconds) throughout other social networking sites and online media.

- **Reddit** – Reddit is a social media site that combines viewer content, ratings, and discussion. Its purpose is "social news," meaning it focuses on things that are entirely member submitted: pictures, links, discussions, videos, and more. Topics of all sorts can be found throughout the site. Each topic is contained in a community known as a "subreddit," which is monitored by community moderators. Content in each subreddit is "voted" on by members, who either vote the content "up" (like) or "down" (dislike). Links that receive enough "up" votes will ascend to the top of their subreddit and eventually gain attention on the front page of the site.

- **Whatsapp** – Whatsapp is also owned by Facebook and does not function in the same form as most of the social media networks mentioned here. It is a VoIP-technology service that functions as both a messenger app and voice message service. It is considered social media because it is used not just for voice calling, but also for sharing photos, documents, video calls, and to specify user locations. Whatsapp is, as a feature, used to connect people in other countries (especially where internet technology is less developed) and for international calling and connection.

- **YouTube** – YouTube is a social media platform devoted to video sharing. Members create video content anywhere from a few minutes to twelve hours in length. These videos are located on creator channels, giving people the option to follow the specific channels where their favorite content is found. For creators, YouTube offers a creator content studio, allowing basic editing of videos in a user's account. Creators also have viewing stats and essential information about their viewers. Content creators must watch for certain things, including copyright infringement and content that may be dangerous or unsuitable for minors.

Using social networking sites for ministry

Social networking is a great forum for internet ministry promotion. That is the bottom line of social networking for ministry purposes: it is a ministry promotion. We can have some fun on there and talk to people that we've known, but the main purpose of our presence is to promote our ministry. This makes social networking a tool for ministry. Our presence online can't be too personal, nor can it be too informal or stiff. We must strive to find the balance between overly social and not social enough. Here are some tips to accomplish this:

- **Watch the nature of the pictures posted online** – A minister with an online presence should do the best they can to represent that presence in all they do. The old adage, "A picture's worth a thousand words" applies heavily in a minister's online presence. Photos should display the minister of God in a positive light: nothing provocative, disorderly, or dishonorable should be featured. Photos also shouldn't be too personal in excessive displays of family life. It's fine to feature a few photos of a family event or some family fun, but displaying more pictures of family than ministry doesn't provide a professional image. Also, make it a point to post a profile picture. It's fine to change it from time to time, but people need to be able to see the minister to whom they are speaking. Pictures should be clear and show the face well.

- **Complete your profile from a ministry standpoint** – People don't know you are in ministry if you don't provide that information. Whatever professional ministry info you can provide, post that, along with your website or website links.

- **Identify yourself** – Some ministers are uncomfortable revealing their calling online. If you want to have an online presence for your ministry, you need to state what your calling is. Many are uncomfortable with using titles, and if that is where you are, that is between you and the Lord. What should not be a secret is what you do in ministry and your ministry calling. If you do not want to put it in your name or online handle, at least state your office in your profile somewhere.

- **Find networks and groups pertaining to ministry** – You can still join ministry networks that are made available for free, hosted by ministries through Ning networks or through webs.com websites. Facebook offers a variety of groups for ministers to participate in and belong. Get out there and participate with other people!

- **Watch spam and spammy applications** – A host of ministries get their accounts hacked for installing applications they should have never installed. Be wary of the various things that come your way on the internet. Never click a link that says you've been captured in a video or that it is a video of you (unless you know for certain it is) and do not open links or attachments of images if you do not know for sure they are what they claim to be.

- **Mark a copyright notice all notes and blogs** – There are both informal and formal forms of copyright. By law, everything we write is protected by copyright. The problem is enforcement if we do not have our work registered. Because of the vast world of electronic publishing, registering a copyright for an informal or informative blog may seem excessive, not to mention get expensive. It is essential, however, that we note work as being our own, and legally holding the rights to that work. At the end of every blog or note should follow a line with the copyright symbol © or (c), your name, and the year, followed by a statement that says, "All rights reserved." It should look like this: © 2011 Jane Smith. All rights reserved. Doing this ensures all your work has the boundary of copyright protection and deters people seeking to infringe on your work.

- **Be careful who you "friend"** – Adding people as friends on social networking sites is key to connecting with people you need to connect. Online ministry work is about just that: connecting for the purposes of ministry online. When you begin this work online, you need to identify your target audience: who are you looking to reach online? Is the internet a means to reach non-believers, minister to believers, or work with other leaders? Answering this question (and perhaps other specifics: youth, men, women, etc.) helps you know who you should add as a friend and who you should not. We all need to beware scammers, spammers, and ministers who just say or do things that don't "feel right." Don't add everyone who sends you a friend invite. Check out people's profiles, pages, information, and websites before you decide to connect to someone online.

- **Avoid talking to minors online that you do not know offline** – The world is funny about adult contact with minors. Something that may seem totally harmless to one person may sound different when posted or sent to someone else online. Accusations can fly easily online and it is important ministers guard themselves from such accusations, even if they are untrue. Do not have contact with minors you do not know.

- **Be careful about your postings** – It is easy to use the internet to vent about something that made you angry just because it made you angry. It is also easy to get into debates, arguments, and heated discussions about things that don't matter. Don't waste time online with things that are not essential and distract from your ministry purpose. Also be careful about revealing very personal details of your private life online.

The following is a list of things you should never post on Facebook (or any social networking site, for that matter):

- **Full date of birth** – It's been said that if someone has a person's social security number, full date of birth, and mother's maiden name, they can find out anything they want about that person. Never post your full birth date online via social networking.

- **Answers to "favorites" questions that are used as security questions** – If you use your favorite color, favorite book, etc. as your security questions to login to a secure website, don't post those things online as part of a fun "favorites" game.

- **Your phone number** – If you want be tele-marketed and called by people you don't like to death, post your phone number. Otherwise, hide it within your settings so it is not visible to anyone but you.

- **Your bank account number** – It's amazing that we have to tell people this, but really...don't post your bank account or your bank information, for that matter...on the internet.

Instant messaging

Instant messaging is an internet means of private communication between parties using an instant messenger program. It is a direct text program, where people can communicate instantly rather than having to wait for messages to transmit via email. Most IM programs also allow people to talk via webcam, voice chat, play games, and share media. Facebook Messenger, Yahoo, Skype, Windows Live Messenger, Pal Talk, and ICQ are all popular instant messaging programs with many facets to them and are great for private communications online. Both MySpace and Facebook also have an instant messaging chat feature. With all things technological, there are things to beware in the instant messaging arena: beware accepting friend requests from people you do not know, avoid clicking on strange links, and be careful with strange files and watch for viruses.

CHAPTER TWENTY-SIX

CATCHING THE LITTLE INTERNET FOXES THAT SPOIL THE VINE

Catch the foxes for us – the little foxes that spoil the vineyard.
Our vineyard is now in bloom.
(Song of Solomon 2:15, ERV)

AS I sit and shake my head yet again this month, I am truly taken aback at the level of total disorder I see among professed ministers on Facebook and other places around the internet. If we claim to be ministers, we must operate in professionalism. Many don't like hearing that ministry should be a professional enterprise, something we do and pursue in a certain way, with certain graces, and certain ethics. How do I know it's an unpopular topic? Because it is so seldom discussed, and when it is, the speaker is often attacked with counter viewpoints. Instead of professionalism, what I see frequently are ministers running rampant, here and there, operating by all sorts of conduct, inconsistent, unprofessional, and unethical. They gossip, run their mouths off, say things they shouldn't in public or in the pulpit. They run around acting like beggars, asking everyone for money and expecting that people will give it just because they ask. They do not edit documents they put online for others to read. They engage in arguments and debates. They post inappropriate pictures of themselves. They post titles they have not earned, and graces which they do not carry. They use their ministry accounts and presences to sell things through pyramid schemes.

I am not expecting people to be perfect. As a leader, I am a big advocate of the fact that we, as leaders, have the right to be people. I myself know that I am far from perfect, have my days where I don't feel like acting very holy, and yes, I don't do everything right. But I also know that there comes a time when, as a leader, I have to step up and show myself as the leader God has called me to be. I have to carry myself with a certain dignity, ethical perspective, and honor. I am also uniquely aware that this concept comes from my training as a leader. What I am seeing in ministry is the simple, basic fact that many ministers clearly do not know how to conduct themselves in a professional manner. We have grown so accustom to relying on gifts and anointing that we've forgotten the simple, basic fact that ministry is about more than your anointing and your gifts: it's also about how you present yourself. From how you dress, to what you ask of people, to how you carry yourself in public, to yes...how you behave on my Facebook page and other places...it affects how your ministry is presented and how it is perceived.

The internet is a big place. There are lots of opportunities to work wonders and have an awesome ministry presence online. The thing we cannot forget is that the way we behave on Facebook through our pages and our conduct in places such as groups and fan pages is a good indication of how you conduct yourself in your work. The way you interact on Facebook and on other internet sites is noticed. We talk about the 'big things:' making sure your pictures are appropriate, not using foul language, and not getting into full-fledged arguments. What we don't talk about is the 'little things' that ministers do online which create a terribly negative persona. They are often regarded as so minor that we don't even consider them to be doing harm - but the reality is that they are causing harm because they turn people off.

The Bible gives us a very interesting teaching in Song of Solomon 2:15: *"Catch the foxes for us— the little foxes that spoil the vineyard. Our vineyard is now in bloom."* (ERV) In the middle of this very important book, we learn the precept that it is the little foxes that spoil the vine. We are always so busy looking at big things, we forget to monitor the little things, and those little things are the things that spoil the work. We are encouraged to 'catch' the little things before they become a problem - because the work is in full bloom. I am not one of those leaders who thinks the internet is inherently evil. I think it is a neutral tool that can be used for good or for bad, and can firsthand say that I was working with a ministry presence online back before anyone else was doing it, way before it was popular - even back when people were still afraid of the internet. I've been through the evolution of internet communication, through dial-up to Ethernet to high-speed, from email to community posting boards to forums to social networking. I have been around and working online since 1998 - which is a feat in and of itself. I have watched the way we approach the internet pass from fear and trembling (remember when we didn't even use our real names?) to a comfort that I sometimes wonder if it has become too lax. Regardless of how the internet has evolved, there is one thing I can't deny: it's important for a ministry that desires to grow and actually go somewhere to have a presence online. If we want to get there, however, we have to mind ourselves and catch those little foxes before they spoil the vine.

Instead of ranting and raving about what's wrong, I am going to provide some things you can do that will make a radical difference in how your ministry is perceived. As the internet is often the first way people encounter a ministry today, it's important that your ministry is perceived as positively as possible. Here are some great ways to mind your 'little foxes' online!

- **Do not add people to a Facebook group (or another group) without their permission.** – I can't count the number of private messages I've received because I left a Facebook group that I was added to without my permission. The messages I receive about this are all the same: They apologize to me if they "offended" me because they added me to the group without permission. Then, they proceed to tell me why they added me to the group without my permission, as if that is going to change something. I feel that I need to clarify something in this example because I know being added to groups without permission is an extremely common issue on Facebook. First of all, I know that I myself have made it explicitly clear on at least twelve public occasions that I do not want to be added to things without my permission. It's been on my Facebook page no less than twelve times to rave reviews, with multiple 'likes' and statements of agreement. If you are starting a group and you would like to belong, come and ask people about it first. That is decency and order. Tell them that you have a group, the name of it, and that you would like to add someone to it. I know a common defense to this is for me to change my settings, but no – I should not have to do that, and there is no viable way I can keep people from adding me to groups without my permission. What should happen is individuals should ask before adding people to a group. This is not hard to do, nor is it too much to ask. Stave off emotional excitement about having a group long enough to come and ask the woman or man of God if you can add them. Or better yet, put a notice about your group in your status and invite people to join if they would like to be added. At one time, I operated a group on Facebook with over three hundred members, none of which were ever added without permission. Operate by decency and order! If you are a leader, respect people's time and interest and do not add anyone to a group without their permission.

- **Do not send people messages to people online telling them how they are feeling.** - This seems to be a big problem online. Given the fact that tone can be extremely difficult to perceive and most people you know online you have never met in person, it is easy to misread someone's thoughts or feelings based on a posting or a status. Despite this fact, people are always going around telling other people how that other person is feeling. Last time I checked, nobody crawled inside anyone else's mind and knows what they are thinking. Personally, I am extraordinarily in touch with how I feel and I don't really like it when someone else tells me how I am feeling, because they are usually wrong. It's not prophetic to tell someone how wounded they are or offended they are online, it's stupid. If you know someone (actually having met or even talked to them online) or are perceiving something in the Spirit, that is clearly different, as it is done out of caring, rather than presumption, and I am not talking about that. Clearly when this is done, it is done in a different context. While I am on the topic at hand, do not use the word "offended" too freely. "Offended" seems to be the word du jour on the net. It is all too common to watch people accuse others of being 'offended'. This is done because offense implies the receiver of the action is somehow in a certain state of fault, rather than the transferred accepting responsibility in full for their actions (possibly causing offense). In the example above, I am not "offended" when I am added to a group without my permission. It does not hurt my feelings or emotionally wound me. What it does do is show a total lack of respect for me as a minister, for my time, and for my request that I not be added to groups without my permission. It shows me that someone does not hold proper respect for me as a person and as a leader. What it does do is make sure the leader who did it will not ever be invited to speak at any of my events, because I can't trust they won't overstep the boundaries of order and authority therein.

- **Don't manipulate leaders online.** - If there is one thing I know I despise, it is when someone comes on and starts telling me how wonderful I am when they have no idea who I am. I'm not talking about being complimented, because people can tell a lot about us from our ministry presence. What I am talking about are the sickly, sweet, saccharin-y individuals who come on and say how anointed you are, how great your ministry must be, and how incredible you are...and then start talking about themselves, or just have to give you the opportunity to network with them, or buy their item...or how you can get your spiritual breakthrough in nine days or less if you just send them money, like their page, or buy their book. Um...no. We, as leaders, know when someone is being genuine, and when someone is just blowing smoke.

- **Don't try to recruit for a pyramid scheme on other people's pages** - I know that we are living in difficult economic times, both among believers and among ministers in the church. I also know these economic difficulties create the perfect opportunity to get involved in pyramid schemes. There is no end to the number of agencies out there who seek to prey upon vulnerable people who are hoping for a financial windfall with seemingly little work. No matter how you may perceive an organization you are selling for, remember decency and order. Do not solicit sales or recruit for a sales company online. It is especially out of order to come to a leader and solicit their support. There are lots of opportunities to sell items - as a vendor. Don't use ministry connections to promote pyramid schemes, multi-level marketing organizations, or sales pitches!

- **Do not promote yourself or your ministry on someone else's fan page.** - A fan page for a ministry, a person, or a business is just that - it is for that ministry, person, or business. It is not for you to promote yourself, what you are doing, an event or leader that you believe in, what you like, or what you feel is important. People who insist on promoting themselves on someone else's fan page are just selfish, and don't tell me it is done for the Kingdom – it is done to try and attract someone else's audience. Your presence on a fan page indicates that you are a supporter of what someone else is doing. Let me say as one with fan pages - it speaks volumes to me when someone is willing to show forth that sign of support - it's a sign of respect. If you want to promote your own areas, beliefs, thoughts, or issues of importance, get your own fan page.

- **Don't ask for money or ask people to support someone you know (that they don't) on somebody's page.** - I am really getting tired of all this begging in the Kingdom. I'm sorry that so many cannot trust God for finances that so many believe they must resort to begging. I know we all hit difficulties, I know there are problems that we all encounter, but I also know that the Bible says to seek first the Kingdom of God, not seek first money from everyone in the Kingdom. Do I have issues from time to time, yes. Have I ever come online and sent out private requests for money, no, I have not. Stop asking people for money. I think what personally galls me is online beggars don't just ask for an offering, they ask for specified amounts - anywhere from oh, say, $50 to $2,000 - and these are the same people who know I books for sale, know I have .mp3 downloads available on Amazon.com for under $5 apiece, not to mention a host of other materials available now and soon available through both ministry and business, and yet they never show a single sign of support to this work financially. They expect me to give, but they do not expect to sow. Then they come on my page and litter my inbox with messages asking me to buy something done by someone else or to support someone else - who I do not even know online and have never even met! I am not sending money to people I do not know and do not trust online. I am surely not giving money to someone

I have never even heard of! I am not sowing into ministries that display disorder online. This is still the internet, and no, no one is entitled to receive from me just because they come and ask me for something. I am not a bank, someone's distant personal covering, or tied to such an individual in some way.

- **Don't solicit to cover people.** - When did people start going to people online and telling them that they should be their covering because "God" appointed it? Then the individual is accused of being out of order when they don't dump their current covering to be under the individual saying it is God's will? If you are a real leader, then your fruit speaks for itself, and that person will be moved by God to be under your leadership if it is within His will. People will come to be covered because God draws them. It's not a magical process that operates via control or manipulation. Covering is not a competition - this isn't "whoever covers the most people wins."

- **Edit your notes and check the spelling in your statuses.** - Yes, we all have an occasional typo, myself included, and I am not talking about this. I am talking about the consistent misuse of words, spelling errors, and grammar that are extraordinarily prevalent online - from Facebook, to blogs, to yes, even people's websites. I've had people argue with me that "People don't take the internet work that serious." Well, do you want to get invited to preach, or not? Do you want to get a book published, or not? If you do, check your spelling and grammar. If your thought is so profound you have to get it down, type it in Word, run spell-check, and then copy it into your status. Doing such will make a huge difference in your presentation.

CHAPTER TWENTY-SEVEN

BLOGGING

Write, therefore, what you have seen,
what is now and what will take place later.
(Revelation 1:19)

BLOGGING is one of the most popular features online. A blog is an online journal that is visible for the world to see. As a result, blogs are a great way to share thoughts, revelations, perspectives, and events with others.

Blogging is often considered to be a public journal. People who blog do so to share something on their minds, a thought, or a revelation they have about something. Some people blog every day, others only when they have an inspired thought. There are blogs on every topic imaginable: current events, cooking, technology, education, crafting, hobbies, religion, spiritual matters, book reviews, and so on and so-forth.

Many ministers do not take up blogging because they think they have to write something every day. Blogging isn't the long version of tweeting, and doesn't serve to give an update of every move made throughout your day. Blogging is, instead, a great forum for the minister to share writings, revelations, and things the Lord places upon your heart to share with others. Most blog sites have free and paid options, depending upon how extensively you want to develop your blog. Many website platforms also allow you to have a blog directly on your website, as also do many social networking sites allow you to post blogs to your profile.

Blogs are often followed by individuals who find what you write or share intriguing. As a blogger, you also have the option to follow other bloggers and their diverse writings. Some people set up different blogs for different themes, while others use one blog to showcase everything they are interested in sharing. However you desire to set up a blog, remember a few key things.

First, blogs should be well-written. This means they should be edited for spelling and grammar. Avoid vulgar language and content. Content is also important: a blog should be used for a specific purpose. Stick to that purpose as much as possible for the continuity. For example, if your blog is for ministry, do not use it to share information about changing the oil in a car. Third, successful internet presence requires a minister have at least one blog and that the blog is updated at least once per month (even if the update is nothing more than an event posting or a prayer or prayer request). Regular blog maintenance shows a ministry is up-to-date and cares about conveying their message to the world on a regular basis. Fourth, blogs should be attractive and eye-appealing. Most blogging sites give you the option to design your blog using various templates. These templates can be modified with your own desired colors, photos, and themes in order to create a design that is unique to your own interests and thoughts.

Blogs are also a great way to share about upcoming events, flyers, photos, and happenings with the world. All blogs provide ways to share text, pictures, video, and other media through their sites. Just like a journal is not always just writing but sometimes pictures and other mementos inserted in along with text, so a blog can serve this purpose as well. Instead of narrowly-defining the way a blog must be, expand the concept of it and view it as another means to provide information to your online audience. Even if you are not a prolific writer, blogging can be a great asset to your ministry presence on the internet.

Blogging sites

The most popular blog sites are WordPress.com, Tumblr.com, wix.com, and blogger.com (operated through Google). WordPress powers a large portion of internet sites in general, and also has options to use their services for website building. Tumblr is frequently used for pictures, videos, and images. Blogger (formerly BlogSpot) allows the integration of YouTube videos and extensive presentation of text. Facebook also offers blogging through its "notes" section, available to each user on their profile page.

Some ideas for using blogs

Still stumbling on the idea of what to do with a blog? In our world today, it's not uncommon to deal with people from a variety of states and countries. Keeping in contact, teaching and training, and dealing with many people in a variety of areas can become quite exhausting. For the majority of my ministry, I have done just this: maintained numerous ministries from a long distance. In my situation as an apostle, the internet has been a blessing to reach out and keep regular communication with the people I am leading. One of the easiest ways I have been able to engage in training, discussion about current events, and get feedback from those I lead in order to discover what they need to learn and share. Here are some practical uses for blogs to create discussion and instruction:

- **Posting Bible studies** – If you are having to train a large number of people at once or even a group of people who are all at a distance, use a blog to post some general Bible studies for training and teaching.

- **Posting teachings** – If you're desiring to teach on something more general, posting a general teaching on a blog is a great way to disseminate that teaching to those you lead, and beyond.

- **Answering questions** – If you are one of those leaders that is always getting lots of questions from people you cover, a blog is a great way to answer these questions, once and for all. It creates a catalog of questions and answers that are easy to access and read whenever a question arises. When someone comes to you with the same question later on, refer them to your blog posting.

- **Addressing ministry issues** – A blog is not the place to address internal issues with someone specific. Those issues are better handled one-on-one, in private. For ministry issues that are more general, a blog is a great way to share thoughts and teaching that relate to things commonly seen in ministry today.

- **Discussing "stream of consciousness" ideas and thoughts** – Blogs can be great places to share thoughts and ideas one may have that teach lessons or help with issues (no matter how random they may seem). They can be great for instruction, personal devotions and spiritual thoughts, or for weaving pop culture ideas with spiritual teachings.

- **Writing a book** – If you've thought about writing a book but seem to trip up with a blank page, a blog is a great way to put many different thoughts into print and generate some interest. You can later take those posts and incorporate them into a longer book.

CHAPTER TWENTY-EIGHT

PODCASTING

We proclaim to you what we have seen and heard,
so that you also may have fellowship with us.
And our fellowship is with the Father and with His Son,
Jesus Christ.
(1 John 1:3)

PODCASTING is the art of sharing an informative broadcast via the internet. It is most often used in the context of a video cast or an audio cast. A podcast may be a clip, a video blog, a broadcasted show, live, or pre-recorded. Podcasting is a wonderful way to establish broadcasting for a new or developing ministry, as many of the options that exist are free or low-cost.

Podcasting seems extravagant and complicated to some. They think being a good podcaster costs a lot of money and requires a lot of time. To be a good podcaster, you need a good webcam, a good backdrop, a headset, recording software, and a telephone or Skype system.

To do a video podcast, you need to have good organization and good direction. Scripting is essential. Don't just "wing it." Plan what you are going to say and take the time to formulate thoughts. Make your words clear and articulate. Learn about the equipment you have and learn about the different ways that the equipment you have can enhance the production you seek to establish. Also consider having a "set." This doesn't mean you have to spend lots of money renovating your location, but it does mean you need to give some thought to how your background will look. Some people prefer to record against a blue or green wall so they can edit in a different background using editing software. For those who do not have this technical skill, recording with a bookcase in the background, a window or curtain, some flowers, a table with a vase, or something else similar can give a beautiful and tasteful look to any situation. During teaching it's important to sit back, as webcams can accentuate the facial features and make it look like you are in "someone's face." Speak as level-toned as possible, avoid screaming, and hold your attention forward. Establish yourself neat and clean, well-dressed, and well-prepared. Depending on the site and means used to promote the podcast, a video is either uploaded to the internet site or is immediately seen by others via a live stream.

Audio podcasting holds to the same principles as video podcasting, minus the visual component. Audio podcasting uses one of three different methods to convey its point: recording software, a telephone, or an internet system like Skype. Using whichever means available, an audio recording is then made that can be shared.

Below are five examples of podcasting sites: three are video podcasting sites, and one is an audio podcasting site. The function and purpose of these different sites helps to establish a minister in podcasting in a powerful and easy to distribute way.

- **YouTube** – YouTube is still the most popular podcasting site in existence, and a great place to post "short clips" of sermons, messages, preaching, advertisements, and commercials for events. YouTube videos are easily accessible and can be easily shared on websites and social networking sites. YouTube videos can be longer than fifteen minutes in length once an account is established for a certain length of time.

- **IBM Cloud Video** – Formerly Ustream.tv, is a live-streaming website for visual podcasting. It takes a little skill to get the settings right for the live recording, and obviously, recording live takes a little practice and skill as well. As a paid site, it offers many features, and can be a great resource for live events, such as conferences, preaching, and workshops.

- **Blog Talk Radio** – Blog Talk Radio was, at one time, an immensely resource for audio podcasting, especially among ministries. This is because the technology was new, innovative, and free. Blog Talk Radio operates through a telephone or by using Skype. Hosts receive a call-in number and pass code to broadcast their programs live or upload audio files to play during the program. A unique feature about Blog Talk is the ability for other people to call in and speak with the host during a live broadcast. Starting in February 2011, Blog Talk Radio began limiting their free accounts to 30 minute programs per day and disallows programming for free accounts during primetime. As a result, many Blog Talk hosts left the airwaves. Now Blog Talk allows a number of different plans and hosting options to hosts at various costs. Despite the changes, Blog Talk Radio still remains a great avenue for podcasting around the internet. It is easy to install a player on a website or social networking site, and it also is easy to connect automatic updates to Facebook, Twitter, and other sites through Blog Talk.

- **Facebook Live** – Sometimes called "going live," Facebook Live is the use of a live stream on an individual's Facebook page to speak to those who follow them. This stream is used for all sorts of things online: programs, reviews, preaching, singing, ministering, and communications, all from one's phone or computer, for free.

- **Spreaker** – An audio podcasting site that is both free

and paid, audio producers can upload their programming and schedule it for a later broadcast or make it available for listening, now. Spreaker features a wide variety of available tools and distributions, for varied prices.

CHAPTER TWENTY-NINE

EMAIL LISTS

*I charge you before the Lord
to have this letter read to all the brothers.
(1 Thessalonians 5:27)*

IN an earlier chapter, we discussed the proper construction and use for emails. One of those uses is to distribute information about ministry events, happenings, and to advertise things people may be interested in. The best way to do this is to maintain a mailing list.

Most ministries prefer to maintain a mailing list consisting of people interested in the events and happenings of the organization. Email lists are impersonal. Even though a minister may know the people on a mailing list, the purpose in sending out a message through an email list is to reach many people with the information. Most email programs and services have the option to maintain an address book, adding various contacts and sending out one email to everyone on the list rather than having to send out separate emails. Emails are sent to a list under the "bcc:" option in an email: the "bcc" stands for "blind carbon copy" and prohibits the recipients from seeing one another's contact information. Emails can be fancy, formal, plain text, or sent in html.

Maintaining an email list can be challenging, but there are some basic components to enhance and maximize the benefit of an email list. Here are some tips to help with the challenges.

- **Do not send out too many emails in a month** – We all know people forget things. With an email list, it's tempting to remind people day after day after day about upcoming events. Doing so renders you annoying to recipients and can get you quickly marked as a "spammer" by internet programs. Unless your specific email purpose is a daily devotion or some sort of daily reflective thought, restrict your emailing to so many times per month – figure a maximum of four times per month, or once per week – to provide necessary updates. Remember, an email list is to provide updates and information, not to motivate people to remember things.

- **When hosting an email list, do not send attachments with them** – The temptation exists to use your email lists for all sorts of things, from sharing forwards to sending cute, little pictures of kittens chasing butterflies. Email blasting indicates you are sending an email, not an attachment. Sending attachments causes your emails to be labeled as spam and many will not open an email attachment, even if it makes it past anti-spam software.

- **Edit emails** – I cannot emphasize enough the importance in editing your emails. Check your spelling and grammar! Sending out a poorly edited and worded email negatively reflects upon a ministry image.

- **Don't abuse an email list** – Since emails are sent to a wide audience, do not use them to settle personal scores or argue with people about personal matters. Issues that are private are not for public distribution through an email list.

- **Be careful with content** – Mass emailings need to be for their expressed purpose. Don't use an email list to send out announcements that would not be of interest to the general body of the list. For example, the majority of people would not care about your child's birthday party. Also refrain from sharing personal information such as telephone numbers or physical addresses.

- **Check recipients frequently** – Update the list often. People's email addresses change, so be sure to remove old "bouncing" email addresses. Let your friends and contacts around the internet know you are updating your list and invite them to join every few months. Also make sure that you give an "opt out" option on each email or notify members once per year that they have the option to be removed from your mailing list.

CHAPTER THIRTY

PUBLISHING AND E-PUBLISHING

Oh, that my words were recorded,
that they were written on a scroll,
that they were inscribed with an iron tool on lead,
or engraved in rock forever!
(Job 19:23-24)

THE world of publishing has changed in massive ways over the past twenty years. The advance of the internet has changed the way information is disseminated, promoted, and presented. Whereas self-publishing used to be a quiet industry utilized only by people who could not get their material legitimately published, self-publishing has become an increasing norm, thanks to the internet.

The mainline publishing industry suffered after a flood of publications introduced to the market never sold, causing publishers to lose money on their investments. This started the close of the publishing industry to new or upcoming authors. As even celebrity books failed to sell and popular books turned out to be fabricated or exaggerated, the publishing industry grew even narrower. As a result of this tide, publishing houses all over the United States started to close or consolidate with other publishers. To many, the publishing industry was thought to be tanking quickly. Instead of tanking, the publishing industry changed. The advance of technologies: e-books, downloadable books, digital magazines, print-on-demand technology, and easier access to layout software began to change the way printing was conceived and delivered.

Today there remain the main two avenues of publishing that have always existed: traditional publishing and self-publishing. The internet has, as can be seen above, changed both radically.

Traditional publishing follows a standard course of action: potential authors formulate a book package for submission to publishing companies. The book package typically consists of something known as a query letter (a one-page letter summarizing the contents of the book and a little about the author's qualifications to write the book), a table of contents, a summary of contents, marketing and target audience information, an author's biography, and a sample of the book (one to three chapters). The package contents vary between publishers, so it is very important to match the desired contents with the correct publisher. It used to be customary that a traditional publisher absorbed all the costs of publication and promotion, introducing the author to the world. With the crunch on the publishing industry, this does still exist, but it is a rare find and difficult to break into. Even traditional publishers break deals with their clients (especially newer ones) to cover financial costs of printing and publication, and most no longer cover advertising or promotional costs. Using a traditional publisher may help sell more copies and make distribution and promotion easier, but there are things one should know about pursuing traditional publishing:

- **Traditional publishers require a contract that locks an author in for a certain period of time**, anywhere from two to five years. Inspect the contents of a contract carefully and ask for clarification on any points that don't make sense or seem to add up.

- **Traditional publishing takes longer than self-publishing**. With a traditional publisher, there is far more emphasis placed on editing, content, and first-run printing than with self-publishing. It can take anywhere from a few months to a year for a traditionally published book to go from acceptance to book form.

- **In traditional publishing, financial arrangements are different than with self-publishing.** In traditional publishing, the author is paid a royalty payment on each copy sold. The amount of that royalty is anywhere from 5% to 60%, depending on the prior arrangements stipulated within the author's contract. Most royalty payments are on retail sales (the lower end of royalty payments) rather than wholesale copies (the higher end of royalty payments) and, as a result, are extremely low per copy. Wholesale copy royalties are usually done when an author has made a substantial financial contribution to the cost of the publication and printing, whereas lower royalty payments are reserved for situations where the publisher has assumed full or most of the cost. In self-publishing, the author assumes all of the printing costs and makes the cost of the profit minus those printing costs. Most of the time, an author must either pay for professional editing and layout services or complete these tasks themselves. Self-publishing also requires the author to assume full responsibility for distribution, promotion, advertising, and often, sales. Distribution for a self-published book is more limited than with a traditional publisher, although the distribution is, long-term, usually more beneficial for the author because the audience is better targeted. If you are not interested so much as in sales as in impact, and are content to do much of the work yourself, self-publishing is a good option.

- **Both traditional and self-publishing options have expanded.** Having a "book" published just doesn't mean what it used to in days gone by. It used to be that being published meant a person's work was printed in a tangible book or periodical and used to be an extremely big deal. Nowadays someone may say they have been "published" but that can mean any number of things: a traditional book, newspaper, or magazine, an e-publication, an e-book, a downloadable book for a digital device, or even a blog. Now print-on-demand technology even creates a situation where being published in book form does not necessarily mean a book is available in a bookstore, but may only be available from a certain online company.

Publishing also functions for periodicals, newsletters, tracts, mini-books, curriculums, and smaller publications that are different from book publishing. Many ministries benefit greatly from publishing different ministry items on a regular basis that help provide information, articles, teachings, advertisements, and updates for readers. The internet offers a variety of digital magazine options. Sites such as magcloud.com and Joomag.com make available both a digital and print option, and magazines can be made free or at a cost to patrons. This takes much of the expense out of traditional printing and costs for periodicals while still giving the traditional option for all of them. It also gives your magazines a wider exposure than traditional methods. Such digital applications make promotions through websites and social networks very, very easy. Magcloud.com also now has a variety of sizes and styles available for publication through their site.

Other sites, such as issuu.com, also offer digital publishing options that are available to others for free. Unlike magcloud.com, issuu allows a variety of documents and file types to stand featured on your storefront page. Some allow you to charge to download or share your documents, and others do not. Always check the conditions, investigate the options, and match the site to your desired posting and materials.

Copyright

I already spoke about copyright a bit earlier. Copyright protection is the legally recognized standard an author, artist, photographer or musician uses to protect their work from being stolen or used without permission. It does serve to ensure the creator of a work is dutifully compensated, but it also ensures more than that. Copyright protects a work, making sure the author holds their full rights in conjunction with that work. A copyright remains in effect for the duration of an author's life plus seventy years beyond their death.

All original work is copyright protected unless it was written prior to 1925. Works written prior to 1925 is in a classification of work known as the public domain. Nowadays, some pictures and writings are specifically released to the public domain, for free usage personal, in print, and in media. Public domain works do not require prior permission to reproduce, in part or in whole, because they are not considered to be copyrighted.

It is important that, when writing official material (especially material for sale), the material in question is legally registered with the United States Copyright Office. This process is usually done online and involves filing the appropriate form with applicable information about the work and the author. To file a standard application online, the process is $35. Some claims with a high volume of public domain or other produced material costs $55. After the claim is processed, the individual who files will receive a certificate of copyright.

Fair use

Fair use is an oft disputed aspect of copyright law which allows others to reference or quote materials without being in violation of copyright. In order to be in accordance with fair use, one must cite the passage as a quotation, credit the author as having written the work, make no changes to the content itself, and must make reference to the book. Fair use allows for music, quotations, literature, and other copyrighted material to be used without prior permission for educational, reviewing, critiquing, citations, and comparative purposes.

CHAPTER THIRTY-ONE

BUSINESS ESSENTIALS

One generation will commend Your works to another;
they will tell of Your mighty acts.
(Psalm 145:4)

WE must be thoroughly prepared for Kingdom business. It is essential to have knowledge of business basics, as we have discussed here. It is also essential to have certain essentials to effectively communicate vision.

Most ministries consider the bigger aspects of business essentials, such as websites and event flyers, but forget about the smaller means which communicate Kingdom business, such as business cards and a logo. Never underestimate the power of that personal touch when interacting with others. The little business essentials make a big difference in the impact we have as we meet others and interact with them on an interpersonal level.

- **Business cards** – Business cards are one of the most effective essentials for ministries. Once extremely expensive, business cards have become affordable and attractive through companies like vistaprint.com. Business cards should contain the minister's name and title, the ministry's name, address, telephone number, email address, and website address. If there is any other applicable information, such as a key

Bible verse, slogan, photo of the minister, or ministry logo, those also can be included.

- **Address labels or an address stamp** – Handwriting a ministry address on envelopes is not only time consuming, it's also tacky. Address labels are also cheap to print or purchase and make a real class-act statement. When it is an option, custom stationery is also nice (although more expensive).

- **Logo** – Every ministry should have a logo that identifies their ministry and its important theme and vision. Logos can be designed using programs available on a home computer or can be professionally made; the results, when one knows what they are doing, can be about the same. The logo should be used as necessary to identify the ministry.

- **Organizational seal** – An organizational seal is an official raised embosser used to officiate documents, certificates, certifications, and licenses. All non-profit organizations are required to have an organizational seal to officiate documents. Embossers and gold foils used for seals are relatively inexpensive and can be purchased through a stationery store. When ordering, you have the option to customize your embosser with your unique ministry information and make it as fancy or simple as you would like.

- **Ministry seal** – A ministry seal is a specified logo for the minister presiding over a ministry. For example, I have a logo-designed seal for official documents, such as ordination papers, that expresses the unique facets and call of my work in ministry. The symbols on it represent the work I do and the pillars of the ministry, as well as my own unique call. Ministry seals can be quite expensive and generic, and it is essential, therefore, that when having a seal designed, communication and specification is made for what one desires.

- **Customized domain name** – We all know the internet is a big place, filled with a veritable plethora of websites, information, and personalities. Your presence on the web is largely dependent on how easy it is for others to find you. Once you have been found, it's important people are able to remember how they can reach you. The most obvious way this is accomplished is through your unique domain name. Domain names are available for purchase at very reasonable rates and are renewable based on how they are purchased (for one year, two years, three years, five years, or ten years). A domain name should reflect something about your work – either your ministry name or an abbreviation of it, your own name if your ministry is named after you, or a program or catchphrase title that relates to your work.

- **PayPal Account and Square or mobile reader** – It is easier than ever to accept payments via internet and mobile phone than ever before. With a growing number of individuals who prefer to make donations or purchase items electronically, having a means to receive electronic payments is a must. PayPal provides merchant services at a low rate, which is deducted from every payment received, thereby eliminating the cost of merchant services through a traditional bank. A Square or other mobile reader gives the option to receive credit card payments by swiping a credit card using a small mobile reader that fits in a smart phone or by typing in the credit card information on the phone. Those who use this method are able to sign and authorize purchases, receive receipts, and immediately transmit funds without using a check or cash.

- **Brochure about the organization's purpose, vision, and mission** – Brochures are readily easy to create and distribute without a lot of expense. A simple brochure made available on a

- **Recordings** – Most ministries benefit from the sale and distribution of audio and video recording on CD or DVD. Recordings are made using recording software and applicable technology to generate the recording. All recordings should be edited (mistakes edited out) and should be labeled applicably and attractively. Prices should be set according to the number of discs in a series. DVDs should be priced higher than CDs. All DVDs and CDs should have an introduction and post information for contact.

- **A record of ministry work, outreach, and events** – Most ministries choose do to this through photo or video documentation. Anytime a ministry has something…photograph or record it! Also take the time to write out summaries of events, who was present, themes, dates, etc. and keep a record of it, that the work of the ministry may be remembered for a long time.

SECTION IV

PRESENTING THE VISION

CHAPTER THIRTY-TWO

THE ESSENCE OF PRESENTATION

I have become its servant by the commission God gave me
to present to you the word of God in its fullness—
the mystery that has been kept hidden for ages and generations,
but is now disclosed to the saints.
(Colossians 1:25-26)

S O far, we've discussed writing the vision, organizing the vision, and communicating the vision. Now we are going to turn our attention to the area of presenting the vision. It's been said that presentation is everything. When working in ministry, presentation may not be everything (as this book can confirm), but it is definitely something that cannot be ignored.

Presenting the vision is all about how the vision manifests in our ministries and how we carry ourselves as ministers. It's a last step to balancing all the necessary facets of a solid ministry. It is the essential application of the information, data, facts, and work we put into ministry. We can present well or we can present poorly. Often how we present ourselves and our ministries can affect how our ministries are perceived. If we have a great vision and great purpose, that needs to be seen in how we present the work of God.

Jesus always presented His vision and His personage well to others. No matter what the audience, situation, or circumstance, Jesus knew how to handle Himself. The same is true of the other leaders of the early church. They might have had their issues and their bad days, but overall, God's leaders have made it a point to present well in accordance with His Kingdom vision. The reason for this is two-fold: they were representatives of the Kingdom of God and also they had a Kingdom message to proclaim. The presentation went hand-in-hand with the message because presentation gives a visual component to the message proclaimed. The same is true today: our presentation of the Kingdom lets people see what we tell them about and also allows them to see that we live what we believe.

There are many different dimensions to presentation. Presentation is how we prepare ourselves, carry ourselves, and handle ourselves. It is how both the church and the world see us when they look at our work and at us. At the same time, it is being aware of the things people look at when they see us and guarding ourselves against judgment and scrutiny. In learning about presentation we learn about what we want to present to the world, what we want to keep private, and how we can best display God's love and power to those we seek to reach with the Gospel.

Presenting the work of ministry is a Kingdom mandate. How we present the message, the Kingdom of God itself, and ourselves as leaders are as important as the message we present. Some today argue that the message is all that matters, but that isn't what the Word of God tells us. As leaders in the Kingdom we must be the best representatives of excellence as much as possible. We must dress the part, speak the part, talk the part, walk the part, and display God's purpose in our lives. While anybody can claim to be a leader within God's Kingdom, not everyone can meet up with the extensive standards God has laid out for His ministers.

Being called to be a leader means putting one's self aside in the work of the Lord. If we are going to be Kingdom leaders, it's time to stop lowering the standards God has established for us and present a professional and unified approach to Kingdom ministry. In this section, we will work to accomplish just that.

CHAPTER THIRTY-THREE

PUBLIC IMAGE

He has made us competent as ministers of a new covenant—
not of the letter but of the Spirit;
for the letter kills, but the Spirit gives life.
(2 Corinthians 3:6)

MINISTRY life is a complicated walk because everyone the world over has their own standards of judgment and concept about what ministry is and how ministers should live. It is even more frustrating to note that the same standards are not upheld for all ministers. Ministers that are regarded as having a celebrity status are given more leniency than ministers who aren't as well-known, and obvious double standards exist between men and women. This makes maintaining a public image for a minister very complicated. People may feel the right to inquire and even pry into a minister's private life, and may probe with very personal questions in attempt to see how a minister "measures up" to their own personal standards.

It is true that we don't do this in other professions, even one where moral standards are considered to be quite high. Ministers shouldn't have things they feel they need to hide, but that is different from believing every area of one's life should be up for public display. Ministers who have been in ministry for quite some time are well aware that people easily misconstrue details, blow things out of proportion, or exaggerate the truth on matters when they think they can run with what, in reality, may be the smallest issue.

There will always be an aspect of a minister's life that someone else can pick apart and turn into something it's not. This can span from someone dragging up ancient history to misconstruing a bad day. Because of this, ministers need to be aware of the image they project to the public. Ministers are public figures as people who stand before groups or work with individuals and that means people seek to have a certain perception about them. The best way to maintain this perception of an individual as a minister and leader is to maintain privacy.

Even though people will be forever curious about the private lives of ministers, ministers of God are entitled to their privacy. There are certain things that nobody has the right to know about, no matter what they may think. If ministers desire to have any privacy, it must be tightly guarded. Protecting privacy is one of the best keys to maintaining a solid public image. This is achieved in the following ways:

- **Be careful about who you take into your confidence** – There are different levels of confidence: things we share with no one but God, things we share publicly, things we share professionally (with other ministers or those we work with), things we share with acquaintances, things we share with friends, and things we share with people we know on an intimate level. Some things are just not up for public consumption, scrutiny, or opinion. Private information should be reserved for those we know well and trust on an intimate level. One must prove they are able to handle having such intimate information via the fact that they are not gossipy and do not tell everything they learn about you to everyone else. This is easy to discern by how an individual responds to having information about others and whether or not they exaggerate or lie about what you know to be true.

- **Don't answer everyone's questions** – Ministers believe they need to be transparent. The truth is, we do need to be transparent, but that transparency has limits. It is not uncommon for people to ask questions beyond the limits of good taste and decency just because they want information – and to do it under the guise of wanting more information about you as a minister. When answering questions, it is a good practice to never answer anything beyond what's a part of a public testimony. Politely decline to answer any questions that are too personal to be answered. If someone persists anyway, make it clear the question is not their business and will not be answered.

- **Be cautious about what you speak in public** – Testimonies are a great, personal journey about our own call and experience with God. It's great to give testimony. It's also important not to give too many details about a testimony. Being inappropriately or unnecessarily graphic in a testimony (explicitly explaining details of drug abuse, medical history, sexual encounters, etc.) gives away private details of one's life that really don't need to be mentioned. Remember, testimony is about giving glory to God – not shocking people. For that reason, testimonies should be prepared rather than spontaneous and, if there is question of subject matter, check with someone before presenting certain details.

- **Watch the "entertainment factor" in preaching and teaching** – It's great to tell stories, relate personal experience, and make a teaching understandable and applicable based on personal example. It's also important to make sure you never go too far with those stories into exposing very personal details of your life. Details of your sex life, for example, don't belong in the pulpit. Don't risk exposing too much about yourself while at the same time making others very uncomfortable.

- **Consider those around you and the company you keep** – This may be considered an obvious facet of ministry, but ministers need to be careful about who they befriend. This is more than just in the sense of behaviors that could be deemed publicly disgraceful or contrary to ministry. Do your friends talk about you behind your back – especially to your enemies? Do they seem to be critical of the ministry decisions you make? Do they argue with you about judgment calls? Being cautious about those we keep around us is about more than just how they look; it is about how they make us look to others and what they say about us when we are not around.

- **Be careful about the amount of contact information you give out** – People will forever manipulate you into giving out a phone number, address, or other personal contact information because they feel entitled to have it. With the vast number of social networking options available today, there is no reason to give strangers your personal contact information if you do not desire them to have it.

CHAPTER THIRTY-FOUR

MINISTRY ORDER

And in the church God has appointed first of all apostles, second prophets, third teachers, then workers of miracles, also those having gifts of healing, those able to help others, those with gifts of administration, and those speaking in different kinds of tongues. Are all apostles? Are all prophets? Are all teachers? Do all work miracles? Do all have gifts of healing? Do all speak in tongues? Do all interpret? But eagerly desire the greater gifts.
(1 Corinthians 12:28-31)

WHEN interacting with other ministers, there is certain order that must be followed. In today's church, most ministers perceive themselves allowed to conduct themselves any which way in any setting. What they do not recognize is they deeply hurt their own chances of being invited to participate in other events or work with other leaders because of the way in which they behave. As much as we do not like to deal with it, there is rank and file within ministry order. We need to be conscious of our attitudes, interactions, and presentations of order when dealing with other ministers. If we are respectful of that order, we will be better leaders in the long-run.

We are very familiar with how to interact with our personal superiors, such as a covering, teacher, or instructor. We know that we are to honor those who teach and train us as our leaders. What we aren't familiar with – and we refuse to tap into on any level – is the reality that submission to a leader is only the beginning of our call and leading within the Kingdom. The Word of God instructs us to *Submit to one another out of reverence for Christ* (Ephesians 5:21). This is not just a command to submit to our personal leader, but to show respect and honor to everyone in the Body.

That having been said, we must pay careful attention to the following interactions within the Body to maintain order:

- **Elders** – The term "elder" is not so much used to indicate age, but to indicate calling and experience. Even though someone may not hold personal covering authority over you, each office of the church serves a definitive function, purpose, and authority that encompass with it the directive and obedience of the entire church. In other words: if you are a part of the church, it doesn't matter if you are a leader or not: you must respect and subscribe to the church's leadership and order. We know from the Bible that the five-fold ministry operates via apostles, prophets, evangelists, pastors, and teachers. When these assemble together and there is a question of authority or issue, the apostle holds the senior rank as the office designed to maintain and implement order (1 Corinthians 9:2, 1 Corinthians 12:28-29). It is not a competitive rank, it does not make the apostle better than everyone else or the main leader in every situation, but it does mean that when an apostle is present, they represent an office of order. The church needs to line up with apostolic order out of a sign of respect for the apostolic gifting and purpose. Prophets are second in authority, as the apostle and prophet form universal offices. Wherever the two go, they have authority; whether or not it is wise to exercise that authority becomes another matter entirely, and not one we will be discussing here. Pastors and teachers represent local authorities, holding authority over local congregations and those they teach, pastor, and instruct, and the evangelist represents an authority somewhere between local and universal. Bishops, elders, and deacons represent appointments rather than five-fold ministry offices, and are subject to apostles, prophets, and pastors. If we say we believe in order, we must respect God's order. It also means we uphold God's order with decency and dignity.

If someone has an issue with an elder in ministry (whether or not that person is their covering), they need to follow Biblical protocol and handle that issue, going to the individual and speaking them about it directly (Matthew 18:15-17). If the issue remains, they are to bring witnesses, and if an issue continues to remain, disassociate with them. Do not use a public forum, gossip, or the pulpit to try and defame an elder. Doing so will open the individual to rebuke – and public rebuke at that – from the elder in question or another leader (1 Timothy 5:20, Titus 1:13, Titus 2:15). It is also unwise to try and battle an elder without just cause. It is natural for us to have disagreements with people. We do not like everyone and that may cause us to have issues with different people. Just because we don't like someone doesn't nullify their legitimate call to their office, nor does it mean you have the right to make a ministerial leadership judgment based on a personal knowledge. Respect the privacy, integrity, and dignity of leaders who are duly called – whether or not you care for them as individuals. If you have issue with false teaching, that is surely to be raised – but we should never try an elder's calling based on a personal dislike.

- **Visionaries/conference hosts** - When we are invited to a conference and we accept the invitation, we are submitting ourselves to the vision and order of that event. The vision, mission, theme, etc. of an event should be noted and we should seek to align ourselves with it rather than trying to align it with our own agendas. If there is some reason we are unable to align with the vision, we should politely decline the event invitation. If we know the host and we are so led, we are welcome to discuss the issue we may have with the event privately – not publicly – with the host. Under no circumstances does any minister have the right to undermine another's event, as in the case of a conference, we must submit ourselves to the vision of the leader. Doing so publicly or within the pulpit extended for the event is the surest way to be dismissed from an event – spoken badly about by attendees and the inviting ministry – and never invited back for any reason whatsoever in the future.

When in a conference event, it's important to maintain respect for the social interactions of the vision as well as the conference itself. Conference participation extends far beyond that of simply attending conference sessions and hiding out in one's hotel room thereafter. It is important to follow the order established: if all speakers are going out for a meal, having a meeting or discussion, gathering for prayer, or called upon to deal with a certain issue, all speakers must attend the meeting. It does not matter if you are uncomfortable with it, dislike another minister in the event, or feel spiritually burdened; order dictates a certain cooperativeness and sociability within the event itself. It is also important to step up and assist in altar work if it is needed if you are not the speaker for a session.

- **Memberships** – It's trendy today to be a member of an organization through a network, a group, a council of churches, a bishopric, a diocese, or other formalized setting. These organizations give ministers an easy way to develop support and connection. What most often don't consider is that joining these organizations means that, in some way, you are required to submit to the leadership which oversees these groups. They may not require to become your immediate covering, but all expect you to submit to their guidelines, participate in their events, and do things according to a certain style, certain regulation, and often, with a certain membership fee or price. There is nothing wrong with participating in a group, but it is essential to understand the purpose of the group, their vision, their intent, and what is expected of you as a member so you can understand your participation therein.

- **Instruction (Bible college/university)** – When we are taught by someone, they become a leader to us in instruction and knowledge. We are to learn of them and respect their knowledge, education, wisdom, and teaching. As a result, we are to act as such. If we can't handle that, we should not be under their instruction. If we have issue with something taught, it is our place to ask for clarity – not to defame our instructors. Schools should be investigated for credibility and teaching instruction prior to admission. If we experience a bad teacher in one way or another – for anything other than personal dislike – we are to take it to the proper authorities within the structure of the school.

- **Interviews/guest spots** – If a minister is invited to do a media interview or be a guest spot on a panel, parameters for such should be clearly laid out prior to the program. The minister being featured/interviewed/serving a guest spot follows the lead of the interviewer/host, within certain parameters. If there is a theme, a specific topic, or a certain direction, the featured minister follows that form. If the featured minister is given a green light, they should seek out the host for any directives associated with that. In an interview, questions should be professional and not too personal. If a question seems to be out of line or in any way driving in an inappropriate direction, the featured minister has the right to politely, but firmly, decline any inappropriate or leading questions.

CHAPTER THIRTY-FIVE

RESPECTING MINISTERIAL OFFICES IN PERSONAL RELATIONSHIPS

Give everyone what you owe him:
If you owe taxes, pay taxes;
if revenue, then revenue;
if respect, then respect;
if honor, then honor.
(Romans 13:7)

MINISTRY today is far more complicated than it has been in other times. We see a host of titles, ministers, claims to calling, ministry styles, and relationships that can complicate events, services, and ultimately, ministries. It's not uncommon to meet ministers who work in ministry with a spouse, a parent, or a child; to meet ministers who work together as friends; or to meet people who work together and have long-standing relationships of one sort or another. Sometimes we see certain interactions in their lives that can cause question as to how to refer to one or the other, or wonder who is really in charge.

No matter the nature of a personal relationship outside of pulpit or ministerial activities, the order of the Kingdom remains in ministry matters. When in ministry events, leaders should be properly addressed by ministry office – not by first names – no matter who is calling whom. Spouses likewise should align with ministry order: if one spouse is an apostle and one spouse is a pastor, the apostle is the elder in a church setting and respect for that office should be acknowledged as such, regardless of gender. The same is true with children and extended relatives. Friends and other personal acquaintances in ministry should refer to one another by ministry office in ministry settings, upholding decency and order, and respecting one another.

Friendships often come forth in ministry settings, as ministry events are often a time when friends are able to see one another and come together to worship the Lord. This is fine as long as ministry does not become an opportunity to become cliquish or exclusive. Ministers should take time to fellowship with one another, engage with one another, love one another, and share with one another both in and out of the pulpit, expanding the bonds of friendship and encouragement as believers in the Lord.

Personal disagreements held by those with personal relationships outside of the pulpit should remain outside of the pulpit. Household issues, personal arguments, politics, and rivalries should be put aside in church. Knowledge of an individual's temperament, opinions, and issues should not be used to intrude on one's authority within an event or church setting. Whether or not one agrees with how an elder in ministry handles an issue based on personal information they have does not pertain to how that minister should handle the issue. Respect should always be shown for individuals who are in ministry, whether or not personal information is obtained by those who work with and fellowship with them.

It is also important that, no matter what the personal nature of a relationship may be, a minister's integrity and dignity are upheld when speaking of that minister to someone else. It is vital that gossip is kept in check. The surest way to disrespect a relationship one has with a leader is to spread stories about them. Spreading rumors based on suspicions, theories, things you've heard other people say about a leader, or something that you've just made up is the surest way to destroy a relationship with a leader. As such rumors can destroy a minister's work, reputation, and established ministry, spreading rumors is a vicious way to end a ministerial association.

CHAPTER THIRTY-SIX

BEING PUNCTUAL

You will arise and have compassion on Zion,
for it is time to show favor to her;
the appointed time has come.
(Psalm 102:13)

DESPITE all of its differences in doctrine, understanding, and codes of morality, most of the modern church has one thing in common: its members are always late. Church service starts late because nobody has shown up yet (including half the worship team and the leadership), ministers are late, events run late. Most of us would never be late for our secular jobs, nor would we show such thorough disrespect to a secular leader, but a good majority of the church thinks it is acceptable to be late when it comes to the things of God.

I have been in church meeting after church meeting that was late, started late, or had to start late because everyone who needed to be present just was not on time. Being late is a sign of disrespect. It shows that whatever we are going to is not important enough to us to be on time. It also tells whoever is hosting the event that we have no respect for them and no ability to budget our time wisely to be punctual. Chronic lateness shows a chronic lack of priorities: that it is simply not important enough to be on time. What does that say about the Kingdom of God and the amazing things God does for His people?

Punctuality is a staple of the business world. If we are about Kingdom business, it should be a staple of what we do as well. We know from Scriptural understanding that God is not late. We also know that God expected His people to do things at appointed times, and showing up late had consequences (Exodus 16:1-30). When someone wanted to receive of the Lord, they did so on time – not late. The same is true of the church today. If we are ministering for our own ministry, ministering for someone else, or attending, it is our place to be on time, if not a little early. If we cannot be on time, we should notify someone as to our circumstance out of courtesy.

Ways to remain punctual

- Keep a calendar and datebook handy to organize all applicable events. Know where you need to be, and when.

- Give yourself plenty of time to arrive at an event, calculating preparation, travel, and other time incidentals.

- Don't schedule meetings, events and activities too close together. If you know that you have to be at one event, do not squeeze in other events within two to three hours of each other. If you are coming from one event to another, make sure you are leaving one event with plenty of time to arrive at the other.

- Do not double book meetings, events, and activities.

- Enlist people to help you prepare and organize events as applicable. Do not feel that you have to do all the preparation work yourself, especially if the preparations involve preparing children or parents for something.

- If you have other people to get ready for an event (such as children or an aging parent) make sure you consider the amount of time it takes to get them ready as well as how long it will take for you to get ready in your preparation time.

- Make sure travel arrangements are made in advance, so there is no scrambling around at the last minute to make travel plans. If you are driving yourself, make sure you have ample gas in your car and your car is in working order. If you are driving with someone else, make sure they are picking you up in plenty of time to arrive.

- Aim to be early for an event rather than right on time.

- Advertise services and events approximately thirty minutes before their set time to begin, to ensure as many people as possible are present for the beginning of the event.

CHAPTER THIRTY-SEVEN

FAMILY IMAGE

Still he and all his family were devout and God-fearing;
he gave generously to those in need and prayed to God regularly.
(Acts 10:2)

THE ideal family concept is rooted strongly within Christianity via the face of its ministers. It doesn't seem to matter that this ideal image is, in actuality, not prophesied – and the Word clarifies that those in the Kingdom will have to make choices between ideal family life and the Lord (Luke 9:61-62, Luke 12:52). While there are some examples of good family image and family cohesiveness (Acts 10:2), these exist because the family chose the Lord. Most Christian groups expect ministers to marry at some point within their lives and maintain family life in addition to ministry work. There is nothing wrong with being married and having a family in ministry, but ministers must consider the expectations a group may have about their family image.

The Apostle Paul makes a powerful argument for both single and married life in 1 Corinthians 7. Theologians have spent years trying to dissect this passage and figure out the precise advice he was trying to give, because in some ways, an untrained reader could find the advice contradictory and confusing. If I were to summarize 1 Corinthians 7, I would say the Apostle Paul is examining the various ways people struggle to find purpose in their lives through personal relationships. The bottom line of every personal matter is simple: both single life and married life have complications to the individual. In today's church, the truth of this is no different. A single minister has to fight the rumors, expectations, and stigmas that surround being single. A married minister has to deal with family life, the responsibilities that go with family life, and an endless parade of advice and opinions about ministry when married. Both can cause questions in others, and both must be prepared to guard their own privacy and defend the privacy of others in ministry, as well. The bottom line of the entire matter: we have the right to make our own choices as pertain to single or married life, whether we are in ministry or not in ministry, and nobody around us has the right to question that choice in our lives.

Single ministers must realize their entire lives are not open to scrutiny and judgment. Much of the time a single minister will feel the need to answer to others or explain things that are just not anyone else's business. If you are single and dating someone, the church is not coming on the date with you and it is not their business who you are dating, why you are dating them, or for how long you are dating them. Do not entertain questions about sexuality, the single "rumor mill" or allow congregants to arrange dates or "fix you up" with friends or relatives. When it comes to matters of marriage and family, allow the Lord to lead you rather than the pressures of the church to do so. If you are content being single, then listen to the Lord's leading in your circumstances. Also, keep in mind that it is important to marry someone for the right reasons rather than to satisfy ministry pressures or to do the thing that seems right to everyone else.

Most ministries expect a minister who is married to display a semblance of their family life before the congregation. It is expected a spouse and children (if any) will be present at certain events and behave in a certain manner while present at ministry events. A minister may also face judgment if a spouse or child behaves in personal conduct considered inappropriate or unseemly. Ministers also need to recognize they do not need to account for age-appropriate behavior, nor do they need to account for the behavior of adult children. It's important ministers are prepared for such if they have a family and do their best to maintain privacy in their families' lives. To many, it doesn't matter if a minister and his family are happy as long as they appear to be so, which is why it is so important to uphold privacy. Do not bring personal family issues before the congregation or go tale-bearing about a spouse or situation because the story will run through the church and come back to you sounding quite different.

CHAPTER THIRTY-EIGHT

LEARNING AND STUDY

Instruct a wise man and he will be wiser still;
teach a righteous man and he will add to his learning.
(Proverbs 9:9)

STUDY used to be a required component for ministry operation and execution. In the days when denominations reigned, seminary education was required for ordination. When trends started to change, two-year Bible colleges and institutes became a long-standing norm. Nowadays it is not uncommon to meet ministers with no formal ministry education or training behind their ministry work. We also see a host of ministers who do not have an ordination or affirmation behind their calling.

Today we hear much about anointing, emphasizing anointing over learning. While the purpose of this book is not to delve into anointing and its intention, anointing is an unction. It is the Holy Spirit working in our lives through our abilities to build the Kingdom of God. Anointing is an essential component of ministry work because it is God's grace by which we operate and flow as He has called. While I would never question the importance of anointing, or the essential nature of anointing working in ministry, I do question those who think anointing replaces the discipline and dedication of ministry education in one's life. There are many components of education that enhance a ministry call and anointing that cannot be substituted, nor ignored.

Understanding of the Word of God and bringing forth God's revelation does not come by reading the Bible as a novel or treating it as any other book one may own. It also does not come about by picking out random verses here and there and trying to make messages on singular verses alone. Ministry is about more than just preaching; it is about impact. So many things go into the proper understanding of God's Word: history, culture, context, language, syntax, idiom, belief, and faith throughout the course of the Bible's pages are all essential to having a thorough understanding of the Word and what is spoken in it. We receive the essential knowledge of these things through our education of all things Biblical.

The Bible tells us that God's people are destroyed for lack of knowledge (Hosea 4:6-9). If we look closely at this passage, the people die from lack of knowledge generation after generation because God's ministers do not set themselves to learn the essentials of God and, therefore, do not teach the things of God. Ministers of God also need to transcend the experience of education into the area of life. So many different things in this world testify to the glory of God and His presence among us, and require us to be well-rounded. The ministers of God have always had affluence in a variety of areas: David was proficient in music, the Apostle Paul had knowledge of Greek philosophy, the Apostle Matthew was a tax collector, Priscilla and Aquila were tent makers, Lydia was a seller of purple cloth, Luke was a physician – and so on. God's people were diverse in their educational backgrounds and understandings because the knowledge they had of so many different things made them better ministers. If we will step back and see this simple fact, it will truly transform our attitudes toward education. A negative attitude toward learning is not a good attitude for a minister to have. It closes the gap for the window of revelation that comes forth from Biblical knowledge and understanding, and also from the practical revelation of God that comes through life and living.

History is also an essential study for the minister because it shows the history of humanity. If we are to understand where we are going, we need to know where we came from. History is full of heroes and heroines, sinners and saints, and as we study the history of both the world and the church, it helps us to better understand why we are here and where we are heading in the future.

Ministers need to be able to speak their native language correctly, using proper grammar, syntax, language, and appropriate dialogue for their audiences. Being too common in speech from the pulpit presents poorly as does being too common in style. Notes, messages, etc. should be well-organized and presented, backed up with the Word and clear in style. Ministers must avoid being too wordy, talking too long, and talking too much.

Every minister should have, at minimum, training for ordination or affirmation, and college or seminary experience from an institution that has a minimum of a Christian Accreditation behind it. There are lots of affordable programs that excel in the things of God and the training necessary to equip for ministry. Making this kind of an investment prepares the minister of God by laying essential foundations for information and learning that will carry a minister all throughout their call.

Things a minister should look for in an educational program

There is no end to the various ministries that claim to offer training, both online and offline. There's a vast difference between taking a class that is simply offered for believers and one that is taken for ministers. There's also a difference between simply taking a series of classes that reveals nothing more than an instructor's opinion about a subject. When examining a ministerial program, use the 1/3 rule: 1/3 for Scripture, 1/3 for protocol, and 1/3 that relates to practicalities of ministry.

- **1/3 Scripture** – Scripture studies are important and should be a necessary component of an educational program for ministers. Scripture should be the foundation of a program overall, but it is important that ministers have the opportunity to delve into the Word from a leadership perspective. A program may focus on specific books or general study as part of this guideline, but 1/3 of the program should be devoted to study of the Word as applicable to leadership.

- **1/3 Protocol** – Protocol remains one of the most overlooked aspects of ministry training. Yes, it's great to be anointed, yes it's great to have a vision, but ministers need to understand how to operate within order in their anointing and exercise their vision within Kingdom operation. Ministers need to know how to interact with ethics with those they lead, how to interact with other leaders, how to interact with their leader, how to interact as part of an organization, and about other various matters of protocol (including attire, shirt colors, robe accessories, and conduct at formal occasions). Even if you do not have a ministry that is very into the pomp and circumstance of ceremonies, it's important to have this information for interactions with ministers who do, especially if you are invited to such an occasion.

- **1/3 Practical Ministry** – Ministry training should be unto the end of practicality. This means ministry training should be something that you can use. Practical ministry training should pertain to ministry business information, specified training in accordance with your call, and social Gospel training, which teaches you how to make your ministry work practical.

Depending on the length and depth of the available program, ministers should also look for a few elements. While not all programs are as basic as the 1/3 rule (which really represents the minimum a program should offer), all longer programs in length should contain:

- Church history
- History of worship
- Foreign language training
- Hebrew and Greek (possibly Latin)
- Christian Counseling
- International Christian perspective
- Spiritual Warfare/Demonology
- Minister's training (altar work, helps, etc.)

CHAPTER THIRTY-NINE

PRESENTING PROCESSED INFORMATION

God has raised this Jesus to life,
and we are all witnesses of the fact.
(Acts 2:32)

THERE used to be a commercial on television for a privacy protection system that states approximately three percent of the population will become victims of identity theft. In their clever advertising, most people become so worried at the prospect of having their identities taken from them, they fail to properly process the statistic given. If three percent of people become victims of identity theft, that means ninety-seven percent of people are never victims of identity theft. If people are able to watch the commercial without being fearful of prospects, they will see the expense offered is not worth the actual risk that pertains to identity theft.

This advertisement is a classic example of the way people do not properly process information due to a lack of critical thinking. Many years ago, critical thinking was something we were supposed to gain from word problems in math and literary reading at school. When presented certain information, we were supposed to be able to draw necessary conclusions about what we discovered. Today we do not see the emphasis on critical thinking that we once did. Many people process information very slowly and still do not understand the whole expanse of an issue because they do not have the necessary skills to process information critically.

Questionable details

Television, internet, news sources, and various media all bombard us with different versions of facts, events, and statistics every single day. Most of these so-called facts are presented vastly different, with a different set of information each time. In a state of trust, we often buy what we are told based on the agency providing the information to us, even if that information is, indeed, incorrect.

There is a vast difference between being a direct witness to something and forming an opinion about an issue based on information provided by a bystander. All media outlets and news forums are created by the word of people who often have second or third-hand information – if not even more than that. Recent media spectacles including high-profile murder cases prove that the media simply does not get it right much of the time. Basing our perspectives on the words of bystanders is not only dangerous, it shows that we do not care enough about the truth to critically think about matters and examine true evidence.

Sorting out truth from myths

The only way we can sort out the truth from the myths in our world today is if we are able to process presented information. Because ministers often repeat what they hear statistically, it is vital we have correct information. We do not live in an era where the media provides us the reliability to simply repeat whatever we hear. Ministers need to have the ability to process information they read and draw conclusions from the things they read and see. It is very easy to spout off things one hears without a thought, and more difficult to present properly discerned and processed information. The world likes to "spout" off study after study, percentages, and various sides of research that appear to prove a point. What we don't often realize is that many studies and research components may be highly inaccurate, specifically slated to prove a certain point with tainted or inaccurate data.

When reading information, we must be careful to research beyond just the immediate. We need to check facts, statistics, and understand what we are reading before we ever share that information with anyone else. If we aren't clear on something, we need to learn more about it. We should research information carefully before presenting it in a message or in writing and should always back up the information we provide with references. If something is your opinion, state it as such. Never alter data or make things up to prove an opinion.

Understanding differences in facts and reporting

There are a variety of different ways in which information – and facts, at that – are reported. It's essential that ministers understand the different ways information is presented, because the sources and presentation of information are essential to the way we interpret what we read, assess, and process.

- **Political** – Politics tend to be a gray area of information processing because in order to gain power, candidates, lobbying groups, and other special-interest political groups tend to promote information that makes their cause, case, or issue look as if it is the biggest priority and most factual. This means that, in the case of political information, facts can often get colored. Because the purpose of political information is to push and promote a specific agenda, it is easy to be drawn into a political cause, thinking it to be spiritual or moral, when its only true purpose is to gain political control.

  For this reason, ministers need to be very careful when reading or using politically-driven materials. Information filtered through these sources is for political purposes, meaning it is not always clear, nor objective. It's also important to emphasize that ministers do not have the right to demand a congregation or other leaders they cover feel a certain way on a political topic. Ministers do not have the right to impose their political candidates, nor do they have the right to tell others how to vote.

- **Moral** – Moral information could be defined as information processed from a story or lesson in order to convey value. As a result, morals often tend to be subjectively interpreted by people. It is not a question of whether or not right and wrong are subjective, but the way they are interpreted tends to be very individual. It is for this reason that moral information is often presented – and processed – in very personal ways.

  When it comes to moral information, it is important to understand the beliefs and opinions of the one presenting the information, as well as considering how it is being interpreted by those who hear the information presented. If moral information is interpreted subjectively, that means those who hear the information will process it as they understand and perceive it.

  Moral issues also relate to the different ways which we view other human beings and their rights as people. Once again, the way people see human rights issues often vary. Overlapping frequently with ethics and politics, the way people see human rights issues closely relates with the way in which people see and understand the essence of moral values.

- **Ethical** – Ethical information relates to matters pertaining to our conduct and interactions with other human beings in a professional and personal setting. Ethics are the ways in which we, as individuals, both professionally and personally, uphold the dignity and respect for ourselves and others. Closely related to moral issues (we could say these are the application of moral issues in action), ethical issues are often based upon the requirements of a profession or job and the subjective interpretations many have about moral issues. Things surrounding end of life, confidentiality of certain professions, and medical experimentation and procedures are all issues that relate to ethics.

Ethical information tends to be slanted toward the views and morals of the individual presenting that information. This means facts may be slanted in the favor of that viewpoint, even though ethics should represent a place of objectivity. Sometimes ethical information represents multiple viewpoints, with the final verdict assessing these different viewpoints in favor of certain ethics and perspectives.

- **Legal** – Legal information pertains to laws, the passage of laws, and those things which people desire to become law or be repealed. Legal information tends to relate to morals, politics, and ethics, as legislation is related to all three of these things. More specifically, legal information is written in its own specific language, which those who are a part of it are quick to understand. As a rule, people without a legal background or much legal understanding are often lost in the face of its contents. As a result, there are those who help to interpret or reduce legal jargon to common language.

Understanding legal information can be quite complicated. Even when it seems clear, it can be convoluted. Many people have strong feelings about legal matters, and this often does cloud one's perspective about the laws. It can also make it more difficult to understand the legal issue on its own.

- **Scientific** – In order to save time, scientific information includes various scientific presentations, including medical, biological, and chemical. Scientific information relates to studies, data, and investigations into things which pertain to our world and the way things in our world come together and function. Scientific information tends to be convoluted and confusing to the average reader, and as so much of it is based on theories, it is often contradictory.

- **Professional** – Professional information relates specifically to the profession in which it is used. I am using this as a general heading for any type of language used in an industry that would not be easily understood by those outside of said profession, and can be easily misconstrued or misunderstood by someone reading it. When processing professional information, a dictionary or inside information is most helpful.

- **Spiritual** – The last type of information is spiritual, which relates to any type of information of a religious, mystical, or otherworldly nature. It can be true or untrue, in accordance with belief or not in accordance with what we ourselves personally believe, and may be objective or not objective. As a result, spiritual information is much like moral information – it is processed by the individual in accordance with their own perspectives and beliefs. It also means much of what we read from a spiritual perspective may be biased in favor of one belief system or another, including tainting or distorting true facts to raise up one system over another.

Sometimes information crosses these different categories. Something may tap into every area above, some is only one of the categories, and some are mixed. Knowing what we are reading helps us to understand what we are reading, and also helps us to sort out when we need to do additional research or abandon something altogether. It is also important to realize the type of information we receive affects how we process it. Things that are of a political nature are interpreted in the light of the law and of the ways the law affects people, not necessarily in a moral way, even though people might want their morals to affect laws. Spiritual information is pertinent to the one giving the information, and what they believe. Someone who is presenting professional information, having a thorough insight into the area or field is going to present their perspective on that job different from someone else.

In short: no source is completely objective when providing information. Every information source tends to have slants and biases, and it's important to cross-check data and facts when in pursuit of the truth. Relying on only one source for all of your data leads one into a world where perspectives too closely resemble a perspective without any objectivity at all.

When presenting information to others

Just because you, as a minister, have a certain perspective as an individual – and process information in that specific way – does not mean you have the right to impose that perspective on everyone else. Differences of opinion will exist about things not pertinent to the Kingdom of God until Jesus comes back. Critical thinking, forming opinions based in facts, and being able to process and convey correct information are all far more relevant to Kingdom interaction than we will probably ever know. This means every minister needs to step back and examine themselves before they ever open their mouths to present information to anyone else. To ensure information presented is accurate and correct, check facts, statistics, and data from a number of sources.

CHAPTER FORTY

DEBATE, DISCUSSION, DIALOGUE, AND DISAGREEMENT

Don't have anything to do with foolish and stupid arguments,
because you know they produce quarrels.
(2 Timothy 2:23)

THE art of Christian debate has long been lost through centuries of authoritarianism and defensive stubbornness. In the New Testament, we see the art of debate as a valued and prized aspect of the ancient culture. Philosophy was all the rage in Greek and Roman culture, each with its own school of thought where students were educated in the art of rhetoric. Long-winded debates, discussions, and dialogues were frequent and common. One individual would present a point, and then another would present a counterpoint, as the discussion went back and forth between parties. That is why we see the early church speaking the truth eloquently and with complexity to large groups of people in the book of Acts: such sites would have been prime locations for discussion and conversion. We don't see people interrupting when the people of God spoke. There was almost always a response after the debate was over from the crowds and others present, either for questioning or for argumentation. Debates and discussions were ordered, following a strict protocol and manner of handle.

Today, we don't find this kind of order in Christian debate and discussion. Most Christians find themselves unprepared to discuss matters of any sort with other Christians, let alone being able to uphold conversations with non-believers. The standard Christian ability to speak with another reduces any discussion to endless arguments, emotional debates, and frustrated and ineffective conversation. Nobody grows or moves on past their own perspectives to see another viewpoint and eventually set aside differences and explore God's Word deeper.

The ministry of apologetics used to be the standard means for the defense of the faith. Biblical scholars spent hours comparing texts, original languages, history, context, traditions, and various methods of interpretation to form a solid approach to Biblical understanding. The art of apologetics, which provided concrete proof for belief beyond a verse here and there, has all but died and been replaced with intense emotionalism and politics. Stepping back and learning about matters helps us to form a more polished approach to our defense and reminds us that we are defending the faith, rather than our emotions. While faith certainly stirs the emotions, neither faith nor ministry, are to be things that operate on emotions. If we are employing emotions in our debates, then we are operating an essential aspect of our ministry via emotions. This must end here and now because it creates a negative witness.

The Bible advises us to avoid needless debates (2 Timothy 2:23, Titus 3:9). This means there is more than one type of debate. A debate can be productive – a learning experience, one that facilitates discussion and interest – or it can be needless. A needless debate is any argumentation that has no purpose to go anywhere. Some people just want to fight or have people think they are right. Sometimes debates get out of hand because they are designed to do so. Some people just don't have the ability to handle a debate-type situation. Sometimes the debate just isn't worth our time. This is where discernment comes in, in a powerful way.

A productive debate seeks to respectfully discuss matters and present viewpoints. It looks at different angles of an issue and examines those issues from research or evidence. Debate is not emotion-based, but presents a reasoned viewpoint of a critique or argument. In productive debate, there is no interruption and everyone is given the opportunity to present the appropriate viewpoint. Productive debate can be very effective in witnessing the Gospel as topics arise and the Word can be used therein to be shown to apply to whatever the topic at hand may be. Remain poised and eloquent, not shouting, name-calling, or interrupting. Present a reasoned argument.

A needless debate has no purpose except to argue with others. Typically it is a random, nonsensical topic that doesn't have any significance and has no power to change anyone's life. In other words, it is a topic that doesn't really have an answer, just random opinions. The purpose is to go back and forth, back and forth, interrupt, create disorder and confusion, and outlet anger. Most of the time, the debate causes a level of frustration that causes a fever-pitch to get someone so out of control, it "seems" to prove the other side's point. Discernment calls us to step away from such debates that are mere traps to discredit the work of the Kingdom.

A discussion is a conversation between two or more people. It is like debate with the exception that discussion is more open, more intimate, than just debating a topic. It is about conversing, sharing, and building. Akin to discussion is dialogue. Dialogue is an "open door" of communication. It is more than a mere conversation: it is a continuing discussion on a matter. In the Kingdom, we need to be prepared to answer questions as the start to dialogue. When people come to us with a question, it is often in search of something beyond an answer. Sometimes people do just want an answer to a question, but much of the time they are looking to talk about something bigger than the mere question. In dialogue, we must listen and truly speak as directed to bring about the necessary revelation within a dialogue.

We also must pay attention to the areas of disagreement in ministry. It is inevitable that we will encounter a minister, ministry, individual, or issue that we will disagree with. How much we agree with someone is not nearly as relevant as how we handle our disagreements. There are a few keys to handling disagreements below, as found below:

- **Is this an essential or non-essential disagreement?** – Ego is a big factor in life. We can try and pretend it isn't, but it is. That having been said, it is amazing the things people magnify because of a bruised ego. Not everyone in the entire world is going to agree with us about every little thing in life. If we are waiting for this to happen, we will have a long and lonely wait. There are some things we cannot unite ourselves unto because they are in contradiction to Kingdom principle. We can't unite with leaders who are out of God's will for leadership, we can't participate in events that mix truth and error, we can't allow ourselves to be abused or mistreated, and we likewise can't expose ourselves to harm by mingling ourselves with error. That having been said, we can put aside personal opinions or differences outside of the realm of truth and work with God's people in the building of His Kingdom. Working with differences of this nature helps us to grow as people and grow in our own viewpoints, recognizing we aren't the only people in the world working in the Kingdom of God.

- **How should I handle this matter?** – Sometimes we need to speak up, and sometimes we need to shut up. Sometimes we need to voice issues and sometimes we need to let them rest. Disagreements can be handled in more than one way. Recognizing this – and stepping back to examine a situation so it can be handled rightly – can make a huge difference in the outcome of a disagreement.

- **What is behind the disagreement?** – Disagreements aren't always about the subject matters that appear on the surface. Sometimes there are deep issues behind disagreements between people that either need to resolve or they need to part ways. If there's something that keeps coming up in every situation that manifests behind the things that manifest, it may be time to do some examination about the situation and people with whom you find yourself involved.

- **Watch tone, language, and control** – Disagreements get out of hand because people get out of hand in an attempt to try and get another person to agree with or see their viewpoint. It doesn't take much for a situation to get totally out of control because of such an emotional rush and high. We can't control other people in disagreement, but we can control ourselves. Watch tone, sarcasm, language, and personal disciplines in disagreement. If a situation is getting too hot to handle, walk away from it, stop talking, leave, or do whatever else is necessary to handle your own level of control. If someone else wants to be disgraceful, leave them to do it alone.

- **Keep order and respect in mind** – Remember the establishment of order we spoke of in an earlier chapter and remember to maintain a specific balance of order when dealing with elders and those who have authority over you. It's also a good practice to maintain respect with anyone in the Body of believers. Just because you don't like what someone has to say does not give you the right to become unruly and behave without self-control. How we carry ourselves in areas of debate, disagreement, dialogue, and discussion is not about anybody but us. We can walk away from a situation with total dignity if we keep ourselves controlled and well-behaved.

CHAPTER FORTY-ONE

INTER-MINISTRY ETIQUETTE

We put no stumbling block in anyone's path,
so that our ministry will not be discredited.
Rather, as servants of God
we commend ourselves in every way...
(2 Corinthians 6:3)

THE way ministry leaders interact with one another is quite different from how they may interact with congregants or ministry followers. This makes inter-ministry etiquette perhaps one of the most important dimensions of ministry work and support.

The Kingdom of God calls its representatives to maturity. Dealing with other ministries is not the place for immature leaders who behave like children. Ministry work needs to bear with it respectability, both in giving and receiving respect. Ministers should always be respectful of one another, both when someone is looking and when someone is not looking. Ministers should never gossip about other ministers behind their backs or seek to disgrace another ministry. As people who uphold the truth, we should not stand behind false ministries or work to further them. We surely are in ministries of correction, and should expose what is untrue. This means, however, that we are honest in truth, not fabricating things because we just don't like someone. Ministers must handle themselves with discipline and courtesy, being willing to participate as the Lord leads. They should dress the part, carry themselves with dignity, and introduce themselves as necessary. When attending a service, ministers should be polite, courteous, and observant of what is going on around them. When invited to another church or ministry to minister, ministers should be present with the people for praise and worship, should deliver God's message, minister in power, and be graceful about financial matters and arrangements.

Over the years, ministry has become increasingly competitive, reducing the amount of support and mutual respect seen among ministers. This has decreased the amount of etiquette and increased the need for ministerial support, which should be a natural part of the courtesy and respect extended between ministers. If you are called to be a minister of God, it is essential you position yourself in this place: one where you can not only be supported by others, but you can support others as well.

Working with other ministries has its challenges as well as its joys. Parameters must be clear when teaming up or working together, and all gifts must be welcome and embraced. Trust must exist between ministers who work together, and anything necessary should be offered and split as applicable. Ministers should foster good-will, friendship, and display God's love among one another, especially when working together.

Ministers need to be supportive of one another because ministry is a difficult walk and life seldom understood by those who are not in it. Ministry is a life unlike any other. Ministers of God do incredible things, walk away from what would seem to be incredible opportunities in life, and spend time persisting through incredible difficulties for what may seem to be little reward in this life. Ministers are often misunderstood by those closest and intimate with them, including spouses, family members, and friends. They often experience powerful stings of rejection and heartache, and face constant issues. Throughout their walk, I would venture most ministers deal with questions about their own call, their own personal struggles, and wonder why things are the way they are for them. The saddest part of this is the fact that so many ministers never share their feelings with other ministers because of fear of rejection. I stand behind my earlier statement that ministers need to be careful about those whom they take in their confidence. At the same time, we need to be people in whom others can confide. Some things that happen in ministry just need to stay in ministry, and the doubts, fears, and difficulties a minister has from time to time should never be revealed as a weapon of retaliation.

CHAPTER FORTY-TWO

INTERFAITH ETIQUETTE

I am talking to you Gentiles.
Inasmuch as I am the apostle to the Gentiles,
I take pride in my ministry.
(Romans 11:13)

T HE word "interfaith" describes the interaction of people of different faith systems. It can mean many different things depending on the individual using the term. Sometimes people use it to denote a belief that every single "faith" in existence is the same as every other, while others denote it in a strict context of the interactions or mingling between people of different faiths. Here I am using it to describe interactions between ministers of Christian belief and those of non-Christian belief.

It's a nice idea to think we can stay among ourselves and never encounter people who believe differently than we do, but we know this is an unrealistic ideal. Not every person we meet will be as open to the Gospel as we might like, and different beliefs will exist in this world right up until Jesus comes back. This means that as Christian ministers operating in this world, we must prepare ourselves to interact with ministers who believe differently than we do about faith matters.

We know the Bible's teachings against mixing or merging religions in personal relationships (Nehemiah 10:30, Malachi 2:11-12, 2 Corinthians 6:14) and the principles about mixing different religious systems together (Exodus 20:23, Exodus 23:23-24, Exodus 34:15, Jeremiah 1:6). The Bible also tells us that we are to love our neighbor and that He desires all nations of the world come to worship Him (Deuteronomy 10:19, Psalm 9:11, Psalm 47:1, Psalm 67:2, Psalm 72:11, Isaiah 56:7, Matthew 22:39, Mark 12:31, Luke 10:27). These two commands are not as opposite as we might think. We can maintain the purity of our faith and interact with others without any spiritual compromise. The key to doing so is remember that, in all things, we are called to be witnesses of our faith.

We often think being a witness of the faith means verbalizing our beliefs and trying to persuade others to accept those beliefs. This is a part of our witness of the faith, but there are other ways that we witness to our faith, as well. The Bible speaks of the believer as being a living letter testifying to the ministry, and interfaith witness is perhaps the best opportunity to do this (2 Corinthians 3:2-3). One of the best ways we can be a positive witness to our faith is to represent the Kingdom well to those who believe. This means that, in loving our neighbor, we respect other people and their right to decide about matters for themselves. We do not have to agree with what others believe or do, and we certainly do not have to participate in the worship of other religions, but we do need to refrain from name-calling, degradation, disrespect, and put-downs. Debate on an intellectual level is fine, sharing and discussing is fine, and learning about other beliefs is essential for establishing a pattern of respect. If we want others to find the Christian ministry respectable, we must be people who are respectable without compromising of the Word.

How do we do this? We represent the best the Gospel has to offer. We present ourselves as we would to any other Christian minister: poised, prepared, eloquent, look the part, and speaking well of the Lord and the call He has placed on our lives. We must know enough of the Word to be prepared to defend the faith as it arises and to witness to people in these situations. We consider their knowledge and ours, and make our representation of the faith solid and respectable.

Behaving with courtesy and respect does not mean we agree with others, but does mean we respect ourselves and our belief systems enough to behave with grace and dignity. If we attend events or functions as we are invited, we represent the Gospel and do not disturb who may be participating in a rite of their own belief systems. Ministers should give off comfort with themselves, not haughtiness. In turn, we extend invitations for others to attend our events without pressure and with respect. In these circumstances, we uphold the dignity of the person and let the environment of God, our worship, love, and respect minister to those in our midst.

SECTION V

EXECUTING AND FULFILLING THE VISION

CHAPTER FORTY-THREE

MAINTAINING LEADERSHIP

For we do not have a High Priest Who is unable to sympathize
with our weaknesses, but we have One Who has been tempted in every way,
just as we are – yet was without sin.
Let us then approach the throne of grace with confidence,
so that we may receive mercy and find grace to help us
in our time of need.
(Hebrews 4:15-16)

THE entirety of this book is about practical business plans and ways you, as the reader, can enhance your ministry and your ministry experience by employing these different business techniques. The remainder of this book, we are going to shift and look at more of the interpersonal aspects of business and at ways to be a good leader. Some of these are professional, but many of them apply in deeply spiritual ways. In this section, we are going to expound upon some of these principles and see how we can put them into action.

Our spiritual lives are not a competition for the professional guidelines we follow as ministers. Even though there are some who believe that, the truth is that the two are a compliment. Nothing represents more of this balance than the call to maintain as a leader. Being a leader does not begin and end at ordination. It is a continual process by which God continues to give us insight and revelation about what we are doing. The leadership process may, at times, take us into new directions and horizons. The longer we are in leadership, the more focus and dedication it takes to persist in the vision. There will be times where little seems to manifest, and others where overflow is persistent. Ministry is a combination of both good and bad, joys and sorrows, and trials and victories. Understanding this balance helps the minister to maintain their leadership consistently through the years.

Maintaining leadership means it's not something you move away from. Maintenance indicates a persistent, continual flow, making sure the position you have as a leader does not dissipate or disappear with time. Maintenance requires practical action, practical spirituality, and yes, practical professionalism. Here we are going to discuss major headings that help Christian ministers to maintain their presence, continue on the race, and never quit as they pursue their calling.

Staying current

When in ministry for more than a few years, it is common to note the various changes that occur in ministry and the world over time. Some of these changes are positive. It's not uncommon to see new teachings and themes emerge that were once obscure and also see new believers come in. The changes that we see, however, we all know are not always positive. Some of the common trends in ministry are false and, therefore, discouraging. People come and go, and with the coming and going of people, we also see society change in ways that are not always for the better. Changes in attitude are close behind in changing times, which often reflect in the values and concepts people have in matters that relate to church and ministry.

It's easy to feel "archaic" or "forgotten" if a minister does not readily accept the changes in culture and attitude. Historically speaking, it often takes the church longer to adapt to changes, even if they are of benefit to the church. It can also be awkward to advocate for a change and come up against opposition from others who are not ready for the change.

Along with changing times and attitudes often comes the shift in what seems "relevant" or "important" to the church. For example: if people are overly preoccupied with prosperity, a teacher advocating the theologically aesthetic life will probably find their teachings rejected by the majority of church members. If a minister's member is not culturally popular in the time in which they are called to give the message, it can easily lead to a leader's disappointment and feeling of total loss when the message is rejected.

Ministers have the responsibility to remain current on modern trends, shifts, and things that are important to people. At this point, the question is not so much whether or not the trends are right or wrong, but to assess and acknowledge they exist. Trends reveal needs, interests, and thoughts people have about their lives and issues that affect their lives. Watching trends helps a Christian minister know the issues that are affecting people and how to best address those issues, especially if the trend itself is not supplying the answer.

Rather than looking at trends as the enemy, it's important to see them as a revealing platform. It helps for leaders to step back and realize that just because something is popular or massive in trend, does not mean it is what's true or represents the balance or perspective God wants us to have on a topic. Every "trend" or teaching that becomes popular started out as an idea someone had. They taught it and taught it until it wound up in the right hands, which led to its spread as a trend. The word "persistence" is key in this instance. Trends have a way of shifting and major popular themes in Christianity also have a way of changing with time.

Contrary to popular belief, not every message is for the masses, either. It's important that every leader know the message God has given them and who that message is for. Jesus had messages that appealed to the masses, then He had words that were for the seventy, then some for the twelve, and some of what He did was only for three – Peter, James, and John – to hear, witness, or see. Some leaders have messages that are for different types of audiences, and some leaders aren't called to have big, huge ministries. The biggest secret to handling changing times and attitudes is to be content and blessed with the work and people God has blessed you with. If you have a great congregation of people, be thankful for that even if it's small. If you are only covering a few people right now, be thankful for having good, solid leaders. Rather than focus on numbers, it is more important to regard impact.

In times like these, it is most blessed and beneficial to realize our God never changes (Malachi 3:6). We need to know what is going on, but not get swept away with every wind of teaching or every massive push that comes up. While things come and go and trends seem to fade in and out, God stands as our constant. Finding the balance between truth (which is eternal) and changing times (which change frequently) will help the minister of God to know exactly where they fit in as things change in the church and society as a whole.

Handling competition

I once saw a T-shirt that read, "I don't have A.D.D., I can focus whenever...Oh look! A chicken!" I think of ministry competition just like this – it seems like there is always someone who is the "chicken" and able to draw attention away from whatever the genuine focus should be. Competition is one of the most disheartening aspects of ministry. Seeing people fight, quarrel, and battle it out in the ministry arena for prestige, control, and domination is a source of discouragement for many. It does not help that the levels of competition have heightened and often become downright dirty. I hear stories of individuals trying to "steal" other people who are rightly covered and attending a ministry (try to get them to attend their ministry), try to get other leaders to come up under their leadership using manipulation and intimidation, or still other instances where people backbite, cajole, or wheedle people in or out of an event for their own purposes.

It hurts to be a minister and feel the deep competitive

sting so prevalent in ministry today. It hurts to watch people you've invested time and spiritual instruction into in a deep way fall prey to individuals who come along out of a spirit of competition and disorder. It also hurts to feel excluded because others are trying to force their way to the top without any regard for the ways in which they do so.

Competition is unfortunate, but it does exist. With an upsurge of people believing they are called (even if they are not), there are more people claiming to be ordained or "called" than ever before. People are sometimes not legitimate in credentials, nor in calling. It can be frustrating to watch people advance or somehow otherwise mistreat you when you know the truth about them. It's also disheartening to be overlooked for things, to see others fooled by wrong, and to feel like everyone is moving forward...except for you.

Competition is easier to handle when we realize those people who come along and seem to "steal thunder" tend to be fleeting. They are around one day, but they do not have the grounding and rooting to remain in ministry long-term. It's easy to sound right, preach right, say the things that seem popular at a given point in history, and advance very quickly in many circles. The sad truth about human nature is it gravitates toward that which is extremely entertaining, even if it's not true. When we are in ministry, we must have perseverance to wait out trends and still be standing. It is essential we focus on the ministry work and assignment God has for each one of us, and not compare ourselves to other ministers. Whatever God has called you to do, you are right for the job. Whatever someone else is doing, while it may affect you, and while you may be called to address it at times, does not stop you from doing what God has called you to do. Always remember that...and realize if you are genuinely called, you will still be here when a fleeting, competitive person leaves.

Unsupportive/uninterested spouses

Being married and in ministry can be a great thing. It can also feel like a terrible thing if you have a spouse that is unsupportive of your call or plain uninterested in it. The majority of questions I get, especially from women (but also from men or individuals who are non-binary) relate to how to handle unsupportive or uninterested spouses. They are often hurt because of it and don't understand why they are experiencing such an immediate and steady opposition from a spouse as they answer God's call.

I discussed earlier the intense pressure ministers face to have a perfect-looking family picture. If someone is a leader, it is commonly expected a leader does not just have their own selves in order, but everyone else around them, as well. Ministers face the challenge of ministry work, ministry stresses, and can also face the challenge of unsupportive family members. Maybe the saddest part of this is how many ministers suffer this sting in silence, not feeling like they can speak of their difficulties. Being in ministry brings with it unique challenges and complications. Warfare is intense, people can be demanding, God may ask things of the minister that separate them from others in their lives, priorities change, and obstacles are abundant. Having a spouse who just doesn't seem to "get it" or, at times, even care, can be deeply hurtful.

As much as having an unsupportive spouse hurts, what often hurts just as much is the way such a situation is treated by the church. People who discover such a situation can blame the minister, tell them they are unqualified to be in ministry, exclude them from events, or make accusations against them as people. This is an unfair response to such a situation, and perpetrates the mentality that ministries have to have perfect-looking marriages, even if they don't. The first thing we need to address is simple: not every marriage is what it seems, and marriages do not have to be perfect. Acknowledging this should be a big "deep breath" for those who have this kind of experience. Being married has complications and it is perfectly normal to have a marriage that is less than perfect. Nobody has a "perfect" marriage. Life happens, and with all the things that come along in life, it's wrong to expect perfection. I believe it is also fundamentally wrong to expect a spouse to be interested in every single thing we do with the same passion and commitment we ourselves have to that thing. No matter what a spouse may do for work, the other spouse may not find themselves particularly interested in it. The most important thing a minister can do is press forward in the calling they have. Even though they may encounter obstacles and doubt, they need to press forward in God's call for them. If the spouse they have is for them, their spouse will accept what they are doing. They might not always like it, it might not be their first choice for it, but they will accept how important this work is to their spouse. There is more in here than it just being ministry. If it's something important to a spouse and the other spouse truly loves that person, then that spouse should come to support it. If that is not the result, the couple needs to re-evaluate their relationship and see what is best for them to do.

The church, especially trusted leaders, need to support whatever is right for that couple. Instead of giving endless advice (whether well-meaning or not), realize people are involved here. If you are in this situation, find someone you trust to help you talk your course of action through. Pray and seek God...and just keep yourself focused on the work God has assigned to you.

Too much stress

It's not a big secret to know many ministers deal with unreasonable and excessive amounts of stress. Between ministry work, demanding and long hours, family life, and sometimes holding down secular employment, ministers always seem on the go. It does not help that ministers often complain about being pulled in too many different directions.

Being the leader means you are the one everyone comes to when they need advice, help, guidance, or all three. It's a true testament to good leadership that you have people who trust you, but there is no doubt such trust can lead to overwhelming responsibility. The most important step a minister can make – both professionally and personally – is set needed boundaries. Being a minister does not mean one becomes subject to the whims and demands of everyone at all times. The more your ministry grows, the larger number of people who will seem to need time and attention, often with urgency (even if no emergency exists). It is vital those who are both under and a part of your ministry recognize the boundaries that are set in place to make sure both you – and they – are properly served and balanced. Boundaries include normal working hours by which counseling, meetings, and other appointments will take place, service times, and understand that just because someone feels they have a need at that moment does not mean it classifies as an emergency. It's important leaders reserve non-emergency situations for normal working or business hours, and leave open availabilities for true emergency situations.

An emergency situation qualifies as: natural disaster (flood, fire, earthquake, etc.), medical emergency (hospitalization, death, suicide, etc.), legal emergency (domestic violence, abusive situation, damage to property) or other situation that demands immediate attention. Situations that, no matter how trying they may be to the individual personally, do not pose an immediate threat to anyone, are not emergencies. In this instant gratification world, it is essential people learn how to wait and also understand that their problems are not emergencies demanding immediate attention in this world. Learning to wait is a powerful Christian principle and also helps leaders develop their own space and time for the sake of avoiding burnout.

Leaders must take time for themselves and their families, if they have families. They must not spend every moment of every day attending to everyone else's problems or issues, and learn it is completely acceptable and beneficial to tell people they have to wait until normal working hours to address issues. Leaders also need to realize their own need for "pouring" in. Giving all the time without ever pouring back in the virtue of the leader causes exhaustion, stress, and burnout. Leaders need good leaders themselves. A true covering is a great resource, as are good friends, periods for retreat and getaways, and spiritual refreshing that ministers to the leader.

Too many emotional attachments and involvements

Traditionally speaking, the professional workplace was a place of business rather than emotions, feelings and personal involvements. With the rise of numerous studies about the mental and emotional morale of the workplace and their impact on the productivity of an office, we now see a different tone in many management and professional environments. It's not uncommon to see people cross professional and personal boundaries, expecting employers to make accommodations for personal problems, and managers who resemble counselors or therapists more than...well...managers. This same attitude of emotional attachment, involvement, and explosion has spilled over into ministry relationships, as well. One of the biggest boundary crossers in ministry today lies in the fact that too many ministers are emotionally involved and attached with the people they cover in an unhealthy way. I'm not talking about affairs or intimate abuses here (as that is a separate issue for another time) but about emotional dependencies and involvements that cause the leader and the member to operate by clouded and non-objective judgment.

In ministry, leaders need to never forget they are just that – leaders. That relationship automatically demands and confronts the realities of certain boundaries. If we are overly involved with the people we are trying to lead, our role as their leaders becomes questionable. This means leaders need to be very careful to remain within ethical boundaries with ministry or church members:

- Do not violate confidentiality.

- Do not engage them in intimate or compromising relationships.

- Do not show favoritism or partiality.

- Avoid emotional intimacies with your flock.

- Maintain objective distance.

- Remember your primary role is to be their leader, not their friend.

- Beware confidences or bringing those under you into your matters and personal issues.

Unsolicited (and unhelpful) advice

It's not uncommon to meet people who have been in ministry a total of five minutes who think they know everything there is to know about it, and then some. Then there are those who are not even in ministry who think they know something about it because they've seen people talk about it on Facebook. It's very common to receive advice that is often unsolicited and usually completely unhelpful from people know nothing of what they are talking about.

It seems as if ministry – and ministry advice – is something many people feel they are entitled to dispense in our modern era. As ministry is now treated like a hobby people do on the side rather than a professional option, too many people think they understand what ministry is like, how it operates, and the unique challenges ministers face, whether or not they have the first clue what ministry is all about. Couple the fact that people are in love with their own opinions today and feel the right to voice those opinions at any time, no matter how inappropriate or unhelpful they may be, and we have a situation where many ministers feel as if they are being written off or, worse, may mislead them if they follow the suggested advice.

Receiving constantly unsolicited and unhelpful suggestions (especially when they are undesired) can feel trite. It may feel like others do not regard you seriously as a minister or consider the issues you encounter as a minister as seriously as those in another profession. This can cause a minister to become isolated, distant, and keep many of the things they are facing bottled up, for fear of judgment or critical response if such matters are shared.

The first key to handling unsolicited and unhelpful advice is to be careful who you share matters with. I understand that we all go through things at times and sometimes our thoughts, feelings, or issues can leak out by accident, but ministers need to be cautious about talking to people just because they seem willing to listen. Ministers also need to exercise good judgment about their postings on social media sites. Everyone on your friends' list does not need to hear about the issues you are having, why you are having them, and should not be consulted in what you need to do about them. You should also be highly guarded against individuals who seem to want to be around you and know all your business when they are not individuals who are classified as friends, mentors, a part of your ministry, or ministry covering.

In keeping with what I just said, I do not believe that ministers are islands or that we should cut ourselves off from the entire church because people mishandle or give out wrong advice. Every leader needs their own leader – their covering – and mentors who can help them through times like these. This is part of why having a leader is so vital, no matter at what level of ministry you may be functioning. A covering is there to protect, guide, and advise, especially when things seem difficult or troublesome. Mentors serve to advise and encourage based on their years of experience in a given area, specific to what we are speaking of here, their years in ministry. It is also important ministers have friends with whom they can speak freely and share issues.

As people who constantly receive unhelpful and unsolicited advice, one of the best ways we can prevent this practice is to resist the temptation to engage in the same kind of behavior. Rather than constantly seek to give people advice, we need to be people who listen when others come to us with problems or issues. Avoid trite sayings or slogans to try and make people feel better (such as "God's got a plan," "You know what the Bible says," or "Stop being negative"). Listen to people in the same way you would want people to listen to you if you were having an issue. Give comfort and support as necessary...but don't give advice based on pop culture church clichés.

Preconceived notions about ministry

When I first accepted the call to ministry, it was a different scene than it is today. Clergy members were considered professionals, who functioned in ministry full-time and were compensated for their time, accordingly. While a pastor or minister might not have been paid as much as an individual in another profession, pastors and ministers were treated as respectable and honorable for the work they did. When travelling somewhere, the offerings they received were more than adequate to cover travel and supply needed income for life and living. Ahhh...the good old days.

In the more than seventeen years I have spent in ministry, I have watched ministry change many times over. The result is where we are now: ministers who often have to keep multiple jobs to maintain their lives and ministries, people expecting ministers to travel long distances at their own expense, involved and complicated honorarium systems (that are often not honored), and burnt out, frustrated, disrespected ministers. I have watched ministry

I went into ministry with many preconceived notions about what it would be like for me. I expected ministry for me to resemble the ministries I saw when I was first a Christian. I believed that ministry would be a professional choice that would, at some point, be easier to handle and that the job would be rewarding, no matter what avenue of ministry I pursued. To say that I find myself disappointed at times about where ministry is today is an understatement. The endlessly difficult people, complex problems, lack of funds and generally disrespectful attitude I receive from others in regard to ministry leaves me feeling like I have wasted my life and my pursuits of the Gospel.

Having come into ministry with a concept of how it "should" be hampered my own ability to handle the changes and disappointments that have come with ministry over the years. No matter how correct or incorrect my concepts might have been, the fact that ministry hasn't measured up has been disappointing at times. I cannot imagine how disappointed people who go into ministry with aspirations of million-dollar honorariums and private jets must be when they find themselves struggling to keep the church doors open and with nasty attitudes in demanding people.

If you've entered into ministry with pre-conceived ideas about how it should be, the odds are good that disappointment will find you. In paralleling what we discussed earlier about unhelpful and unsolicited advice, it is important to have good, solid leadership, friendships, and mentors who can help guide you through the developments of ministry and the changes that come with a long-term decision to serve God through the years. Training in ministry (from a Biblical, ancient, and modern perspective) helps ministers to see how ministry has and does change and be better prepared for different changes as they arise. It also helps to share with ministers who are in ministry and learn from their challenges and difficulties.

Disorder

It is impossible to operate effective ministry in chaos. We are not just people who operate things in this world, but ministers who exercise authority in God's Kingdom. Because we are in a Kingdom, we must acknowledge and know the following things about Kingdoms:

- Kingdoms are run by the king, who has the ultimate authority, final say, and only unquestionable rule in the dominion they have.

- Kingdoms function as the king establishes and installs governors or leaders who are able to follow the edicts and execute the directives of the king. The king's officials are a reflection of the king, not of their own dissentions.

- Kingdoms are not a democracy. The king's officials are appointed officials, not elected offices. It doesn't matter how you feel about the king's directives; you follow them.

- Dissenters cannot consider themselves a part of the Kingdom; they are either kicked out, banished, or executed for treason.

We are getting lost on essential matters of order today because people treat the Kingdom of God as if it is a democracy. Any time someone thinks they have a better idea than someone else, a new revelation, or even a thought, people feel the right to voice that opinion as if it is a fact or an eternal truth. When they are met with opposition (i.e. order) to their new-found approaches to revelation, they fuss and cry abuse and injustice. Leaders have allowed this sort of mess to go on far too long, fearing bad reputation, lack of funds, or trouble from people who are out of order and behave improperly because they don't respect authority.

There is nothing wrong with authority. The sooner we realize this, the sooner we will see the church in a more ordered and functional state. Nobody in the church has the right to behave outside of God's order, and we need to stop thinking that we have some sort of God-given ability to check the entire world as a result of a private revelation.

Being in ministry of any sort still requires accountability and ethics, and operating as some sort of Lone Ranger-style minister is going to, without fail, get someone in trouble every time. For this reason, ministers not only have the right, but the expectation, to implement order in their ministries. Some general guidelines for order are as follows:

- **Church ministers and main church authorities are found in the five-fold ministry** – Apostles, prophets, evangelists, pastors, and teachers

- **Covering offices** – Apostles (leaders of all types and appointments of all types); prophets (other prophets); pastors (members of the church who are not in ministry; elders and deacons)

- **Non-covering offices** – Evangelists and teachers

- **Appointments** – Bishops (assist apostles, and by extension, the rest of the five-fold); elders (installed by apostles, assist pastors); deacons (appointed by apostles; assist the entire five-fold and congregations).

- **Works of the church** – Service-oriented work that is most often operated via volunteer opportunities given to the non-clergy (laity) members of a church or ministry (such as nursery, cleaning the church, community evangelism, etc.).

Ministers need to be people who exercise the authority given to them in the context of their office or appointment. If you are in a situation as a minister where you are having issues with your congregation or members as pertain to order, the first thing to do is step back and assess what is going on and exercise the needed authority to get the situation back into a place of order. Instead of fearing financial loss or bad reputation, a leader needs to step up and lead, correcting the wrong that is done and preventing it from infiltrating the rest of the congregation or ministry. People should be taught to respect leaders, not engaging in gossip or in rebellion against church leadership. If there are disagreements with leaders, they should be handled privately, asking for clarity and understanding rather than having a "know-at-all" type of attitude. Members, participants, trainees, and individuals of all types who have some participation in a ministry should have a healthy sense of appreciation toward their leadership, recognizing the sacrifices and discipline it takes to be chosen by God for such a work.

If disorder comes as a result of dealing with other ministers or ministries who are somehow in partnership, covering your ministry, or are in friendship or association with, such relationships need to be terminated. We classify these today as being "messy" people, and people who generate mess try to involve others in their messes. Some good ways to tell if a minister is operating in a disordered manner include:

- **Find out who their leader is** – "Messy" leaders tend to avoid personal disciplines and guidance in their ministries. If someone is consistently without a leader or outright rejects the concept of accountability and covering in their own ministries, odds are good they are people who have a trail of mess behind them. (Note: the way people describe covering and leadership may use different terms and may be a little different from the way you understand it. A different concept of the same basic understanding is not mess. It's just a use of different terms).

- **What kind of ministry they operate** – Ministry visions and directives shouldn't change every four to six months. A ministry's vision should stick to the vision, with some moderate adjustments here and there as ministers try things to help bring the vision to fruition. If you are dealing with a leader who seems to be changing the vision multiple times, changing their ministries all the time, and changing their activities, you are most likely dealing with someone who is trying to find a niche in ministry rather than answering God's calling on their lives.

- **Find out who their friends are** – I've said it before, and I'll say it again – "Birds of a feather smell the same." The associations people have (especially the close associations) tell you a lot about who that person is and how that person is going to handle matters as they arise. If someone has close friends who are constantly in messy situations, the odds are good they are in them, as well.

- **What kind of leader is he/she** – Ministers almost always deal with someone who seeks to challenge their authority at some point in time or another. Ministers do deal with attacks, they do trust the wrong people, and they do encounter an unfair dose of injustice and betrayal. That having been said, this should not be the "norm" among those a minister covers. Leaders will have individuals who stay with them for years and others who are only there a short time, but a loyalty and respect for that leader should be the norm, with difficult individuals a side point. When difficulties arise, leaders should handle the matter with dignity and protocol, always implementing order.

Manipulation and control

Television commercials. Telemarketers. Infomercials. Store clerks. Advertising. Pop psychology. Manipulation and control are two facets of society that cannot be ignored, because they are the very manner by which items are sold, products are endorsed, and people are coerced into doing things, every single day. Those who believe manipulation and control should not be a part of the church are correct, but are very misguided if they believe such is not prevalent in church today. The manner in which many famous preachers teach, the repetitive nature of their teachings, and sometimes even the clothing or gestures they use are all techniques carefully designed to gain a person's trust and, eventually, money.

We could talk all day long about manipulation and control, and the various reasons why it is difficult to handle. More importantly, I think we need to recognize when we are being controlled or manipulated by other people. Manipulation and control does not always come in the obvious package of a David Koresh or Warren Jeffs. The best way to avoid manipulation is to make it clear you are not for sale and the best way to avoid control is to make it clear you cannot be bought.

It's not a secret that ministers today are over-extended and stressed out. We lack resources and help we can rely on. It is this feeling of stress and lack that people who seek to take advantage of a situation prey upon. In manipulation, someone will think they can deceive you into something because you believe that thing is for your benefit. They make you believe they have the answer to all your problems, situations, and woes. In control, people think they can own you and, subsequently, your ministry as well, through money or other means that relate to money. If it is clear that you are not desperate enough for whatever it is they offer and not lured by money, manipulation and control quickly fade from the scene.

Ministers today are being lost because people come along who offer the entire world, make it seem as if the answer to their prayers is that one singular person. No one person is the solution to our problems. The church operating as it should, that is the answer to ministry's problems and issues. Each and every ministry functioned without that individual, and will continue to function if an individual decides to move on. Never accept the lures of manipulation and control.

Cliques

I've described ministry as "junior high with Bibles." Our clothes are better, our shoes are better...but in many ways, ministers tend to act just as we did in our younger days. One of the most obvious facets of this is the clique, whereby a group of ministers exclusively hang out with their group, never expanding out, and never allowing anyone else in. It can be frustrating as ministers who are not in the reserved "inner circle" are passed up for events or looked down upon because they do not measure up to the clique's standards.

Before I say any more, I want to reiterate that it is important to assess those with whom you work with on a spiritual level, considering professionalism, integrity of character and ministry, and leadership ability. You do not want to be dealing with people of poor reputation, character, or integrity when doing ministry. We also recognize that different people have different relationships with others, and sometimes you may look to a group of people or some friends you have for a specific reason. This is not what we are talking about here. Also, there is nothing wrong with deciding not to associate with someone for a perfectly justifiable reason, regardless of whether or not they are in ministry. There is something wrong, however, with socializing with people just to be seen, with ministers who are only of a certain social strata or status, and with judging ministers by class or association.

I compare it to junior high behavior for a reason: cliquish behavior is immature. It signifies someone who hasn't moved out of their immature need to be accepted and socially judged by who they "hang out" with. Building ministries upon this precept eventually causes the ministries involved to collapse upon themselves, because they never socialize outside of their own immediate circles. The best avoidance to involving with cliques is to surround yourself with supportive ministers and friends who are of a variety of backgrounds and who know how to judge and assess situations and people based on spiritual discernment rather than social status.

CHAPTER FORTY-FOUR

◄►

STAYING ENCOURAGED

I long to see you so that I may impart to you some spiritual gift
to make you strong – that is,
that you and I may be mutually encouraged by each other's faith.
(Romans 1:11-12)

IN the last chapter, we discussed issues that affect a
leader's ability to maintain their leadership – and ways
they can regain that maintenance for the issues at hand.
The issues addressed were common complaints ministers
have about ministry today and things that affect their ability
to move their ministries forward. Some of what we talked
about in the last chapter carries over into this one, which
will look primarily at the minister's call to stay encouraged.

Despite the many positive chants we hear echoed in
churches today, ministry is still a difficult walk, with many
obstacles, trials, and considerations to take in. These issues
only increase as a minister moves up in their ministerial
abilities and expand their vision. It is also difficult to balance
the many different facets of life with ministry, such as
family, personal time, rest, and relaxation. Ministry takes
much time, focus, and discipline, which means it's easy to
get burnt out and discouraged.

I do believe that discouragement does come to every
leader, but there are ways we can avoid its snares and keep
from moving from discouragement to a constant state of
depression. Here are some ways leaders can remain

319

encouraged and balanced to avoid burnout:

- **Time off** – Church leaders are guilty of not taking enough time off or enough time for themselves. We are used to being needed and that turns into a thought process that if we take time for ourselves, something bad will happen. The Bible frequently mentions times when Jesus went off by Himself for a little while (Matthew 14:23, Luke 5:16), and nothing bad happened while He was gone. Leaders need time to themselves; to sort things out with God; with their families; and to just relax and take a breather from other people's problems and issues. Leaders should have one day off per week in which they are unavailable for appointments and ministry-related duties (excluding emergencies) and a vacation each year that is at least one week long in which they are away from the mainline duties of the ministry and able to refresh themselves.

- **Avoid getting caught up in the emotional dramas and states of others** – Ministers often see the worst, rather than the best, that humanity has to offer. We see people at their worst emotionally and spiritually, and sometimes mentally and physically, as well. We are the first line of defense people come to when they have needs, and the needs they have may range from the sublime to the seriously taxing and complicated. Even though we hear about drama and help people sort their dramas out, we need to avoid getting caught up in their dramas and emotional states. It is advisable to wait to return calls from people who are very worked up for a non-serious reason (someone in the hospital, illness, death, etc.), especially if they are repeatedly encountering drama. Maintain leadership boundaries at all times; uphold objectivity and make sure general matters (such as this) are handled during available or "business hours" only, rather than every single time someone has an issue or drama.

- **Stick to "available" or "business" hours** – Most businesses do not operate 24/7, but operate during a set availability. People know they can receive necessary services at those hours, and if they have a need after those hours, they will have to wait until regular hours to reach someone. This established boundary lets people know they have to wait sometimes and that they will be attended to within the established boundaries of the business. Ministers can learn a lot from this practice. Being available 24/7 to people does not teach them to handle their own issues or that waiting is sometimes an inevitable part of one's spiritual walk. Yes, ministers do need to be available all the time within certain contact points at all times for emergencies which do sometimes arise in ministry, but they do not need to be available to everyone at all times.

- **Good fellowship** – Leaders need to be more than go-to people and event moderators or hosts; they also need to embrace the joys of being able to fellowship with other believers. Sometimes it's great to just attend an event, go out to dinner, or hang out with people as a believer, a Christian, and not specifically need to be in charge as a leader.

- **Events just for leaders** – Leaders are believers, but as leaders, they do have their own unique set of spiritual needs. Leaders should be encouraged to participate in conferences that are specifically for leaders, leadership development, and leadership's needs. It is a great way to fellowship and also a great way to meet other leaders who can support and edify in the leadership call.

- **Devotional time** – Beyond just having time off or time away from ministry, leaders need to have their own devotional time with God that consists of whatever way in which they best reach out to God, to worship and serve Him. Whether it is devotional reading or reading of spiritual books, regular Bible devotional reading, or just quiet time with God in prayer, leaders must never, ever skimp on their devotional time.

- **Staff/assistants who share the vision** – It is tempting to just take anyone and everyone who comes along and offers to "help" with a ministry...but avoid this temptation. The staff or assistants who work with a minister are those who are closest to that minister, which means your staff or assistants are going to be those who are closest to you. They know about your good and bad days, they see you at your worst as well as your best, and they know you in a way that others who follow your ministry do not. Pay careful attention to those who are so closely connected to you and who work so close with you. Make sure they are supportive of the vision that you have and of the ministry at hand, understanding all that God has entrusted to you and that they too see the relevance and importance in the work.

- **Celebrations** – Never feel guilty for celebrating the advances of ministry. Don't forget to celebrate the good things that come along in ministry! Church anniversaries, leaders' birthdays and ministry anniversaries, and other special occasions that relate to a ministry or church and its leadership are important landmarks in the walk of ministry. Marking these occasions gives the opportunity to not just celebrate the leader, but also celebrate the ministry, giving everyone the opportunity to participate and realize they are an essential part of the work.

CHAPTER FORTY-FIVE

FELLOWSHIP AND NETWORKING

They devoted themselves to the apostles' teaching and to the fellowship,
to the breaking of bread and to prayer.
Everyone was filled with awe,
and many wonders and miraculous signs were done by the apostles.
All the believers were together and had everything in common.
(Acts 2:42-44)

ONCE upon a time, "fellowship" was a common facet of church ministry, especially in the American south. Churches would visit one another, especially if they were all a part of a common network, association, or organization. Over the past twenty years, the emphasis on the local church drew people away from fellowship and association with other churches and instead of moving outside of the local church, many people remain drawn in to their own exclusive circles, never experiencing the joys of true fellowship and interaction with other believers. "Fellowship" is foreign to many Christians today, even though it is an important and essential aspect of ministry relationship.

On the other hand, we hear a lot about "networking" today, but nobody ever explains what it is. Networking is often used in place of fellowship today, as people believe it is the answer to building solid ministry. The results, however, have not been an expansion of ministry or ministry growth, but more competition in ministry. Where people do not understand the proper context of networking, it is being lost in a mire of ministry emotionalism and disorder.

Fellowship and networking are both needed for professional ministry, but each in their own context. They provide for us the balance needed between the spiritual and the professional, to establish clergy as both a spiritual and career entity. If we want both to be effective, however, we need to understand what they are, how they work, and how they can benefit us as ministry leaders.

What is fellowship?

The word "fellowship" is from the Greek word *koinonia*, which means "communion" fellowship, sharing in common, something widespread, familiar and ordinary."[1] If we are to understand "fellowship" in a true Biblical context, fellowship is:

- The gathering together for physical communion, by which the elements of bread and wine are broken and poured out in remembrance of the Lord's death.

- The spiritual principle of unity found in communion, by which believers are one in Christ.

- The "sharing in common" of believers, reminding us that the church is bigger than just our immediate local church.

- The gathering of the church, whether by specific organization or by general grouping, for the specific event of blessing God and blessing one another.

- Coming together with other believers to share in worship, study, and prayer.

- Coming together over the "common and ordinary" things of everyday, such as a meal, a gathering, a social event, or a get-together.

From the definitions above, we can see that fellowship is not the formal understanding of visiting different services from your own on Sunday morning (although there is nothing wrong with doing this and there is certainly room for such a practice in the definition above). Fellowship is a spiritual principle, guiding the unity and growth of the church. It is what keeps us together, giving us opportunities to bless God, to bless one another, and to recognize we are all one body despite the differences we may have about earthly matters or ideals.

Why is fellowship so vital for leaders?

Leaders are used to being the people "in charge" of everything. It's easy to detach one's self from the Body of Christ and fail to recognize how important it is to be a part of the Body, even as a leader. Leaders are called to serve the Body as leaders, but they are still a part of the Body, just as governmental leaders are still a part of the nation they serve. Leaders need to have the opportunity to embrace this idea of being a part of something greater than themselves that comes through fellowship.

It's also important for leaders to remember that "fellowship" and "being church" is about more than just running services or attending churchy-type functions. Worship services, prayer meetings and calls, etc. are all a part of fellowship, and are, yes, all a sign of our unity with one another. Part of the Christian call, however, is to embrace faith in the "ordinary:" in the everyday things: eating, talking, walking, working, sleeping, caring, and reaching out to one another. Never neglect the transformation of these ordinary things as acts of faith! These are commonalities not just of Christians, but of people everywhere, reminding us that the everyday, ordinary things are great ways to reach out to others. Fellowship unites us to God; it unites us to other believers; and it provides common ground, by which we are able to witness to others.

What is networking?

Networking is a business term which refers to making connections profitable for business purposes. In networking, one attends events, meets people, hands out business cards, and joins themselves to others in business who may be beneficial to their work purposes and outcomes. Networking's purpose is strictly for outcome: for the end result of how your services can benefit someone else and how someone else's services can benefit you.

Networking is not a substitute for fellowship. It is not a spiritual principle. There is no unifying purpose behind it, and we cannot use it in place of the necessary spiritual principle of fellowship that helps to unite the body.

Why is networking important for ministers?

Networking is an important precept for ministers on the business-end of ministry. In years gone by, ministry needs were handled exclusively by members of that ministry. For example, if legal advice was needed, a lawyer in the congregation stepped up and offered their services. Nowadays, people expect to be paid for everything and that means people do not readily offer their services to non-profit organizations as they once did. When a ministry has a need, that means they need to call upon those they know in the business community to handle the job and do it as efficiently and inexpensively as possible. In a day where we lack volunteers, ministers need as many options as possible to solve problems and issues that arise.

Using both for the benefit of ministry

In summary, fellowship serves to meet important spiritual needs, while networking meets practical, business-end needs for ministers. Don't neglect one while accentuating the other, or trying to use the other to substitute for the other. Keeping both in their proper perspective, fellowship can help a minister to grow spiritually and networking can help the ministry to gain business asset and purpose.

CHAPTER FORTY-SIX

PROFESSIONAL MINISTRY ATTIRE

But when the king came in to see the guests,
he noticed a man there who was not wearing wedding clothes.
'Friend,' he asked, 'how did you get in here without wedding clothes?'
The man was speechless. Then the king told the attendants,
'Tie him hand and foot, and throw him outside, into the darkness,
where there will be weeping and gnashing of teeth.'
For many are invited, but few are chosen.
(Matthew 22:11-14)

ONE thing that drives me up the wall is attending an event and seeing leaders improperly dressed. Given deciding what one wore to a service used to be simpler than it is now, we still need to make sure we are properly attired and properly representing ourselves in our clothing when we are present for ministry events. I am the first one to admit that with the new implementations many ministries have, determining how to dress for an event can be confusing at times – but we still need to be people who align ourselves with order and dress appropriately for each and every event.

The following is a reprint from my book, *Ministry School Boot Camp: Training For Helps Ministries, Appointments And Beyond.* While the book was written for those first going into ministry and for those who are working in appointment or helps ministries, the advice and guidelines for attire are the same for those who are in Ephesians 4:11 ministry.

Different types of attire

When it comes to attire, a lot of different terms get thrown around today. Many of them are unfamiliar to people, especially in the context of a church setting. Here are the terms as pertain to attire, and what they mean.

- **Formal (black tie)** – A black tie event calls for ultra-formal apparel: ball gowns and formal dresses for women, tuxedos for men, and applicable attire that falls somewhere in between for non-binary or gender non-conforming individuals.

- **Business** – Professional attire based around suits and ties (either two-piece suits or three-piece suits), pantsuits, skirt suits, and dresses. Colors tend to be dark or neutral.

- **Business Casual** – Informal business attire that centers around comfort, while maintaining a professional appearance. Business casual includes trousers or slacks, button-down shirts or polo shirts, or knit skirts and tops.

- **Casual** – Informal clothing that includes jeans and t-shirts.

- **Church** – Formal church clothing that resembles business wear, but tends to be more colorful and a little fancier than business attire. This includes suits, pantsuits, skirt suits, or dresses in any color of one's choosing, with matching accessories, such as hats, shoes, and handkerchiefs.

- **Civic** – Civic attire is a term applied to the traditional collar and shirt worn by many denominational ministers. We will speak more of civic attire later.

- **Ceremonial** – Church attire, usually reserved for formal occasions, that involves robes and garments found in high Protestant churches, such as Anglican, Lutheran, or Episcopalian. We will speak more of ceremonial attire later.

General clothing guidelines

As you are dressing for ministry and church events, no matter what the attire may be, the following guidelines should be followed:

- Whether you identify as male, female, non-binary, or gender non-conforming, it is your responsibility to learn how to dress for ministry in a way that you are both comfortable with and is appropriate for each situation that arises. In such situations, it is best to have a minister who understands such unique circumstances and helps support you while educating and encouraging you in proper attire for each situation that will arise in ministry.

- When you are in different situations in ministry, attire may vary or change, depending on the requirements therein. Proper advice should be offered for situations in which gender roles are enforced or a lack of protocol for non-binary or non-conforming individuals exists.

- What you wear as a minister should reflect the activity you are doing as a minister. Just as the priests of old did not just go before God wearing anything they pleased, so too we cannot minister wearing whatever we please. The clothes worn for ministry work while in church should not be clothes worn for other purposes, such as mowing the lawn or taking out the garbage. When planning an outfit, remember the outline above. If you are preaching or ministering, attire should reflect more formal wear; teaching, business meetings, and workshops should reflect business attire; ceremonies should reflect ceremonial and civic attire; and street evangelism should reflect casual wear, just as examples.

- Clothing should typically be matched to the activity at hand, as well. For example, seminars may call for business or business casual, while an evening service may call for church clothing. An ordination may call for civic and ceremonial attire. When in question as to attire, it is best to ask your leader.
- Clothing should not be too tight, too short, too low-cut, or too revealing. Use good judgment when planning attire.

- All garments should be wrinkle-free, neat, clean, and well cared for. Garments should not have holes, rips, or tears.

- When wearing garments that have buttons, make sure buttons are sewn on, and not missing. When wearing attire that contains jewels or rhinestones, make sure jewels and rhinestones are not missing. If they are, replacing them is an easy and inexpensive store-bought fix: get a bag of them at any department or craft store and glue or cement them back on your garment.

- Avoid t-shirts and other garments with graphics, prints, images, slogans, or sayings that are inappropriate or may be deemed offensive.

- Shoes should be matched to the outfit – they should not clash, nor should they be inappropriate to the activity at hand. For example, if you are doing street ministry and the attire is casual, it is not appropriate to wear designer-name stilettos. If you are in church attire, it is not appropriate to wear sneakers. If there is a health reason why certain footwear must be worn, let your leader know in advance.

Civic attire

Civic attire is, in many ways, making a comeback in many ministry circles. Even though it may not be an attire required on a regular basis, it is important to know the basics of civic attire.

It should be noted that the specifics on civic attire may vary between denominations and, at times, even ministries. What is considered appropriate or standard among one group may be totally inappropriate in another. Here we give guidelines, but if there is an instance where specifics are in question, it is best to consult with someone who can provide the specific answers.

The standard of civic attire is the white collar worn by the minister. There are two options for the collar: either a tab collar, which fits inside the neck of the shirt, or a full collar, which is worn around the entirety of the neck. Some traditions forbid the full collar to be worn by an individual who is not ordained as a pastor, apostle, or appointed as an elder (in this instance, a tab collar is required). Others require the tab collar when one is a licensed minister, but not an ordained minister.

There is then the shirt itself, which is worn with the white collar. The traditional and standard colors for a clergy shirt are white and black, which may be worn by any and all members of the clergy. In travel, black is the traditional color, although any color shirt with a collar may be worn as part of street wear.

- **Apostle** – Red (sometimes fuchsia or purple)
- **Prophet** – White (sometimes royal blue or navy blue)
- **Evangelist** – Gray
- **Pastor** – Royal blue or green
- **Teacher** – Light blue, green, or yellow
- **Bishop** – Fuchsia or purple
- **Elders** – Maroon

- **Ministers** – Black

When dressed in civic attire, one must wear a black suit, one complete with jacket and pants or a skirt. Many denominations and church associations require women to wear a skirt of appropriate, below-the-knee length when in civic attire (they forbid or frown on women wearing pants when in civics). Exceptions to wearing a skirt are social activism, justice, or work done outside of the church. In such instances, black dress pants are a must. Pants require black socks and shoes, and skirts, black pantyhose and formal dress shoes. Jewelry should be kept to a minimal, with the exception of a silver or gold cross, worn with a specific color cord (that should be specified by the ministry).

Ceremonial attire

Ceremonial attire varies depending on the church or ministry you are dealing with. It also varies depending upon the event at hand. Ceremonial attire can be very simple or very elaborate. Below are some of the basics of ceremonial pieces and what they are.

- **Cassock Robe** – A basic preaching robe that buttons up the front and is worn like a long jacket. Cassock robes are worn for preaching or for more formal events by those who are not much for robes on a regular basis. They come in a variety of colors and styles.

- **Chasuble** – The outer garment worn in a formal setting that slips over the head and is free-fitting on both sides, without sleeves. They come in many colors and match the liturgical season or feast color of the day.

- **Alb** – The plain white garment worn as the base of all formal ceremonial attire in liturgical circles.

- **Cincture** – A rope band worn around the waist of an alb.

- **Stole** – A colorful and embroidered scarf that hangs around the neck and down the front of the body, usually fringed at the end. It is worn under the chasuble.

- **Prayer shawl/mantle** – A garment for prayer worn wrapped around the shoulders and back, meeting in the front of the body. A prayer shawl may represent a traditional Jewish appearance, with the fringes and Hebrew lettering, or may be knitted or modern, made to represent more of a modern interpretation of the garment.

- **Mitre** – The large hat worn by a bishop in liturgical churches and, in some circles, an apostle.

- **Yarmulke** – The small pink or red skullcap worn by Jewish men and sometimes Messianic adherents.

- **Cope** – the outer-cape worn to match the liturgical cassock worn by a minister. Traditionally used for outdoor functions.

When civic and ceremonial attire are appropriate

Most ministries do not require their ministers to be in full civic attire for regular services, conferences, seminars, or general events. Civic and ceremonial attire are usually reserved for ceremonial occasions, such as dedications, communion, weddings, funerals, and ordinations. Even in these instances, civic attire may not be required according to every group or polity.

Civic attire is never appropriate for daytime seminars, forums, or other events that center around academic events.

The call to wear white

In traditional Pentecostalism, wearing white was considered customary to formal civic and ceremonial attire. This was especially true for female preachers and ministers. In some ministries, white garments (suits, dresses, plain robes, etc.) is considered formal ministerial wear and more customary than wearing the formal ministerial attire. When called to wear white for an event, it is inappropriate to think civic attire or ceremonial attire can serve as a substitute – one must show up wearing white. In keeping with this, the attire should be pure white – not off white, ecru, beige, or darker shades. The white is used to represent purity in Christ, redemption from sin, and echoes the principle of being dressed in white by God in the last day.

Garments every minister should have

The following is a list of garments every minister should have in order to be fully prepared for all duties at hand.

- At least one church suit and dress (for those who identify as female) for ministering on church occasions
- At least one business suit of a dark color for business attire occasions
- At least one outfit that can be considered business casual
- One black cleric's collar shirt with tab collar (for ministers, elders and deacons) and one full collar (for bishops, apostles, prophets, evangelists, pastors, and teachers).
- If in an Ephesians 4:11 ministry office, the necessary color cleric's collar shirt
- Both a tab collar and a full collar
- One basic black suit, with either pants or a skirt
- Basic black socks (for pants) or pantyhose (for skirts)
- Black dress shoes or black pumps
- One basic cassock robe in a color to be determined by

ministry or necessity (recommended color: black)

CHAPTER FORTY-SEVEN

TEAMWORK (GOOD LEADERS GO FIRST)

Two are better than one,
because they have a good return for their work;
if one falls down, his friend can help him up.
But pity the man who falls and has no one to help him up!
(Ecclesiastes 4:9-10)

WHAT does it mean to be a good leader? There's extensive teaching available today for people who believe they may be called to leadership, but seldom do we hear the qualities and principles that display a good leader's character. One can think they are called to leadership based on the teachings they hear, and not be cut out for leadership at all. When leadership teaching is so basic and generic in nature, it is hard to determine the true nitty-gritty facets of leadership that make a leader the best at what they do to step out in the lead.

The basic principle behind leadership is the ability to motivate, encourage, and discipline others to follow behind them unto the end of a project, goal, or objective. I do believe that leaders are born with the ability to lead, but certain training and disciplines of life help that leader to become a good, solid leader, weathering the difficulties that come with the territory. Being a good leader in church is much like being a good leader in any other situation: leaders must consider both the empowerment of the people and the productivity of the environment, and align the various elements involved so all can focus on the goals present.

If you are called to leadership, you know how important teamwork is. Being a leader means that you are a part of a team, as the captain of that team. Anyone involved as a captain of the team knows that being a captain is not a simple matter of barking orders or being a burdensome taskmaster, lording control over the team members. Good captains see their work as a part of the team, building it up, and training all involved to function as a singular unit. In good teamwork, we find good operations, and good leaders behind those operations to promote the necessary teamwork and spirit to continue toward effective function.

In order to facilitate proper teamwork, good leaders must go first. This means a good leader must have their own necessary preparatory foundations to bring forth all that is needed to create a team and lead other people. This is just as true in a church setting as any other, and we, as leaders, must take those important steps to go first in the process of building integrated participation in church.

Not everyone is called to be a leader...and that is all right

There is a picture circulating on Facebook that reads, "Good leaders don't create followers. They create other leaders." I think this sounds good to many people, but the reality is that it's just not true. Some people are called to leadership, and some people are just not. Different types of leaders exist to handle both those who are called to leadership, and those who are not. Teams cannot operate with everyone trying to be a captain or coach or function with everyone being trained to be a captain. While leadership training is necessary for those who are genuinely called to be leaders, it is not necessary for those who are not called to leadership. Those who are not called to leadership need to be trained to do different things so that every aspect of the team can function efficiently.

So, the first thing leaders need to relieve themselves of is the pressure to turn every person they work with into a leader. Pressuring people into leadership roles, especially if they are not called and not prepared for them, doesn't create proper leadership, it creates mess. As a leader, relax; let people discern for themselves some of what God is doing in their lives. Let them come and talk to you and share about it, and go from there instead of pushing the issue all the time.

Also, just because someone hangs a shingle outside of a church doesn't mean they are called to fill the leadership role they are attempting to fill. Some people are pressured into ministry roles and positions due to trends and the involvement of former leaders. Sometimes people don't have enough information to discern their office, although they do discern they are called to do something. In days gone by, to-be-leaders were first put in positions of helps ministries in order to build their skills and develop grace and humility to prepare them for the work of ministry. Nowadays, many churches forego that all-important process in favor of quick promotion. Quick promotions do more harm than good and create a situation where a leader often has to backtrack a minister's experiences to help them discern what they may truly be called to be.

Different types of church leadership

We know that the five-fold ministry consists of apostles, prophets, evangelists, pastors, and teachers, but many are confused about the differences in authority found therein. If we are to break it down simply, the difference comes down to who leads who and what type of leadership one exercises. The following is taken from my book, *Ministry School Boot Camp: Training For Helps Ministries, Appointments, And Beyond*:

Within the five-fold ministry, there are two types of authority: universal authority and limited authority. This very simple principle is often misunderstood in the modern church and, as a result, often distorted. Understanding the principles behind universal authority and limited authority helps to better understand realms of leadership and adopted ministerial roles when in a certain setting.

341

Universal authorities are leaders who have authority in any church, anywhere in the world. Even though this authority may not be exercised at all times (and, it may, in fact, be unwise to exercise it at times), a universal authority has authority that moves beyond the local realm. The way a universal authority may be exercised may be different depending on the office, but the bottom line is that a universal authority has authority beyond a local congregation.

Universal authorities within the five-fold ministry are:

- Apostles
- Prophets

Authorities with a universal scope but without formalized church authority (meaning they are not superior to either leaders with local or universal authority, but run parallel with a different purpose) include:

- Evangelists
- Teachers

Limited authorities are those authorities within a church setting who have authority exclusively on a local level. While such a leader would be respected and acknowledged as such, they do not hold authority over other congregations other than the one which they preside. These include:

- Pastors

Understanding the sphere of leadership gives us an idea of how the chain of command works. Even though a leader may not be a personal authority over someone, when an apostle or prophet is present in a church, they represent the superior offices. Their authority, words, and instruction are to be universally accepted, as they are given in proper order. It is inappropriate for a pastor to be giving a directive in a church by which they are not presiding. Evangelists and teachers have the right to correct and rebuke, but do not represent church authority as relates to structure and discipline. It is also understood that these offices operate within the bounds of order, and address specific matters relating to leadership, helps, discipline, and other issues through the proper channels of order, which are those that relate to the leadership already in place.

I have included this section because it clarifies the differences in the offices and the authority therein. If we are leaders, we must first know the type of leader we are in the Kingdom and we must know who we will be covering in the Kingdom. For example, as an apostle, I know my job is to cover other five-fold ministry leaders. This means I need to be prepared to see how we, as a ministry, are able to operate best as a team and how each leader I train is best equipped to serve as the captains of their own ministries. This is different from a pastor, who is not working with people who are leaders and are not training for ministry. Knowing who you are and who you are training is essential to how to train them and how to motivate them.

Having a clear vision

Captains or coaches of sports teams know the goal of their work is to bring the various players together to play the sport of choice. In ministry, the goal of our work is to bring the various people we cover together so they can function in the Kingdom as they are duly called. Leaders need to be clear about what they do, why they do it, and the big picture vision of what is to be accomplished. Leaders need to be able to articulate the vision in many different ways, to different audiences and to different groups of people. With a clear vision, leaders are able to implement necessary steps to bring that vision to pass while explaining that vision to those who need to understand it.

Good leaders are also good followers

I know it's kind of cliché, but it is true that the best leaders also know how to follow and support the visions of others. Good leaders in church have leaders of their own, have come up through the ranks, believe in obedience and know how to conduct themselves accordingly with accountability and honor. Being a good follower means leaders understand what it's like to follow a leader and know what it's like to participate in a vision, in something greater than one's self. This gives a leader the necessary grounding to lead well, without abusiveness and knowing the important balance needed between discipline and encouragement.

Taking the necessary time to care

It amazes me the number of people who complain that their leaders are consistently unavailable to them. There are leaders who refuse to take phone calls, talk to, counsel, or share with their people. While I am the first who believes we need to set boundaries and limits on just how available we are all the time (because yes, a leader's time does need to be respected as leaders have multiple people to help), leaders cannot deny their people the necessary time and care in their own spiritual development. Good leaders let their people know they do care about them, and are willing to invest time to help them.

Get your hands dirty!

Many people believe leadership is desirable because they think it means leaders don't have to do any work. They believe leadership is about sitting in heavy robes on a platform, looking down on others as they bark orders. This is not what true leadership is about, at all! In using the same analogy of a sports team, team captains and coaches are present at every practice, instructing, demonstrating, and sometimes, even playing along as they train the players for their upcoming games. Leaders cannot fear being involved and working alongside those they are training. The best leaders are aware of what is going on, are involved and participating, so they know exactly what needs to be addressed, and why.

Celebrate with your people

One of the best experiences leaders can have is to celebrate with their people, especially in the joys of ministry life. Never forget to invite those who participate and work with you to enjoy the bounty of the harvest: ordinations, church anniversaries, special services, and special occasions – especially to those who have been with you the longest and are the most dedicated to the vision.

CHAPTER FORTY-EIGHT

<figure>◀━◆━▶</figure>

CONFLICT/RESOLUTION

Salt is good, but if it loses its saltiness,
how can you make it salty again?
Have salt in yourselves,
and be at peace with each other.
(Mark 9:50)

ON July 29, 2014, my Facebook status read: "When did people get so messy? #smh." Many people identified with this statement, especially leaders in ministry. It seems as if every time we turn around, there is a new mess to behold, clean up, and manage. Many leaders complain about the endless amount of issues they seem to be forced to face as part of ministry today: everything from people's messy relationship break-ups to administrative issues. When problems arise between people, it seems as if the minister is the one stuck in the middle, left to serve as the referee for the issues at hand.

Ministers of every sort today need to have some background in a principle known as conflict/resolution. This principle acknowledges conflict exists and there are general guidelines that can be modified to fit each situation to bring conflicting situations to a state of peace, or resolution. When situations are resolved, it does not mean that everyone in the situation is happy with the outcome, but that the conflict of the situation ceases to be a main point of contention between people. Here we are going to talk about the process and specific techniques that you can use in order to help with the conflict/resolution process.

What is conflict/resolution?

Conflict/resolution is the ability to handle situations of a conflicting nature, whereby people are at odds, and bring the situations to a successful and satisfactory resolution.

Why learn about conflict/resolution?

- Conflicts are a part of the world in which we live.

- Whether or not the world should be a part of church matters, issues in people's lives often spill over into their relationship with God and with church.

- We will inevitably be in situations where we conflict with others.

- We will inevitably be in situations where others conflict with us.

- We will inevitably be in situations where others are in conflict, and we, as leaders need to step into the situation as mediators and bring the solution to a resolution.

Why should ministers know about conflict/resolution?

As ministers of God, it is vitally important we know how to handle people and how to handle situations that arise in the course of interpersonal human interaction. Not everyone we know is going to always get along with us, nor will we always get along with them. Not everyone under our ministries will always get along, like each other, and work well together. It's nice to adhere to naive expectations of ministerial interaction, with the hopes that everything and everyone is just going to behave in a delightful manner all the time...but reality will quickly reveal the truth that ministry is not all sunshine and roses between individuals. As divine representatives, we should be able to act with justice and fairness to bring about resolution to conflict-ridden situations. Christians, having received divine sanctification, should be able to resolve issues among themselves, without having to rely on courts or other worldly avenues to solve their problems. Leaders stand as executives prepared to do just that.

Identifying the parties involved in conflict/resolution

- **The accuser(s)** – The individual or individuals who make an accusation against an individual or individuals about some matter; those who bring forth the conflict.

- **The accused** – The individual or individuals who is/are accused of something; those who respond to the conflict.

- **The moderator** – The individual who serves as a neutral party to represent justice, fairness, equity and resolution in a situation where the accuser(s) and accused cannot reach a resolution without outside assistance.

- **The witness(es)** – The individual or individuals who stand as "involving parties" in a circumstance, either by firsthand knowledge or character justification.

Examples of conflict/resolution in the Bible

- **Abram and Lot separate (Genesis 13:1-18)** – Abram and Lot were faced with who was going to receive what parcel of land. In an effort to end the potential mess that could ensue, Abram agreed to let Lot pick which land he wanted first.

- **The judges serving for the disputes of the Israelites (Exodus 18:13-26)** – Disputes and conflicts are not new to life. Even in Biblical times when people had far less than we have today, people disputed over property lines, landmarks, items, animals, injuries, and other matters. God established the judges system to help out Moses, who was growing weary from dealing with the Israelites all the time by himself. People are emotional when they are upset or feel they have been wronged, and objective parties are needed to bring the conflicting situation to a positive resolution.

- **Having offense against your brother (Matthew 5:21-24)** – The Word encourages us to handle matters quickly and to admit when we have done wrong in a situation. Many conflicts could be resolved if, instead of having an attitude, we could discuss with each other, apologize, and ask for forgiveness when we have done wrong.

- **Settling matters quickly with adversaries (Matthew 5:25-26)** – Many conflicts could be avoided if we would avoid being so swayed by our feelings when dealing with others, and would simply show one another common courtesy.

- **Settling disputes with one another rather than in secular courts (1 Corinthians 6:1-11)** – We discussed this principle in an earlier chapter.

Identifying situations where conflict may arise

- Interactions with family members

- Doctrinal, political, philosophical or social disagreements

- Jealousy, envy, rivalry or competition

- Emotionally-sensitive issues, subjects or situations

- Disagreements of opinion

- Intimate knowledge of others

- Personal offenses

- Being physically impaired (i.e., drugs or alcohol)

- Stress

- Disappointment or depression

- Mental illness

- Circumstantial failure

- Miscommunication or misunderstanding

- Anywhere two or more people gather, work together, or are expected to function as some semblance or unit

How to identify conflict within ourselves and others

When situations arise that cause stress, difficulty, or frustration, it is safe to say and assume you are in a situation of conflict. Interpersonal relationships, interacting with others (especially those whom we are closest to, such as family members), disagreeing with others' behavior, general disagreements or arguments, and observing behaviors that can somehow be problematic are all potential situations for conflict to arise. As it is a part of living and interacting with others, it is safe to say we will all encounter conflicts and go through periods of conflict in our lives.

Comprehensive ways to resolve conflict when a mediator is unavailable

There will be times when conflict arises and there is no one available to help mediate the situation. When such arises, it is important that we take effective steps to resolve such a situation as quickly and with as much integrity as possible:

- **Temporarily remove yourself from the situation and assess it objectively** – It's amazing how different things can look and sound when we step back from them for a little bit. Feelings, emotions, opinions, and perceived attacks can cause issues to seem different than they really are. With a little objectivity, a situation can seem quite different.

- **Do not act or speak emotionally; exercise self-control** – Emotions can cause us to feel justified in behaving in ways that are unseemly and cause a situation to escalate into a complete mess. As much as you might want to say something just to voice your opinion or be mean…exercise silence. Remember, you do have the right to remain silent, because in these situations, anything you say can and will be used against you!

- **Try discussing the issue in a non-threatening manner, offering peaceful discussion and brainstorming to resolve the situation** – Bringing peace to a situation means offering peace, not waiting for someone else to go first. If you want a situation resolved, you need to be one to offer peace in place of emotional heat.

- **Offer a compromise and solutions to a difficult, or conflicting, stressful situation** – Many situations can be resolved if people would only be willing to compromise or find solutions. Today, people make everything a "right fight" and that means their concept of "compromise" is someone else seeing things their way. True compromise occurs when people come together and meet somewhere in the middle of both viewpoints, with both sides giving some on their own perspectives for the sake of the issue at hand. Solutions are offered from both sides to help bring about a compromise that will benefit both sides and keep attention on the issue at hand. The goal of compromise is to bring a sense of fairness and justice to all parties involved.

- **If you are in the wrong on a matter, apologize immediately, asking for forgiveness** – When people feel wronged, it changes their state of mind. If you know you are behind the conflict, the proper thing to do is fess up, apologize, and ask for forgiveness.

Areas where one cannot compromise

There are instances where compromise is not an option. Although these are not prevalent in every situation, it is important that the boundaries on these matters are respected in a debate or conflict. It is even more important that, instead of trying to use your bottom lines as an excuse all the time to win arguments and avoid compromise, that you only call on them in situations that obviously call them out as relevant.

- Unsubstantiated accusations made without substance, proof, or evidence

- Illegal or immoral behavior

- Bullying

- Abuse or mistreatment

- Personalization of issues

- Dishonesty

- Manipulation

- "Dumping" or transference of blame without cause

- Foul or abusive language

- Abusive behavior

Methods to handle conflicts as a mediator between two or more parties

- **Remain objective, considering all sides** – The worst thing you can do is seem as if you are favoring one side over another based on connection rather than facts. Position yourself to help resolve the conflict and make things better for the two people involved, not just to benefit one or gain favor with one of them.

- **Do not accept unsubstantiated accusations of others** – If there is a case of character attack or accusation, require proof that such a thing happened. When people are backed into a corner (especially in the case of conflicts), people are quick to lie about issues and fabricate or exaggerate matters. Don't accept any accusations without proof.

- **If it is an option, bring both parties together to discuss options, facilitate problem-solving, and discover ways of compromise** – A mediator's primary job is to help other people work out their issues by providing the safe atmosphere for them to do so. While there are times where, as leaders, we must intervene and exercise authority and discipline, it is good to let people work out their differences themselves if at all possible.

- **Do not allow the discussion to be empty accusations, emotionally-charged, or an endless stretch of back-and-forth disagreements** – People need a few minutes to voice their side of the story, but they do not need to endlessly drag on and on about what they feel as pertains to the situation. Don't waste time allowing an endless amount of whining to occur, as people argue back and forth without resolution.

- **Establish an atmosphere of maturity, responsibility, accountability and self-discipline** – Make it clear this isn't going to work if everyone goes back and forth, wastes time complaining, and transferring blame. If people want a resolution, each needs to behave with maturity, responsibility, accountability, and self-discipline.

- **Listen, without making judgments; do not speak in haste** – When people go through a situation that is rift with conflict, people most often want to feel they are being heard. They, most likely, feel an injustice has occurred against them and they want someone to validate the wrong done to them. Whether the wrong is actual or fabricated, listening is the best way to make sure a situation can move past the initial stages of emotional need to the stage necessary for problem solving.

- **Expect all uphold certain standards, especially proper conduct and language; do not allow coarse or abusive conduct between the parties** – Just because people are angry or otherwise emotional does not give them the right to behave in any abusive manner.

- **Never make the assumption that the problem will go away on its own** – It's nice to pretend a problem will go away, but that doesn't help problems to go away. If a conflict is severe, it needs to be addressed sooner than later.

- **If the parties cannot seem to resolve the matter on their own, take the initiative to bring resolution to the**

situation – It is best to let people resolve issues on their own, if at all possible. If a situation persists, however, with no resolution, leaders must intervene to resolve the situation cleanly and efficiently, stepping up as necessary.

In summary

- Conflict is a part of life; resolution is also a part of life.

- Don't ignore conflicting situations; step up and work toward resolution.

- Never underestimate the power of solid leadership and genuine communication unto the end of forgiveness.

- Resolution represents God's justice and fairness toward us.

CHAPTER FORTY-NINE

EXPANDING THE VISION

Jabez cried out to the God of Israel,
"Oh, that You would bless me and enlarge my territory!
Let Your hand be with me,
and keep me from harm so that I will be free from pain."
And God granted his request.
(1 Chronicles 4:10)

MOST people go into ministry with very lofty aspirations about what they will do and what they believe will come out of it. Especially in our modern times, many of those dreams and visions fall by the wayside, for the reason that the minister is totally unprepared with what they will have to do in order to meet those goals and visions. Even when a vision partially manifests, it is often difficult to take the vision beyond a certain point. With financial difficulties, endless walls and unhelpful people, and a general sense of "this is the way it has to be done" present in church today, it's easily to stand still in ministry instead of moving forward.

It's God's will that the Kingdom expands. We are commanded to proclaim the Gospel to all the world, in every nation, under heaven. What we will be discussing in this final chapter of the book is the necessary foundations to expanding the vision God has given to you into its fullness. This doesn't mean that you have to take the vision God gave you and turn it into something else, or take multiple steps beyond what God has promised; quite the contrary. It is a necessary look at how you can, as a minister, be doing and functioning all God has revealed to you, one step at a time.

Understanding expansion

If we watch the posts of social networking sites, it would seem that everyone is expected to expand all the time. Becoming "bigger and better" is the desired goal and encouragement of many, and much of the "word" we hear revolves around worldly expansions. Expansion is not necessarily about getting bigger in a worldly sense, but, as I said earlier, doing more of what God has given for you to do, however that is accomplished. If there is something you can do better, more of, or an aspect of your ministry that has been on hold because it hasn't been the right time to develop it, you will, at some point in time (if not right now) go through a season when you are called to expand your work and all you are doing. Expand doesn't necessarily mean getting "bigger and better," but increasing ability, scope, focus, and, most importantly, impact. We need to walk within God's timing and have more of an impact on those we are called to influence with the Gospel through the work and legacy of God's Kingdom.

Being comfortable in your own calling

Ministers today need to refrain from the pressures to be "like everyone else." You are called to do what God has called you to do, and you do not have to be like the minister down the street, the minister on television, or the minister in some other country. If you are being true to what God has called you to do, then you need to remain in His will. Not every minister is called to have a mega-ministry, be on television, and travel all over the world. If you are not called to do these things...then don't do them, and don't feel pressured to do them. If we were to average out percentages, the number of mega-church and mega-ministry leaders in the church are far less than those who are solidly overseeing churches and ministries on a smaller scale. We also need to realize that just because a leader is on television or doing something that seems "big" in a worldly sense doesn't mean they are doing it properly or teaching rightly. If you are where God has you to be, then rejoice in that, and don't bow to the pressures to become something else. Expanding your vision doesn't mean becoming like another ministry or trying to fit in with someone else's concept of "expansion." It means that you grow what you are already doing and it continues to fit with what God has already said to you.

Sticking with what God told you from the beginning

When it doesn't seem like the vision God has given to us is working out, it may be tempting to try different things out. Those that change what they are doing every couple of months prove right there that whatever they are doing is not what God originally told them to do. When a vision is clear and someone clearly understands what God has called them to do, they are going to stick with it, not contrive it into many different parts, hoping it will become the "thing" that will work out. God doesn't call us like that. While we may not understand everything about our calling or how to accomplish it all, we can't expand a vision or take it to a next level if we keep changing it all the time. If you are persevering with what God has given to you and revealed to you from the beginning, then you are doing good – and getting ready for expansion.

Recognizing times and seasons

Times and seasons bring God's *karios* (eternity time) into *chronos* (chronological, time-line time). This means that when we recognize the spiritual times and seasons we are in, we are better able to identify what we need to do in those times as ministers of God.

In Biblical language, the terms "times" and "seasons" can have many meanings. A "time" can refer to a period of approximately one year, consisting of twelve thirty-day months (360 days). It can also just relate to how it is most commonly used – an indefinite period of time in which God is doing something, and we are unaware of when it will end. A "season" most often refers to a fixed period of time, usually having something to do (either beginning or ending) with a special occasion, such as beginning with planting and ending with harvest or beginning with a new moon and ending with a specified feast day. From this analysis, times and seasons are spiritual entities in which we recognize God is doing something. We may or may not know how long it will be, but we are able to recognize that God is working in some specific way for the benefit of His people in that period.

In relation to ministry visions, all of us are in times and seasons as we move forward with the assignments God gives to us. We may be in a period for a while where we actively pursue one aspect of our ministry, and then we recognize that season has ended, to which we follow God's guiding to pursue a different aspect of it. We know via times and seasons when we are ready to expand, if we are in a season of waiting or expectation, and what exactly we are supposed to do in terms of steps and movement at all points based on the times and seasons.

This means – there will be times when you are supposed to wait, times when you are supposed to move, and yes, times when you are supposed to expand. Some seasons are for planning future seasons, some times are for growing and quiet, and still others are for things that involve more work and more growth in your work. Being connected to discerning sources helps you to know what season you are in and what you should be doing in that time.

Knowing what season you are in and operating in that season is a part of being comfortable in your own calling and sticking with what you are called to do. You aren't going to be called to do something you aren't qualified to do because it's a new or different season. The way you operate may change a little bit, but you won't acquire a whole new ministry just because the times or seasons have shifted.

Are you ready to expand?

Most people think they want to expand, but before you answer that, there are many things to think about. The first is, as we just discussed, discerning times and seasons and assessing where you are in the vision and where you are at spiritually. Before deciding it's time to expand, it's time to seek God and make sure, especially if you haven't had a specific word from Him about it.

Planning for the future

How far do you think ahead? I know many ministers who think only from Sunday to Sunday in terms of their ministries. It is such a struggle to pay the immediate bills that paying the rent is a constant and intimidating struggle. There are no thoughts to what is coming next or what will be happening in a month, six months, or year down the road.

If we want to approach expansion properly, we need to have the proper tools and thought processes for expansion. We need to be ready to launch out into whatever God has for us in the times and seasons to come. That means we need to have an expansion mindset that helps us to think about the future. Thinking about the future is about more than daydreaming about preaching before tens of millions of people. Thinking about the future is thinking about the different things you would like to do and accomplish within your ministry over three different specified periods of time: six months, one year, and five years. Some people go as far as to plan ten years ahead, but I think that's a little too far, as things can change much in a ten-year period of time. Obviously, the five-year goals are the most flexible, with the six-month goals being the most definitive. Some things to consider when planning include:

- Changes made to the regular schedule (different times for services, new regular events, classes, etc.)

- Board meetings

- Staff meetings

- Recurring special events

- Starting special events

- One-time special events

In expansion, every minister needs the following items to keep track of events and plans:

- **Date book/day planner** – I actually recommend every leader have two date books/date planners: a larger one that can stay on a desk or in an office (this is the main one with complete details and information) and a smaller one that can travel (with the main information in it, only less detailed and smaller). Yes, I am the first to admit it can be difficult to keep track of everything that comes up, but it is important the minister of God knows what is going on at all times, is familiar with their schedule, and is able to plan accordingly not just for themselves, but for their ministries, as well.

- **Event calendar** – Every ministry should release three different versions of their events calendar: one to the general body of a ministry; one to the ministers of a ministry; and one to the staff of a ministry. Each one should contain the relevant information as pertinent to each audience. How you choose to release this is dependent upon the needs of the ministry and the number of activities you have going on, but many ministries choose to release a yearly general calendar in January and monthly event calendars after that.

- **Tentative event calendar** – A tentative event calendar is one to be circulated among ministry ministers and staff for a period of at least three years in advance. It details dates for annual and special events, meetings planned that far in advance, and other general times by which ministers and staff should plan to prepare for and be available. These events are not necessarily written in stone, and the tentative calendar may go through revision and updating. As a result, a tentative event calendar should be released at least once per year.

The fiscal year

A fiscal year is a business term used to describe the twelve-month period an organization uses for its financial budgeting and reporting. It is distinguished from a calendar year in that it may not begin on January 1st and end on December 31st, although there are certainly organizations that do operate fiscal years in this time frame. Fiscal, or financial, years operate as an organization plans and sets up their desired goals and agendas for that period and operate how much money they will need in order to accomplish all they seek to do in that period of time. They may run from July 1st through June 30th, January 1st through December 31st, April 1st through March 31st, or any other year-long period of time that is established for that organization's function.

If it's time for expansion, thinking in terms of the fiscal year is essential for this end. It gives a minister the ability to think in terms of financial planning, limits, and budgeting to the end of seeing how expansion can work, step by step. Expansion doesn't happen all at once in a business sense. There is no grand explosion, only careful planning within the available funds and limits an organization has. Having a good sense of financial planning and fiscal responsibility is essential to ensure the vision will expand and be provided for, making more possible than previously realized.

Annual fiscal reporting

Most non-profit organizations release an annual report of their donations, earnings, and spending each fiscal year, with a special section about how the money was used to benefit or better those touched by the organization. Fiscal reports are an important part of understanding the relationship between donors and organizations, because it is important for those who have given to see their money was put to a purposeful and good use. The fiscal report does not have to be long and detailed, but should break down the amount of money an organization had at the beginning of a fiscal year, the amount of donations given to the organization, the amount of money that was spent, and the existing balance at the beginning of the new fiscal year. Fiscal reports should also include information about the organization and any changes made to it, the ways the organization impacted those it is designed to affect, contact information, and a list of the organization's board members.

Applying for grants

Because the world of non-profit has exploded in the past several years, there are far more organizations, causes, and ministries to give to than in years past. As a result, many non-profit organizations are turning to the world of grants and grant money to fund their projects and fill in the gaps caused by minimal donations.

Grant-writing demands a book all by itself, and I will not be using this book to delve very deeply into the world of grant writing, because it is very extensive and complicated. Many organizations think obtaining a grant is the answer to all their financial issues, but the truth about obtaining grants is more complicated than this. Yes, grants are money given for the purpose of a specific charitable cause or educational endeavor, but obtaining a grant is not an easy process. It requires either a trained professional who knows what they are doing in the grant writing process or a very dedicated individual who is a part of the ministry and knows how to write about and present the organization in a way that will impact the grant organization in a favorable way. A few things to know about the grant process:

- **Grant requirements are very individualized** – There are a few basics to every grant writing proposal, which we outlined earlier in this book (the business proposal). Those basics are foundational to grant applications, but the similarities in process from one grant to another end right there. Grant organizations establish their own criteria based on the type of grant given and the specifications of that grant. Closing dates, application processes, and availability all vary from one organization to another. It is important, therefore, that if you are seeking out a grant, you are careful to pay attention to the specifications on that application process. There is no "I'll apply anyway even though I don't have the right materials" leeway with a grant.

- **Grants are specific** – Grant organizations have very specified processes and criteria to determine eligibility. If you want to receive a grant, you need to make sure you meet all criteria to receive the grant. Matching your organization's needs to a grant is a large part of the process, and cannot be ignored. Also, the money given by a grant is for a specific purpose, and must be used for that specific purpose – and none other.

- **Grant organizations are accepting fewer applications, especially from grassroots organizations and faith-based organizations** – Have you ever wondered why big businesses seem to run charitable fundraisers for the same big-name organizations over and over again, while it's nearly impossible to get assistance from a local store for a smaller event? The reason is because big businesses want to ensure their donations go to reputable sources that they can establish a long-term relationship with, while smaller organizations are considered higher risk for profit failure and dissolution. Given the rate churches close at these days, it's no wonder people are often hesitant to give to smaller organizations. They believe that if they give to an organization and it falls apart a year later, they have wasted their money. Grant organizations are thinking the same way as big businesses when it comes to giving. They want to ensure their grant money is used as it was allotted and that it has served its purpose (evident by post-reports), not that it was given and the organization has now gone out of business. If you want to get a grant, it's important to do the things mentioned above in terms of matching your organization to the appropriate grant and making sure all requirements are met.

- **Additional registrations may be needed** – If you are applying for a grant through many organizations (including the federal government), nonprofit organizations are required to provide additional identification markers. One such marker is a DUNS (Data Universal Number System) number. This number is a tracking system which identifies the various financial and business aspects of an organization, including credit reliability, history of payment, and other general information that relates to how likely an organization is to fare with its finances. DUNS numbers are typically assigned when an organization incorporates, and if an organization does not have one, they can obtain one by request through Dun & Bradstreet. Organizations should also register with SAM, the System of Award and Management, by which grant money is often tracked. In order to register for SAM, one must first have a DUNS number. Most grant organizations also require at least one Authorized Organization Representative (AOR) to contact during the grant process.

- **Beware grant writers** – Grant writers can serve as a great resource in a grant process. Trying to find, apply for, and wait on a grant can be a long and complicated task. For many in ministry, they simply do not have that kind of time to invest in, but still need to receive the grant funding. For this, many turn to professional grant writers, individuals who charge a fee to match, prepare, and write the grant for an organization. There is nothing wrong with using a grant writer, but it's important that you do your homework before deciding to use one. There are many grant writers who charge fees far and above what they should and who do not know any more about the process than the average person. Check reputations, websites, going rates, and word-of-mouth recommendations before agreeing to pay someone to write a grant for your organization.

Learning from the past

In expansion, it's important to apply all the wisdom you have acquired as a minister over the years. We are not called to constantly look back, but to learn from what we have been through, and move forward with what we have learned. Expansion may seem like a daunting task, but if you consider where you once were, you had to expand to reach the point you are at now. It is God's will that we continue to grow in our understanding of spiritual matters, that our work and ministries grow, that our lives grow, and that we are abundant and flourish. With every failure or disappointment, there is a new opportunity and new beginning to start again, trusting God, and discover a better way to expand what He has given you. Let me encourage you in your work and ministries! It's not easy, but we all know, if we are called, God has equipped us for the tasks and work at hand...and God does provide for what He asks us to do.

Do not fear ministry. Do not fear change in ministry. Do not fear expansion. On the contrary, rejoice, because God has given you an awesome task that is only given to a few this side of heaven. Never forget that many are called, but few are chosen (Matthew 22:14).

ASSIGNMENTS

1. Prepare a Business proposal, composed of the following elements:
   a. Vision Statement
   b. Mission Statement
   c. Statement of Faith
   d. Statement of Activities and Operations
   e. Brief example of bylaws
   f. An estimated budget

(If you already have a business proposal package, please submit it to us as per the assignment.)

2. Prepare a media kit, composed of the following elements:
   a. An introduction letter
   b. Minister's biography
   c. Minister's media profile
   d. Minister's academic profile
   e. About the ministry

(If you already have a media kit, please submit it to us as per the assignment.)

3. Prepare a resume

(If you already have a resume, please update it and submit it to us as per the assignment.)

4. Prepare a CV.

5. Write a sample ministry letter and a ministry email (can be the same content, just formatted differently for each)

6. Create a flow chart, depicting the process of ministry logistics.

7. Write an essay (3-6 sentences, minimum) displaying an understanding of the criteria to be 501(c)(3), the process involved, and what is required for a minister to maintain non-profit status.

8. Having read the criteria of charities around the world, explain in detail (3-6 sentences) some common facets to becoming a charity in other countries.

9. List documents every minister must have, and why having these documents is so important.

10. List necessary business skills for ministry and why each skill is important for ministry today.

11. Define what the following terms mean in 1-3 sentences each:

   a. Mortgage
   b. Loan
   c. Contract
   d. Lawsuit
   e. Arbitration

12. Write an essay (3-6 sentences, minimum) on the honorarium definition, purpose, and process. Why do these documents exist? Why are they important? When are such documents inappropriate?

13. Make a weekly schedule (including Saturdays and Sundays) displaying ministry activities in a 9AM-5PM office setting. Reserve Saturdays and Sundays for retreats, seminars, conferences, and services.

14. Plan an imaginary conference event from start to finish, using the guidelines within the book.

15. Draft the basics of a ministry website (page information and basic contents) for a website for your ministry. If you already have a ministry website, please submit the domain name for us.

16. Define the following terms in 1-3 sentences each:

    a. Blog
    b. Podcasting
    c. Traditional publishing
    d. Self-publishing
    e. E-publishing
    f. Copyright
    g. Fair use

17. Write an essay (3-6 sentences, minimum) about both ministry order and respecting ministerial offices in personal relationships, and how the two overlap and often interact.

18. List some different ways ministers can benefit themselves and maintain their leadership over time, especially when handling difficult scenarios.

19. Detail proper and appropriate ministry attire via essay (3-6 sentences).

20. Detail how you would handle the following five scenarios. Be specific!

a. A fellow minister comes to you with a problem they are having in their marriage. They suspect their spouse is unhappy with their ministry walk and is having an affair. They come to you because they feel they can trust you. In the process, you learn of personal details pertaining to their life and marriage, including their arguments, discords, and other issues. When another minister comes to you asking what is going on with the minister with the problem, what do you do?

b. A local Muslim Imam contacts your ministry, wanting to know more about what you believe. They come because another Christian group harasses the local Mosque, protesting and picketing during times of prayer, claiming they are all terrorists. They want to know if all Christians think all Muslims are terrorists. How do you present your faith to this minister, and how do you address the issue at hand?

c. Someone considering you for an event comes to you, inquiring about various things in your personal life. They want to know about your marital status and various other things that relate therein. You are uncomfortable with this line of questioning. They make it known if you do not answer them, you will not speak for any of their events in the future. How do you handle this situation?

d. Two of the ministers under your ministry are very, anointed...but never get along. Constantly fighting, you have discovered the conflict has resulted because one of the people involved dated the other individual's significant other after the two had broken up. Given the nature of this conflict, how do you bring it to a resolution?

e. It's time for the end-of-year annual report, and planning for next year. How do you handle such a meeting? Draft minutes and notes for this meeting, complete with descriptions of the necessary discussions to have.

REFERENCES

Chapter 3

[1]"How To Draw Up A Budget Using Microsoft Excel."
http://www.associatedcontent.com/article/297066/how_to_draw_up_a_bu
dget_using_microsoft.html?cat=15. Accessed on November 15, 2011.

Chapter 9

[1]"Logistics."http://en.wikipedia.org/wiki/Logistics. Accessed on January
22, 2013.

Chapter 10

[1]"Exempt Purposes - Internal Revenue Code Section 501(c)(3)."
http://www.irs.gov/charities/charitable/article/0,,id=175418,00.html.
Accessed on December 1, 2011.

[2]"Exemption Requirements - Section 501(c)(3) Organizations"
http://www.irs.gov/charities/charitable/article/0,,id=96099,00.html.
Accessed on December 1, 2011.

Chapter 11

[1]""Register My Charity."
https://www.acnc.gov.au/ACNC/Register_my_charity/Why_register/Reg_T
ax_conc/ACNC/Edu/Char_con_avail.aspx. Accessed on July 26, 2014.

[2]"Brazil." http://2013.emergingforum.org/country/brazil/. Accessed on July 25, 2014.

[3]NGO Law Monitor: Cambodia." http://www.icnl.org/research/monitor/cambodia.html. http://www.cra-arc.gc.ca/chrts-gvng/chrts/pplyng/rgstrtn/menu-eng.html. Accessed on July 25, 2014.

[4]"Applying For Registration." http://www.cra-arc.gc.ca/chrts-gvng/chrts/pplyng/menu-eng.html. Accessed on July 25, 2014.

[5]"Setting Up International Nonprofit Organizations in China." http://www.chinabusinessreview.com/setting-up-international-nonprofit-organizations-in-china/. Accessed on July 25, 2014.

[6]"Three-Self Patriotic Movement." http://en.wikipedia.org/wiki/Three-Self_Patriotic_Movement. Accessed on July 25, 2014.

[7]"Start An NGO In Ghana: Register." http://www.g-lish.org/ngo-work/start-an-ngo-in-ghana-register. Accessed on July 29, 2014.

[8]"Council on Foundations: Guatemala." http://www.cof.org/content/guatemala. Accessed on July 28, 2014.

[9]"More NGOs Per Square Mile Than Any Other Country..." http://oneworld.org/2013/01/10/more-ngos-per-square-mile-than-any-other-country. Accessed on July 28, 2014.

[10]"A Tax Guide For Charitable Institutions and Trusts of a Public Character." http://www.ird.gov.hk/eng/tax/ach_tgc.htm. Accessed on July 26, 2014.

[11]"NGOs India." http://www.ngosindia.com/resources/ngo_registration1.php. Accessed on July 26, 2014.

[12]"How Does Indonesia Control Its Charitable Organizations?" http://www.ehow.com/how-does_5548459_indonesia-control-its-charitable-organizations.html. Accessed on July 28, 2014.

[13]"Tax Administration Jamaica's Role under the New Charities Act."

http://www.jamaicatax.gov.jm/index.php/2012-05-14-21-25-44/charities. Accessed on July 28, 2014.

[14]"Non-Profit Organisations In Japan: Charity At Home." http://www.economist.com/node/18929259. Accessed on July 27, 2014.

[15]"Registering An NGO/Charitable Organisation In Kenya." http://kenyanlawyer.blogspot.com/2010/11/registering-ngo-charitable-organisation.html. Accessed on July 27, 2014.

[16]"NGO Law Monitor: Mexico." http://www.icnl.org/research/monitor/mexico.html. Accessed on July 29, 2014.

[17]"How To Establish A Charitable Foundation In Nigeria." http://www.wikihow.com/Establish-a-Charitable-Foundation-in-Nigeria. Accessed on July 27, 2014.

[18]"Law Of Charitable Foundations In Pakistan." http://allatiflaw.wordpress.com/2008/06/09/law-of-charitable-foundations-in-pakistan/. Accessed on July 28, 2014.

[19]"Register A Non-Profit Organization In Poland." http://www.bridgewest.eu/article/register-non-profit-organization-poland. Accessed July 28, 2014.

[20]"How To Register A Foundation In the Philippines." http://businesstips.ph/how-to-register-a-foundation-in-the-philippines/. Accessed July 29, 2014.

[21]"Russia: Council On Foundations." http://www.cof.org/content/russia. Accessed on July 29, 2014.

[22]"NGO Law Monitor: Rwanda." http://www.icnl.org/research/monitor/rwanda.html. Accessed on July 29, 2014.

[23]"The Charity Essentials In Singapore." http://www.lexology.com/library/detail.aspx?g=d01f7c0c-7163-4107-9120-1312a5fa6ec2. Accessed July 29, 2014.

[24]"Thailand Foundation Registration." http://www.siam-legal.com/Business-in-Thailand/thailand-foundation.php. Accessed July 29, 2014.

[25]"Set Up A Charity." https://www.gov.uk/setting-up-charity/register-with-hmrc. Accessed on July 29, 2014.

Chapter 14

[1]"Legal Requirements For A Contract." http://smallbusiness.yahoo.com/r-article-a-1431-m-1-sc-11-legal_requirements_for_a_contract-i. Accessed on December 11, 2011.

[2]Ibid.

[3]Ibid.

[4]Ibid.

Chapter 25

[1]"Facebook." http://en.wikipedia.org/wiki/Facebook. Accessed on August 7, 2014.

Chapter 45

[1]"What Is True Biblical Fellowship? Message 1." http://bible-truth.org/msg123.html. Accessed on July 29, 2014.

About the Author

$$\blacktriangleleft\!\!\Longrightarrow$$

Dr. Lee Ann B. Marino, Ph.D., D.Min., D.D.

And when He was demanded of the Pharisees,
when the Kingdom of God should come,
He answered them and said,
The Kingdom of God cometh not with observation:
Neither shall they say,
Lo here! or, lo there!
for, behold, the Kingdom of God is within you.
(Luke 17:20-21, KJV)

Dr. Lee Ann B. Marino, Ph.D., D.Min., D.D. (she/her) is "everyone's favorite theologian" leading Gen X, Millennials, and Gen Z with expertise in leadership training, queer and feminist theology, general religion, and apostolic theology. A graduate of Apostolic Preachers College, Dr. Marino has served in ministry since 1998 and was ordained as a pastor in 2002 and an apostle in 2010. She founded what is now Spitfire Apostolic Ministries in 2004. Under her ministry heading Dr. Marino is founder and overseer of

Sanctuary International Fellowship Tabernacle – SIFT (the original home of National Coming Out Sunday) and Chancellor of Apostolic University.

Affectionately nicknamed "the Spitfire," Dr. Marino has spent over two decades as an "apostle, preacher, and teacher" (2 Timothy 1:11), exercising her personal mandate to become "all things to all people" (1 Corinthians 9:22). Her embrace of spiritual issues (both technical and intimate) has found its home among both seekers and believers, those who desire spiritual answers to today's issues.

Dr. Marino has preached throughout the United States, Puerto Rico, and Europe in hundreds of religious services and experiences throughout the years. A history maker in her own right, she has spent over two decades in advocacy, education, and work for and within minority spiritual communities (including African American, Hispanic, and LGBTQ+). She has also served as the first woman on all-male synods, councils, and panels, as well as the first preacher or speaker welcomed of a different race, sexual orientation, or identity among diverse communities. Today, Dr. Marino's work extends to over one hundred countries as she hosts the popular *Kingdom Now* podcast, which is in the top twenty percentile of all podcasts worldwide. She is also the author of over thirty books and the popular Patheos column, *Leadership on Fire*. To date, she has had four bestselling titles within their subject matter: *Understanding Demonology, Spiritual Warfare, Healing, and Deliverance: A Manual for the Christian Minister; Ministry School Boot Camp: Training for Helps Ministries, Appointments, and Beyond; Surrounded By So Great a Cloud of Witnesses: Women of Faith Who Revolutionized History;* and *Ministering to LGBTQs – and Those Who Love Them.*

As a public icon and social media influencer, Dr. Marino advocates for healthy body image (curvy/full-figured), queer representation (as a demisexual/aromantic), and albinism awareness, as a model. Known to those she works with, she is spiritual mom, teacher, leader, professor, confidant, and friend. She continues to transform, receiving new teaching, revelation, and insight in this thing we call "ministry."

Through years of spiritual growth and maturity, Dr. Marino stands as herself, here to present what God has given to her for any who have an ear to hear.

For more information, visit her website at kingdompowernow.org.

www.ingramcontent.com/pod-product-compliance
Lightning Source LLC
Chambersburg PA
CBHW062358090426
42740CB00010B/1321